# PEIRCE

Other interview books from Automatic Press ♦ V|P

**Formal Philosophy**
edited by Vincent F. Hendricks & John Symons November 2005

**Masses of Formal Philosophy**
edited by Vincent F. Hendricks & John Symons October 2006

**Philosophy of Technology: 5 Questions**
edited by Jan-Kyrre Berg Olsen & Evan Selinger February 2007

**Game Theory: 5 Questions**
edited by Vincent F. Hendricks & Pelle Guldborg Hansen April 2007

**Philosophy of Mathematics: 5 Questions**
edited by Vincent F. Hendricks & Hannes Leitgeb January 2008

**Epistemology: 5 Questions**
edited by Vincent F. Hendricks & Duncan Pritchard September 2008

**Narrative Theories and Poetics: 5 Questions**
edited by Peer F. Bundbaard, Henrik Skov Nielsen & Frederik Stjernfelt 2012

**Philosophical Practice: 5 Questions**
edited by Jeanette Bresson Ladegaard Knox &
Jan Kyrre Berg Olsen Friis January 2013

**Intellectual History: 5 Questions**
edited by Morten Haugaard Jeppesen, Frederik Stjernfelt & Mikkel Thorup
May 2013

**Philosophy of Nursing: 5 Questions**
edited by Anette Forss, Christine Ceci & John S. Drummod
October 2013

**Science and Religion: 5 Questions**
edited by Gregg D. Caruso March 2014

See all published and forthcoming books in the 5 Questions series at
www.vince-inc.com

# PEIRCE:
# 5 QUESTIONS

EDITED BY

*FRANCESCO BELLUCCI,*
*AHTI-VEIKKO PIETARINEN &*
*FREDERIK STJERNFELT*

Automatic Press ◆ ⊻̅P

Automatic Press ♦ V|P

Information on this title: ww.vince-inc.com

© Automatic Press / VIP 2014

This publication is in copyright. Subject to statuary exception and to the provisions of relevant collective licensing agreements, no reproduction of any part may take place without the written permission of the publisher.

First published 2014

Printed in the United States of America
and the United Kingdom

ISBN-10 / 87-92130-52-6
ISBN-13 / 978-87-92130-52-5

The publisher has no responsibilities for the persistence or accuracy of URLs for external or third oarty Internet Web sites referred to in this publication and does not guarantee that any content on such Web sites is, or will remain, accurate or appropriate.

Cover design by
Vincent F. Hendricks

# Contents

| | |
|---|---|
| Preface | iii |
| Acknowledgements | v |
| 1. Fernando Andacht | 1 |
| 2. Douglas Anderson | 15 |
| 3. Victor R. Baker | 19 |
| 4. Mats Bergman | 37 |
| 5. Vincent Colapietro | 45 |
| 6. Marcel Danesi | 53 |
| 7. André De Tienne | 59 |
| 8. Cornelis de Waal | 69 |
| 9. Terrence W. Deacon | 73 |
| 10. Susan Haack | 81 |
| 11. Leila Haaparanta | 97 |
| 12. Jaakko Hintikka | 101 |
| 13. Michael H. G. Hoffmann | 105 |
| 14. Christopher Hookway | 119 |
| 15. Nathan Houser | 123 |
| 16. Masato Ishida | 135 |
| 17. Jiang Yi | 143 |
| 18. Isaac Levi | 149 |
| 19. Giovanni Maddalena | 153 |
| 20. Rosa Mayorga | 165 |
| 21. Cheryl Misak | 169 |
| 22. Ilkka Niiniluoto | 171 |
| 23. Winfried Nöth | 175 |
| 24. Jaime Nubiola | 181 |
| 25. Sami Paavola | 189 |
| 26. Helmut Pape | 195 |
| 27. Ahti-Veikko Pietarinen | 207 |

| | |
|---|---:|
| 28. Nicholas Rescher | 225 |
| 29. Lucia Santaella | 229 |
| 30. Demetra Sfendoni-Mentzou | 239 |
| 31. Sun-Joo Shin | 251 |
| 32. T. L. Short | 257 |
| 33. Frederik Stjernfelt | 267 |
| 34. Claudine Tiercelin | 273 |
| 35. Fernando Zalamea | 279 |
| **About the Editors** | **283** |

# Preface

♦

April 19, 1914, the American philosopher Charles Sanders Peirce died in his large, lonesome house in Milford, Pennsylvania. He had not held an academic position since 1883 and had lived the last third of his life in financial distress, increasingly isolated and finally ill. Despite this fact, the last two decades of his life proved the intellectually most fruitful part of his already very productive life. Especially in the years after the turn of the century, Peirce virtually exploded in the last comprehensive articulation of his philosophy, integrating logic, pragmatism and semiotics in a detailed architecture which increasingly attracts investigators from all over the globe, not only for historical reasons but also with the aim of extracting insights and ideas relevant for contemporary purposes. Among his uncanny predictions is the one from 1908 that states that his late system illustrates "a development of thought not likely to be independently reproduced in a century" (MS 300).

At the centenary of Peirce's death, it appeared obvious to us to provide a guide to this ongoing investigation in the handy shape of the Five Questions book series. This format gives, at the same time, the introduction to central persons in a field, to central questions, institutional relations, and open issues. In this volume we have collected a large share of active philosophers, logicians, scientists, semioticians, intellectual historians etc. with an active interest in Charles Peirce's thought. It gives, we believe, an impressive picture of the variety of Peircean themes under current development in many different directions.

We thank the contributors for coping with a tight deadline and the Automatic Press for a quick publication.

May 2014
*Francesco Bellucci,*
*Ahti-Veikko Pietarinen &*
*Frederik Stjernfelt*
*Editors*

# Acknowledgements

We would like to thank Automatic Press ♦$\frac{V}{I}$P, especially editor-in-chief Vincent F. Hendricks and associate editor Henrik Boensvang, for their enthusiastic support of this project and their assistance in bringing it to fruition.

May 2014
*Francesco Bellucci,*
*Ahti-Veikko Pietarinen &*
*Frederik Stjernfelt*

# 1

# Fernando Andacht

Full Professor
Department of Communication, University of Ottawa

---

**1. Why were you initially drawn to Peirce?**
I would like to think of the beginning of my interest and fascination with matters Peircean as a radical conversion that took place not on the road to Damascus but on the highway to Barcelona, twenty-seven years ago. It all happened in the boreal, sultry summer of 1987, shortly after the publication of my first book in Uruguay, *El paisaje de los Signos. Semiótica y sociedad uruguaya contemporánea*, in that same year. A semiotic association founded by researchers of the Universitat Autònoma de Barcelona invited me to participate in the International Forum of Semiotic and Communication. The event was organized by the Universidad de Granada, which is located in Andalusia, Spain's fascinating deep south. One of the landmarks of that gorgeous city famous for its unique architecture is the stunning Alhambra Palace, which is part of the rich heritage left by the Arabic presence in Andalusia during the Middle Ages. A nice coincidence about this beautiful setting is that Peirce visited this architectonic jewel on November 7, 1870 (Nubiola, 1998), while on his way to Sicily, as a member of a scientific expedition to observe a solar eclipse that would take place in December of that year.

After my presentation, one of the participants of the conference approached me and kindly discussed my paper in some detail. It was the French-Catalonian mathematician Robert Marty, of the Université de Perpignan, a specialist in Peircean semiotic, as I would soon find out. He worked with the group of semioticians gathered around Gérard Deledalle, a European philosopher and a renowned Peirce scholar. One of Marty's critical comments was the conspicuous absence of Peircean semiotic from my analysis of society. To me this lack was as normal or natural as my native Spanish language. I had been trained as a linguist, first at the Department of Linguistics of the School Humanities and Sciences of the State University in Montevideo, and then at the Department of Linguistics of Ohio University, in Athens, USA. At both institutions, I had studied the semiological school that originated from the pioneer structuralist approach to (mostly verbal) signs of Swiss linguist Ferdinand de Saussure. Thus semiology – and not semiotic – was the natural way in which I – as well as most Latin American scholars in those years – approached any kind of meaning phenomena, whether in communication, culture or society. My only acquaintance with Peirce had been an all too brief presentation in an introductory course of linguistics, just a passing reference to the icon-index-symbol sign classification. That was all, and for me until that very hot month of August 1987 in Andalusia, that was enough. My next stop was Barcelona, and Marty kindly offered me a ride in his car, on his way to Perpignan. In those almost 9 hours of road travel, I underwent what, almost a quarter century later, I can describe as a fascinating crash course on the relevance of triadic semiotic for the study of life, whether cultural or natural. To make a long and enthralling story short, the road trip finished with Marty's generous offer to send me the Appendix of a book in progress, *L'Algèbre des signes. Essai de sémiotique scientifique d'après C. S. Peirce* (J. Benjamins, 1990). In it, Marty had collected 76 definitions of signs that he had culled from the published and unpublished work by Peirce. A month or so later – that was the time of snail mail only – I had in my hands that precious chronological series of thoughts on signs produced by Peirce. After having read the evolution of the key semiotic notions, an account that was far more nourishing than my description of it can now show, I was hooked. Therefore the next logical step was to go to the National Library in Montevideo to get more semiotic sustenance, and as luck would have it, the eight volumes of the *Collected Papers* were there, waiting patiently for the would-be-semiotician in me to find them, and dive deep into the almost half century of painstaking rediscovery of the logic of signs. The rest is (the) history of my intellectual development. After that fortunate encounter "it has never been in my power to study communication, culture and society except as a study of semiotic", if I may use the words of Peirce's candid intellectual confession to Lady Welby in his mature years, in a letter dated December 23, 1908. In every book, article, talk, or media event in which I became involved, I felt that I was fortunate to find myself under the auspices of that intricate palace of reflections that Peirce built to shelter all kinds of signs, and most decisively, the logical process of sign action. Peirce's discovery has illuminated the path of my inquiry into the ways of those ubiquitous and usually taken for granted living constituent elements of our life whose role is to make it possible in every conceivable way.

## 2. What do you consider your contribution to the field?

Although it is not an easy task to evaluate the impact that one's work, published and otherwise – lectures, applied research and media divulgation of research results – may have had in the field, I will give it a try. If I had to define the kind of Peircean semiotic that I have been working with for the past three decades, I would say it is a *conversational* sort of semiotic. By a 'conversational' semiotic I do not mean a study related to the linguistic school that examines discourse units such as 'turn-taking'; rather, it is akin to Oakeshott's (1959) "conversation of mankind" idea, an exchange which harbors "a diversity of voices that acknowledge each other and enjoy an oblique relationship". It is also related to what Ransdell (2000) insightfully described as the Socratic "conversational art" or "*tekhné*" in the matrix of Peircean thought. In my own case, the kind of semiotic practice that I endeavored to carry out involved the media audience, the radio listeners of a column in which I did a triadic semiotic analysis of political communication in election campaigns for many years. It also included the various academic audiences with which I endeavored to establish a dialogue derived from an inquiry based on Peirce's lifelong reflection on signs. Another useful concept of Oakeshott (1933) is his "modes of experience", which is based on the premise that "experience as such admits of no final or absolute division"; it serves me to describe the thrilling and heterogeneous sign exchange I had for almost three decades.

I discovered that there was so much to learn in my effort to engage the anonymous media audience and the students from sundry educational institutions (Social Sciences, Design School, Communication Studies). Besides there were the many organizations, both private and public, on whose behalf I carried out applied research in the areas of public opinion, marketing and media programming for over a decade, in Uruguay and Argentina. While I was teaching, writing and doing research in a wide range of academic and non-academic environments, I was determined to plunge Peircean semiotic theory deep into the chaotic stream of the life world as it happens and as it is almost instantaneously represented by mass media. This was both the result of the severe problems to make ends meet in Latin American academia, particularly in Uruguay, where I lived until 2002, and also of my resolve to spread as broadly as possible the ideas over which Peirce toiled for most of his adult life.

The title of one of my books is an attempt to express and draw a balance of those years: *An indisciplinary path to communication: semiotic and mass media* (Andacht, 2001). I wrote '*in*disciplinary' and not '*inter*disciplinary'. The latter is both the correct (and trendy) word used to criticize the rigid traditional boundaries of canonical academic disciplines. The reason for using a neologism in the title – in fact, in Spanish and in English the noun 'indiscipline' denotes bad behavior – lies in my conviction that a semiotic approach to the study of mass media, culture and society can trigger the imagination of those fields, and of any other, for that matter, by challenging the borders of all disciplines. As there is no possible inquiry without the intercession of signs, of interpretation, then Peircean triadic semiotic theory is a most suitable approach to the generation of meaning in every area of knowledge.

One further reason for calling my semiotic approach 'conversational' lies in my interest in integrating the terminology and epistemology of Peirce's logic of signs into the analytical consideration of various sociocultural phenomena. One of the biggest challenges for me was to fulfill a distinctive and different social function from that of a commentator of culture, e.g., a newspaper journalist, of someone who writes or talks about what is going on now with the words that are basically the same as those used in their everyday life by the people who watch/read/listen to her. Both in my writings and in the diffusion of knowledge that I began in 1989, I took pains to define every technical term I used, and never employed it figuratively, as a mere metaphor to express something that I could also be saying in simpler terms.

What I deem to be the most fruitful influence of my work, in my own country, Uruguay, and also in the region (Brazil, Argentina, Chile) started in the mid 80s of the past century, when a group of keen sociology undergraduate students invited me to give a lecture at an academic event that they had organized in the Uruguayan State University. After my presentation, they came to see me to find out why semiotic was not part of their curriculum. Profiting from the University system of co-government of students, professors and alumni, that enthusiastic group elaborated a proposal to have semiotic as an optional course in the social sciences curriculum. After a daunting bureaucratic battle, it became one, which I taught for over a decade. In 1989, I was invited to work with a team of social scientists in applied research on Public Opinion, Marketing and Media. My job included giving a seminar for journalists. One of them had a weekday morning news and general information radio program called *En Perspectiva*; he asked me if I would like to have a weekly column to do a semiotic analysis of the political campaign of that year. I did not hesitate; it was a rare chance to present to a mass audience – the target of that radio program was ideal, the educated middle class – a semiotic take on a topic in which traditionally Uruguayan people have been very keen, namely, politics and especially the workings of propaganda. The outcome exceeded my most positive expectations: I continued with the column "Behind the campaign" until I left Uruguay, in 2002. Some elections later, the producers were uploading on the web not only the podcast of my talks, but also and most usefully the videos, photographs of propaganda posters, jingles and segments of electoral debates that I analyzed on my radio column.

Also in the mid 80s, I was appointed semiotic lecturer of the first School of Design, which was created in Uruguay through a donation and technical support of the Italian government. Once again, I took up the challenge to enter into a dialogue with a new, rather unknown area of knowledge, with students whose aim was to change the visible and serviceable face of the world, the creators of design in all its shapes, colors and materials. It was a wonderful surprise to discover the curiosity and keen interest in matters semiotic of those students. The final project of the 1$^{st}$ year course, which I taught for eight years, involved creating every component for the design of a city park, for instance. So students would come to me with genuine doubts, assorted queries that would have delighted Peirce, given his pragmatic maxim on how meaning should be studied by considering its general consequences, those effects "that might conceivably have practical bearings" (CP 5.2). They wanted to find out what difference it made if they chose one design over another for those who were going to live in the environment that they were creating. The etymology of 'theory' is related to the activity of the *theoros*, the person whose special task in ancient Greece was to carefully observe an important event and then report on it to the community (Nagy, 2013: 625). This concept derives from the verb *'theorein'*, to consider, to speculate, to gaze at something, so I can say that these students engaged passionately in semiotic theory, insofar as they observed painstakingly the working of iconic, indexical and symbolic signs, so as to better understand the life of design and to act creatively upon the world. There was nothing artificial or 'merely' theoretical, to evoke again, Peirce's (CP 3.460) critique of nominalism, in these students' real interest and enthusiasm to learn triadic semiotic so as to include it in their actual design projects.

Regarding my published work, I think there are two distinct phases. For almost a decade – 1992 to 2001 – my publications were the result of my adoption of the framework of triadic semiotic to carry out an inquiry into the social imagination, insofar as its workings can be observed in the media, particularly television (talk shows, news programs, humor, propaganda and publicity). I analyzed marginal socio-political events that seldom reached the media or when they did, they were shown in a bizarre way, for instance, the first Uruguayan gay pride march, in the austral winter of 1993 (Andacht 1996). To develop my conversational use of Peircean semiotic, I observed mediated daily life in all its messy, murky flow, and tried to build some bridges with the work of Goffman

(Andacht 1993), Bateson, Castoriadis and Kolakowski (Andacht 1992). From that period are my books, *Entre Signos de Asombro. Antimanual para iniciarse a la semiótica.* (1993), *Paisaje de Pasiones. Pequeño tratado sobre las pasiones en Mesocracia.* (1996), and the already mentioned *Un camino interdisciplinario hacia la comunicación: medios masivos y semiótica* (2001).

The second phase in my published work goes from 2003 to the present. What set it off was a minor tremor in the audiovisual landscape that took place at the end of the 20th century, namely, the launching of the TV reality show, *Big Brother,* in Holland, which soon after became a globalized, s glocal success. It most definitely altered the path of my inquiry. Its improbable popularity in Latin America (Argentina, Uruguay and Brazil) together with the negative though predictable reaction of media critics, and a glacial silence from academia in that part of the world influenced my decision. That glaring absence of a scholarly response to this kind of media production – in contrast with the abundant literature in Europe, particularly in England –motivated me to start studying this cultural phenomenon. One monograph, several journal articles and book chapters later, I dare say that Peircean semiotic proved extremely useful, specifically the indexical sign – based upon which I created the analytical concept of the reality show genre's *index appeal* – together with Peirce's notion of reality, the phaneroscopic categories, and a scholastic term that seems ill at ease in the company of a mundane TV show, namely, *haecceitas.* Peirce borrowed this scholastic term from Duns Scotus to account for the outward clash or resistance of the real in semiosis, and thus one of its essential components. It was central element of my media analysis. In brief, what began as a semiotic study of a television fad and of the large global audience of reality shows such as *Big Brother* created by the Dutch entertainment industry ended up in the analysis of other factuality genres, including new-fangled documentaries, many of which are nowadays watched on the internet. From this period come, for example, my book *El reality show: una perspectiva analítica* (Andacht, 2003b) and the first text on the Latin American reception of *Big Brother*: "Fight, love and tears: an analysis of the reception of Big Brother in Latin America" (Andacht, 2004). The latter is included in a volume on the internationalization of this "media event", as Scannell (2002) describes by. Then this interest became a research project on the representation of reality in audiovisual media funded by the Social Sciences and Humanities Research Council (SSHRC) of Canada. In two recent chapters, I tried to understand the relevance of this new-fangled kind of reality TV in today's mediascape: "On the media representation of reality: Peirce and Auerbach, two unlikely visitors of the house of *Big Brother*" (Andacht, 2010) and "The dance of identification: the signs of the self in the age of Reality Television" (Andacht, 2012). This stage of my work is a further instance of the 'conversational' or 'dialogic' semiotic. The latter term should not be construed in a strictly Bakhtinian sense, rather in a way that is akin to Oakeshott's "conversation of mankind". I would like to believe that my work belongs to what Peirce called a "preliminary inquiry", one that "contemplates phenomena as they are, simply opens its eyes and describes what it sees" (CP 5.37).

### 3. What is the proper role of Peirce's work in relation to philosophy and other academic disciplines?

Given my academic training, I would like to speak of Peirce's relevance in relationship to the social sciences, and foremost among them though not exclusively, to communication and media studies. In two articles published in Brazil (Andacht, 2005, 2010a, 2013) I tried to point out the negative influence of a too often taken for granted adoption of social constructionism as the hegemonic theoretical framework to analyze mass media. Much of that research is based on dualism, namely, "the philosophy that performs its analyses with an axe, leaving, as the ultimate elements, unrelated chunks of being, this is most hostile to synechism" (CP 7.570). Instead of using the fourth method to attain a belief, the scientific one, according to Peirce (CP 5.384), most of those studies rely on the other three methods, and quite often on the third in the presentation of "The fixation of belief": the adoption of a theory because its "fundamental propositions seemed 'agreeable to reason.'" (CP 5.382). In the case of the academic publications that I considered, it is the acceptance of a theory that assumes that reality is "the mental construction" of those who believe they have discovered and investigated it' (Turrisi, 2002, p. 126). Such a choice serves to express the scholars' search not of "that which agrees with experience, but that which (they) find (themselves) inclined to believe" (CP 5.382). The cause of this flawed and biased upshot of media inquiry is that the observation and experience of reality take a second place to the researchers' firm convictions about what is wrong – morally or politically – with the media, and that brings to the fore the other two methods to attain belief: tenacity and authority. Peirce's conception of an autonomous and teleological sign action can effectively remove this block of the road of inquiry, and thus help in the task of building up a reliable methodology for the study of the media. The excessive, unwarranted use of a verbal form derived from Berger & Luckmann's (1966) classic text, namely, 'to construct', as an analytical term to examine the media harks back to "the unmasking turn of mind" idea, which was first formulated in a 1925 article by Hungarian-born sociologist Karl

Mannheim (Hacking, 1999). What these scholars are studying is not a construction, in the obvious, ordinary sense in which any artefact involves human intervention (design, imagination, technology), and thereby the effort of specialists to construct it. The purport of '(to) construct' in that context is a massive deceit whose exposure is the main or maybe the only possible task for those researchers.

By bringing in Peircean semiotic to the methodology of media studies, we would gain a scientific way of dealing with genuine doubts regarding the actual working of mass media. Instead of adopting a theory based on an a priori belief – the supposedly Machiavellian purposes of all media – there would be a genuine inquiry. Representation and interpretation are involved in producing and consuming all kinds of media, so it is inevitable that sign classification, and the anti-psychologism that Peirce cultivated for the semiotic by positing notions such as the interpretant – which is a sign – instead of considering the human, psychological creature – the interpreter – as an central component of the semiotic triad, makes a Peircean epistemology an appropriate tool to understand the practices fostered by mass media. From the tough semiotic habits that are embodied in media genres to the powerful, fleeting flights of the imagination, which are responsible for creativity in today's horizontal realm of social networking websites, all such human activity may be fruitfully studied as part of the evolving, logical process of sign action.

## 4. What do you consider the most important topics and/or contributions in the field of Peirce studies?

My discovery of Peirce's thought in 1987 was soon followed by another intellectual epiphany: I came across the work of whom I consider the logician's finest exegete: Joseph Ransdell (1931-2010). It was an article on the iconic sign (Ransdell 1986), one of his many superb explanations of the kernel of triadic semiotic, a work to which this specialist in Peirce dedicated his whole life. Then, as a Fulbright scholar at the Research Center for Language and Semiotic Studies, at Indiana University, I received another wondrous semiotic gift in my road to Peirce: *The meaning in things. The Basic Ideas of C. Peirce's semiotic*, Ransdell's monograph in progress on triadic semiotic, a book manuscript that he never finished, mostly because he put so much generous energy in building up an on-line forum for Peircean scholars from all over the world, the website *Arisbe* (http://www.cspeirce.com/), which is still generating fine exchanges today. Ransdell's take on iconicity is a pathbreaking approach, because it brings to the fore the epistemological value of the kind of sign that the Cartesian rationalist bias of our civilization has belittled in favor of the mighty symbolic sign, typically, the word. Ransdell's exegesis is precious for analyzing media, since they rely heavily on the iconic (visual and aural) and often share this tendency to underestimate the iconic, as I try to demonstrate in a very recent paper (Andacht, 2013a). The iconophobic frame of mind refuses to consider the work of iconic signs as being relevant when it comes to the growth of reasonableness; it was dubbed "the curmudgeon spirit" by Ransdell (in Andacht, 2003a).

Another fundamental insight in matters Peircean is Colapietro's (1989) landmark monograph *Peirce's Approach to the Self*. It had a great influence in my thinking on human identity (Andacht 2008, Andacht & Michel 2005), and in my understanding the purport of construing human beings as signs. Far from being an instance of anti-humanism, this is a genuine instance of Peirce's community-based construal of meaning, of his non-individualistic sense of humanity. Liszka's elaborate reflection on *The semiotic of myth* (1989) furnished the key analytical tool that I needed to deal with a term that is too often used in a vague, almost ungraspable sense by many social scientists, namely, 'the social imaginary' (Andacht 1998a, Andacht 1998b). By adopting Liszka's concepts of 'markedness', which he drew from the Prague school of phonology, and of 'transvaluation', which he took from Shapiro's Peircean-based linguistic analysis, and which Liszka masterfully applied to the structuralist theory of myth from a Peircean perspective, I was able to consider issues such as the imagined community which is a nation, and also people's use of public signs as the way to believe that they fully belong to this territory. To stay alive every nation must rely on sign processes, as much as on borders and on a common language (or more than one).

In the south of the world, my abode for many years, the work of Brazilian scholar Lucia Santaella has been a source of inspiration. Santaella is a semiotic powerhouse: besides the prodigious amount of energy that she pours tirelessly into her brilliant Peircean research on semiotic theory and on its implications for communication, culture and art, there is her formidable organizing effort to keep semiotic institutionally alive. Of the latter, I would like to mention just one fine example, namely, the impressive bi-annual international Advanced Seminar on Peirce Philosophy and Semiotics, which is held at the Catholic University of São Paulo (PUCSP), and which gathers top scholars from all over the world. I met Santaella during my stay as a Fulbright scholar in Bloomington in 1992, and I am happy to say that she is an admired fellow traveller in the Peircean realm, as well as a fine friend from whom I can always learn.

## 5. What are the most important open problems in this field and what are the prospects/avenues for progress?

A key issue regarding the growth of symbols, particularly those related to semiotic itself, as a fundamental body of knowledge first developed by Peirce for almost half a century of ceaseless labor, and then taken up by scholars and scientists from many fields, from biology to literature, is the inclusion of semiotic as part of the curriculum in secondary and university studies. With the same right as other traditional areas of knowledge, the logic of signs could and should be an integral part of our educational system. As a growing body of scholarship cogently shows, the inclusion of Peirce's architectonic system of thought could benefit students from the humanities (see Andacht 2004a), the social and the natural sciences. Its importance as an epistemological framework merits its being transferred from the exclusively philosophical institutional setting, so that we could have a bolder, more expansive distribution of semiotic across all fields of knowledge. What was feared in the 60s of the 20th century as the 'semiological imperialism' in relationship with the school of structuralism and its almost exclusive focus on linguistic signs should be reformulated in terms of the far more encompassing, not verbocentric triadic logic of signs or semiotic. This is a pressing institutional problem: how to locate that vast body of reflection on the way of signs within the present institutions of higher learning. Only then will Peirce's gift to the world be truly and fruitfully shared by all those who are embarked in the endless journey of inquiry.

From my own experience, I can foresee much progress in the development of the school of psychology known as "the semiotic self" (Wiley, 1994), which is an outgrowth of the monograph by Colapietro (1989), which I discussed above, and which has now spawned a growing school of thought that has points of contact but also important differences with "the dialogical self" (Hermans & Gieser, 2012; Michel, Andacht & Gomes, 2008). To conceive of human identity as being inseparable from its capacity to generate meaning, that is, as an evolving system of signs, comes close to Peirce's vision of the self as a generation of *interpretants*, as opposed to an internal entity locked up in "a box of flesh and blood" (CP 7.591), as Peirce argued in his critique of William James's *The Principles of Psychology* (1891). Far from having that kind of material isolation, Peirce considers that human beings are endowed with the power of "receiv(ing) and transmit(ting) ideal influence, of which (each one of us is) a vehicle" (CP 1.212).

Another area that I imagine would welcome and profit much from adopting triadic semiotic in its methodology is the field of study of mediated communication. The daunting growth of all manner of exchange of knowledge, and the fast diffusion of images, sounds and texts in the internet, in ways that we simply could not foresee at the end of the 20$^{th}$ century, even after the onset of Web 2.0 in 1999, constitute an ideal ground for using the teleology driven, evolving system of signs as an analytical framework. Last but not least, the world's audience fascination with what I have described as 'the semiotic perspiration' of human beings, namely, the indexical signs that the body exudes in the interaction order (Goffman, 1983), when people are face to face – and also screen to screen, in our virtual, heavily mediated environment – in both a manifold of reality TV formats, as well as in the new-fangled documentary films, is a most favorable environment for the study of "the cooperation of three subjects" or "tri-relative influence" (CP 5.484) that Peirce called semiosis, with particular emphasis on the social function of indexicality. I consider the latter to be the main attraction of the globalized appetite for the authentic, which audiences believe can become visible, almost tangible, thanks to the kind of sign that "like a pointing finger exercises a real physiological force over the attention, like the power of a mesmerizer, and directs it to a particular object of sense." (CP 8. 41).

From my research on this type of audiovisual formats, including some reception studies, where members of the audience discussed what they found interesting or relevant in factuality programming, I conclude that it is the index appeal of the genre that bears the promise of a close contact for its viewers. It is a *para-tactile relation* or interaction, to paraphrase a notion proposed in a pioneering article by Horton & Wohl (1956), "the para-social relationship", which is a personal bond akin to an imaginary friendship with the personalities of television. In the case of this indexical television genre, there is the illusory contact with a group of anonymous people who must deal with strangers in a mediated interaction order, and who in that process cannot help producing an inordinate amount of indexicality, which is then interpreted by the audience as a more or less reliable evidence of authenticity, of what could be true about these people, despite the overtly artificial environment and the strongly commercial nature of these television programs.

**References**

Andacht, F. (2013a). The Lure of the Powerful, Freewheeling Icon: On Ransdell's Analysis of Iconicity. *Transactions of the Charles S. Peirce Society: A Quarterly Journal in American Philosophy*, 49/4, pp. 509-532.

Andacht, F. (2013). ¿Qué puede aportar la semiótica triádica al estudio de la comunicación mediática? *Galáxia. Revista do Programa de Pós-*

*Graduação em Comunicação e Semiótica, 13/25*, 24 – 37.

Andacht, F. (2012). The dance of identification: the signs of the self in the age of Reality Television. In R. Luppicini (Ed.), *Handbook of Research on Technoself: Identity in a Technological Society* (pp. 360 – 381). Hershey: IGI-Global.

Andacht, F. (2010a). On the integration of the differentiated: a Peircean outlook on Latin American identity. *Semeiosis. Transdisciplinary Journal of Semiotics, 1*. (http://www.semeiosis.com.br/en/on-the-integration-of-the-differentia ted/ - ixzz1Bb8sbRWY)

Andacht, F. (2010). On the media representation of reality: Peirce and Auerbach, two unlikely visitors of the house of Big Brother. In S. Bauwel & N. Carpentier (eds.), *Trans-Reality peeping around the corner: Metaperspectives on reality television* (pp. 37-64). Totowa, New Jersey: Rowman & Littlefield Publishers.

Andacht, F. (2008). Self y creatividad en el pragmatismo de C.S. Peirce: "la incidencia del instante presente en la conducta". *Utopia y Praxis Latinoamericana, 13/40*, 39 – 65.

Andacht, F. (2005). A síndrome de prometeu: um obstáculo no desenvolvimento do campo da comunicação. *Intexto, 2/13*, 1 – 15.

Andacht, F. (2004a). The forking and symmetrical sign inquiries of Borges and Peirce. *Recherches Sémiotiques. Semiotic Inquiry, 24/1-2-3*, 197 – 218.

Andacht, F. (2004). Fight, love and tears: an analysis of the reception of Big Brother in Latin America. In E. Mathijs, & J. Jones (eds.), *Big Brother International. Formats, critics and publics* (pp. 123 – 139). London: Wallflower Press.

Andacht, F. (2003a). Iconicity revisited: an interview with Joseph Ransdell, *Recherches Sémiotiques - Semiotic Inquiry, 23*, 221– 240.

Andacht, F. (2003b). *El reality show: una perspectiva analítica*. Buenos Aires: Grupo Editorial Norma.

Andacht, F. (2001). *Un camino interdisciplinario hacia la comunicación: medios masivos y* semiótica. Bogotá: Cátedra Unesco/ Pontificia Universidad Javeriana,

Andacht, F. (1998a). A semiotic framework for the social imaginary. *KODIKAS/ CODE. Ars Semiotica, 21*, 3 - 18.

Andacht, F. (1998b). On the relevance of the imagination in the semiotic of C. S. Peirce. *Versus. Quaderni di studi semiotici, 80-81*, 201 - 228.

Andacht, F. (1997). Media coverage of the unreasonable in the land of hyper-reason. In W. Nöth (Ed.), *Semiotics of the media. State of the art, projects and perspectives* (pp. 801-815). Mouton de Gruyter, Berlin, New York.

Andacht, F. (1996). *Paisaje de Pasiones. Pequeño tratado sobre las pasiones en Mesocracia*. Montevideo: Fin de Siglo.

Andacht, F. (1993). *Entre Signos de Asombro. Antimanual para iniciarse a la semiótica*. Montevideo: Trilce.

Andacht, F. (1992). *Signos Reales del Uruguay Imaginario*, Montevideo: Trilce

Andacht, F. (1993). Aristotle, Peirce and Goffman in a new frame. In M. Balat, J. Deledalle-Rhodes & G. Deledalle (eds.), *Signs of humanity. Proceedings of the IVth. Congress of the International Association of Semiotic Studies* (pp.1465-1473). Berlin: Mouton de Gruyter.

Andacht, F. (1987). *El paisaje de los signos. Semiótica y Sociedad Uruguaya Contemporánea*. Montevideo: Montesexto.

Andacht, F. & Michel, M. (2005). A Semiotic Reflection on Self-Interpretation and Identity. *Theory and Psychology, 15/1,* 51 – 75.

Berger, P. & Luckmann, T. (1966). *The Social Construction of Reality: A Treatise on the Sociology of Knowledge*. New York: Anchor Books.

Colapietro, V. (1989). *Peirce's Approach to the Self: A Semiotic Perspective on Human Subjectivity*. Albany: SUNY Press.

Goffman, E. (1983). The Interaction Order. *American Sociological Review*, *48*, 1-17.

Hacking, I. (1999). *The social construction of what?* Cambridge: Harvard University Press,

Hermans, H.J.M., & Gieser, T. (eds.) (2012). *Handbook of Dialogical Self Theory*. Cambridge: Cambridge University Press.

Horton, D. and Wohl, R. (1956). Mass Communication and Para-social Interaction: Observations on Intimacy at a Distance, *Psychiatry*, *19*, 215-29.

Liszka, J. J. (1989). *The semiotic of myth: A critical study of the symbol*. Bloomington: Indiana University Press.

Michel, M., Andacht, F. & Gomes, W. (2008). The Relevance of Secondness to the Psychological Study of the Dialogical Self. *International Journal for Dialogical Science. 3/1,* 301-334.

Nagy, G. (2013). *The Ancient Greek Hero in 24 Hours*. Cambridge,

MA.: Belknap Press.

Nubiola, Jaime (1998). C. S. Peirce and the Hispanic Philosophy of the Twentieth Century. *Transactions of the Charles S. Peirce Society*, 24/1, 31-49.

Oakeshott, M. (1959). *The Voice of Poetry in the Conversation of Mankind*. London: Bowes and Bowes.

Oakeshott, M. (1933). *Experience and its modes*. Cambridge: Cambridge University Press.

Peirce, C. S. (1931-58). *The Collected Papers of Charles S. Peirce*. Vol. I-VI, C. Hartshorne & P. Weiss (eds.), Vol. VII-VIII, A. Burks (Ed.). Cambridge, Mass.: Harvard University Press.

Ransdell, J. (2000). Peirce and the Socratic Tradition. *Transactions of the Charles S. Peirce Society. 36/3*, 341-356.

Ransdell, J. (1986). On Peirce's Conception of the Iconic Sign. In P. Bouissac, et al. (eds.), *Iconicity: Essays on the Nature of Culture, Festschrift for Thomas A. Sebeok* (pp. 51-74). Tübingen: Stauffenburg Verlag.

Scannell, P. (2002). Big Brother as a Television Event. *Television & New Media*, 3/3, 271-282.

Turrisi, P. (2002) The role of Peirce's pragmatism in education, *Cognitio*, 3, 122–35.

Wiley, N. (1994). *The semiotic self*. Chicago: University of Chicago Press.

# 2

# Douglas Anderson

Professor of Philosophy
Southern Illinois University Carbondale

---

**1. Why were you initially drawn to Peirce?**

I was initially drawn to the work of Charles Peirce for two central reasons. When I was younger, I was fascinated both by early Greek philosophy and by American philosophy. Peirce was one of the few American thinkers who wrote extensively and technically about Plato and Aristotle. I found his translations and interpretations of some of Plato's dialogues, for example, intriguing. The second reason had to do with my interest in creativity. Peirce was a practicing scientist yet he never argued for a scientific "recipe" for knowing. Instead, he turned to patient receptivity as modeled by artists and to imaginative hypothesizing as the bases for developing human inquiry. This stood in stark contrast to most of the positivism, deductivism, and confirmation theory of the twentieth century.

**2. What do you consider your contribution to the field?**

I do not believe I have made any special contributions to the field of Peirce studies. I have been interested in pretty much everything he had to say. What I have done that may in part be different from other interpreters is simply to allow him to speak for himself. For example, I have not tried to fit Peirce into an image of twenty-first century naturalism or philosophy of science. When I write about Peirce's religiosity or his connections to Schelling and Emerson, it is not because I *want* him to be religious or to work under the influence, in part, of romantic idealism. It is instead because he makes those claims himself for better or worse. His was a versatile mind. "Evolutionary Love" is, for example, a wild essay. But such wildness was actually not unusual for Peirce as anyone who reads his manuscripts and letters may attest. My contribution, looked at this way, has simply been to take the wild side of Peirce as seriously as the side that fits the needs of twentieth century naturalism. I am most interested in how he tried to get all of this to hang together to create what we call Peircean philosophy.

### 3. What is the proper role of Peirce's work in relation to philosophy and other academic disciplines?

Though I am neither a full blown "Peircean" nor a pragmatist, I believe that Peirce's work constitutes a Copernican turn in philosophy that is even more radical than that of Kant. Time will tell. Kant, in his way, brought rationalism and empiricism into relation. Peirce, in a more fully synthetic way, brought them together in a down to earth way by rejecting the modernist deductivism that held them at odds. As for other disciplines, Peirce contributed to many directly—logic, algebra, geometry, statistics, linguistics, astronomy, and so on. His philosophy also presents all the sciences with a new model for inquiry—one that originates in perception/observation and abduction. This, he believed, fit more closely to actual scientific practices than did, for example, Karl Pearson's more modern scheme that continued to consider the world to be a closed system. When I look at the pathetic "scientific" studies presently conducted in fields like education, political science, and psychology, I believe Peirce's thought has much to offer that might wean these disciplines of the recipe and "body of knowledge" version of science to which they have become habituated. For Peirce, science was constituted not by a set of static beliefs but by the process of inquiry that attempts to overcome our living doubts and tries to answer the actual questions that confront us at any given time.

### 4. What do you consider the most important topics and/or contributions in the field of Peirce studies?

I think Peirce made many important contributions and we may not yet know what all of these are. Some of his contributions I find most interesting and generally useful are:

a. His account of abductive inference and his move away from the geometric model of modern thought. This has been a difficult turn for contemporary thinkers to make.

b. His emphasis on statistical reasoning that leads to general rather than specific conclusions. Unlike Laplace or Pearson, for example, Peirce believed that statistical reasoning was important not just because of human finitude but because it reflected the tychistic nature of the world.

c. Peirce's new "scholastic" realism makes better sense of the social and cultural power of ideas and habits. Traditional and contemporary nominalisms either deny this power or leave it unexplained.

d. The richness of Peirce's semeiotic leads us well beyond "linguistic analysis" with its focus on stripped down conventions of formal human languages. For Peirce, these languages were one important mode of sign activity but his general theory reached out to encompass all modes of sign activity. This includes modes that explore the sign relations between and among all organisms and ultimately between organisms and the environment at large.

e. Peirce's development of what he called "critical common sensism" is, I think, an underrated feature of his work. Here he tried to make sense of how ideas can be both effective cultural guides and at the same time be open to historical criticism and development. If we take our instinctive notion of "justice," for example, we can through critical common sensism see how its use in the U.S. in the nineteenth century underwrote both slavery and systemic sexism but also, gradually, enabled abolitionists and feminists to resist these institutions. Justice as a common sense notion is general and requires ongoing historical assessment of its specific deployments. In recent years, for example, some have begun to ask if "justice" might be relevant for discussions of the lives of nonhuman animals.

## 5. What are the most important open problems in this field and what are the prospects/avenues for progress?

There are many issues Peirce considered that remain open and interesting—his account of continuity, his theory of inquiry, his structuring of the normative sciences. Three strike me as of most interest. First, Peirce described the move from perception to abductive inference as continuous. It will be interesting to see what future empirical studies have to say about this hypothesis. Second, Peirce's work in statistics and logic opened avenues for their use in dynamic and growing systems. These areas have already been developed and it would appear there are even more possibilities on this front, some of which may be foreshadowed in Peirce's writings. Finally, in both logic and scientific inquiry Peirce developed accounts of indeterminacy—generality and vagueness. These accounts, if at all accurate, hold interesting consequences both for logic and for our actual practices of inquiry and communication. Peirce's notion of vagueness, for example, can help make sense of how different cultures merge and meld historically. At cultural borders entities and practices are more likely to be both/and rather than either/or. And his notion of generality allows us to take basic ideas and allow them to grow with historical developments. So, for example, "art" has no fixed and final definition but its meaning must grow with actual developments in human experience and history. Impressionist paintings were initially excluded from the meaning of art but have come to define a special genre of art.

In closing, I think it is important not to overdetermine Peirce's work in any one direction. Its depth and range, I think, have not yet been fully explored. He was the consummate "American scholar," drawing on all of his traditions and at the same time creatively rethinking and revising them to meet the actual experiences he encountered in life.

**Some favorite readings:**

Richard Smyth, *Reading Peirce Reading*, Rowman and Littlefield, 1997.

Manley Thompson, *The Pragmatic Philosophy of C. S. Peirce*, University of Chicago Press, 1953.

Carl Hausman, *Charles S. Peirce's Evolutionary Philosophy*, Cambridge University Press, 1997.

Peter Skagestad, *The Road of Inquiry*, Columbia University Press, 1981.

**Selected Publications**

1. *Strands of System: An Introduction to the Philosophy of C. S. Peirce*, Purdue University Press, 1995.

2. *Conversations on Peirce: Reals and Ideals* (with Carl Hausman), Fordham University Press, 2012.

3. "Peirce: Pragmatism and Nature after Hegel," in *The History of Continental Philosophy*, Volume 2, ed. Alan D. Schrift, Acumen, 2010, pp. 217-238.

4. Four essays on Peirce and pragmatism in *El Pragmatismo norteamericano: un mundo de posibilidades*, Departamento de Psicoanalisis, Universidad de Antioquia, 2013. Titles: "Los Tres Gringos Ciegos," "Los Origenes del Pragmatismo: desde Peirce hasta James y Dewey," "Los Animales que Usan Signos," and "La Abduccion segun Peirce," pp. 1-102.

# 3

# Victor R. Baker

Regents' Professor (and Professor of Planetary Sciences and Geosciences)

Department of Hydrology and Water Resources, The University of Arizona

---

**1. Why were you initially drawn to Peirce?**

I was drawn to Peirce in much the same way that Peirce was drawn to philosophy. As a scientist I became interested in the things that other scientists commonly presume (without thinking about them) when they go about the business of doing their science. For me the science of interest, from my first memories, has always been geology, though I could never decide just what kind of geologist I wanted to be. Very early trips to the American Museum of Natural History possibly instilled this interest, but it was also nurtured by experiences living in and moving across various parts of the northeastern and northwestern U.S., followed by high school years in Europe. In eighth grade I made a flour-and-salt relief model of Washington state, depicting both its giant volcanic mountains and the immense network of dry channel ways cut into the basalt bedrock of its east-central plateaus. The origin of these channels would later become the subject of my Ph.D. dissertation at the University of Colorado.

While living in Germany during my high school years I traveled extensively, becoming interested in the history and cultures of Europe, as well as its geology. Greece held a particular fascination, and I probably sensed there the spirit of the place that gave birth to Western philosophy. The high-school years in Europe were followed by undergraduate university studies (in geology, of course). For my humanities emphasis (a requirement for science majors), I chose history, which is quite appropriate in that geology is the most historical of all the sciences. In this regard I think I instinctively rejected what I would later learn to be a claim made by R. G. Collingwood (in his book *The Idea of History*), who followed Hegel in asserting that geological history could not to be true history at all, in that it merely relates "events" without any connection to the history of thought. Much later I learned from Peirce that geology is all about a semiosis that is constituent of thought in a much richer and broader sense of idealism than what was understood either by Hegel or Collingwood. Time may be "events" to the physicist (and those philosophers who naively equate all "science" to physics), but to the geologist "time" is a wondrous flow of all the actual experiences of the planet, a flow through which one can gain an understanding via the "traces" of that experience in rocks, fossils, landforms, and landscapes.

In the late 1960s geology was undergoing a kind of scientific revolution. I found that the work of Thomas Kuhn was invoked in this regard, though this was more for the implied glory of being part of a "scientific revolution" than as a reflection informed by actual understanding of its philosophical relevance. Also, in the early 1960s, like the many scientists who only give very limited thought to works of philosophy, I became quite intrigued with the views of Karl Popper, which were introduced to me in an undergraduate petrology course. Popper's ideas about "bold conjectures" in science seemed to glorify the enterprise, and this had considerable appeal to one who was just getting into the nitty gritty of doing a science. Moreover, the emphasis on falsifiability, which both Popper and I later found to have been anticipated by Peirce, acted as kind of revelation to me about the importance of a philosophical perspective to the doing of one's science.

In graduate school I managed to avoid the rush to participate in the plate-tectonic "revolution" (I was always changing my mind on what kind of geology to do). Instead I was drawn back to my eighth grade fascination with those strange eastern Washington channels, which comprised a region known as the Channeled Scabland. My Ph.D. dissertation focused on what was once thought to be an outrageous hypothesis: that the Channeled Scabland had been very rapidly eroded into solid rock by immense cataclysmic flooding (see Baker, 1973). This dissertation topic was to lead me more directly to philosophical concerns, and those would eventually lead me to Peirce.

As a result of my dissertation work, I became convinced that the formulation of hypotheses, suggested by the anomalies that the scientist encounters in nature, was not just a matter of idle conjecture, but was instead the most important component of scientific reasoning. Indeed such hypothesizing was what made geology a science. However, I found that this was not the view expressed in the prevailing philosophy of science (POS) literature, and that geology was not a subject that received any attention in that literature. The latter was dominated by its presumption that physics provided the exemplar for all science. Moreover, this presumption reinforced an all-to-common prejudice among those many scientists who read superficially in the POS literature, as exemplified by Ernst Rutherford's quip: "All science is either physics or stamp collecting."

As a life-long devotee of geology, my encounters with this scientistic/physicalist attitude motivated me to learn more philosophy, and to discover in the process that nearly every well-argued philosophical viewpoint can be contrasted with a totally opposite philosophical viewpoint that is usually equally as well argued, and that this contrary viewpoint is commonly buried in those recesses of the philosophical literature that are not usually accessed by advocates for the various forms of scientistism/ physicalism. I might also add that subsequent experience made me more sympathetic to what may have motivated Rutherford and those sharing his opinions about science and physics. In thinking about the practical consequences of their viewpoint, I have observed in my many interactions with physicists that, when some actually try to do real geology, the results of their uninformed, inexperienced efforts really do indeed generally amount to the intellectual equivalent of "stamp collecting."

After my graduate work I took an appointment as an assistant professor in the Department of Geological Sciences, The University of Texas at Austin. Although I was hired to work in the area of environmental geology, a major scientific discovery in 1973 set me on a completely new track. The spacecraft Mariner 9 generated thousands of high quality images of the planet Mars. Some of those pictures revealed immense channels cut into the cratered surface of that planet. I soon became involved in the rapid development of hypotheses for the origin of features on that planet (see Baker and Milton, 1974), yet again leading to a change in my geological specialty.

As I developed an analogy between the Channeled Scabland region and the immense channeled bedrock regions of Mars (see Baker, 1978, 1982), I became even more interested in how the methodology of hypotheses worked in geology. I was fortunate to be able to interview J. Harlen Bretz, who had originally formulated the cataclysmic flooding hypothesis in the 1920s. From this I learned much about this process of hypothesizing in geology, discovering in actual geological practice what I later learned from Peirce to describe as abductive inference. I have since written much about this topic, using as a prime example the 50-year long history of scientific debates over the origin of the Channeled Scabland (see Baker 1978, 1981, 1999, 2008).

In the 1980s I moved from Texas to The University of Arizona, where I continue to be jointly appointed in 3 departments: Geosciences, Planetary Sciences, and Hydrology and Water Resources (still undecided as to what kind of geologist I want to be). My scientific work at Arizona became divided between the rapid pace of planetary discoveries, mainly involving the surfaces of Mars and Venus, and the challenge of achieving an understanding of the nature of extreme flooding phenomena on Earth, including the hazards posed to life and property. I continued to grapple with philosophical issues in geology (see Baker, 1882, 1985, 1988). Then, a critical inspiration for my philosophy of geology program came with the publication in 1988 of the English translation of a 1982 book *Theorie der Geowissenshaft* by geologist Wolf von Engelhardt and philosopher Jorge Zimmermann (Von Engelhardt and Zimmermann, 1988). This book included an extensive section entitled "Abductive Inference in the Earth Sciences" that relied heavily on methodologies described by Peirce. This provided the stimulus to set me on a search for more insights to gleaned from Peirce's writings.

The late 1980s and early 1990s were an ideal period for a philosophical outsider to get interested in Peirce studies. The 1989 Charles Sanders Peirce Sesquicentennial Congress had resulted in many new publications that did much to erase the damage that had been done to understanding Peirce, at least for outsiders like myself, by the confusing impression conveyed in the *Collected Papers*. The Peirce Edition Project was also in full operation, and beginning its monumental task of organizing all of Peirce's writings. I devoured the material that was appearing in the early 1990s, including books by Delaney (1993), Houser and Kloesel (1992), Hoopes (1991), and Ketner (1992).

Especially helpful to me in this period was the first published biography of Peirce, Joe Brent's 1993 *Charles Sanders Peirce: A Life*. Because I occasionally went to Washington, D.C., for meetings related to my NASA research and for various advisory and review panels, I was able to meet several times with Joe Brent, who was always very kind in helping with my Peirce studies. Though criticized by some of the "purists" among Peirce scholars, Brent's biographical scholarship, long delayed in its fruition by the arcane maneuverings of the academy, provided just the kind of chronological order and temporal context that allowed me to achieve a sense of the whole pattern to Peirce's thought, even though many more details would still have to be learned.

In my initial reading of Peirce's classic 1878 paper "How to Make Our Ideas Clear" I was struck, as any geologist would be, by the example that Peirce chose to use in the paragraph that followed his famous statement of the pragmatic maxim. In their beginning coursework, geologists get introduced to the simplest test for mineral identification: the scratching of one mineral by another in order to determine relative hardness. Many years later, as I sat in on a college philosophy course dealing with Peirce and pragmatism, I was struck by how much philosophical concern was expended on such a simple commonsense idea, one that becomes instinctive to any geologist: that the meaning of hardness for identifying Earth's mineral building blocks lies simply in the actual scratch testing of those minerals.

In 1996 I was invited to give a keynote address at the Hungarian Academy of Sciences at the opening of a conference of The International Association of Geomorphologists. While in Budapest I was also able to meet with Thomas Sebeok, who at the time was in residence at the Institute for Advanced Studies (Collegium Budapest). Upon hearing of my interests in regard to Peirce, Sebeok encouraged me to delve much further into both philosophy and semiotics, with the one caution that I should always let Peirce be my guide in such matters. Regrettably I had only a few such opportunities to meet with Professor Sebeok before his death in 2001.

Another encouragement for my Peirce studies came from the late Max Fisch of Indiana University. When I wrote to him in the early 1990s about my general interest in Peirce studies, Max responded with enthusiasm, providing me with a file of information relating to Peirce's very important unpublished 1897 report on a geological controversy concerning the origin of slaty cleavage in rocks. Peirce's 1897 report to the U.S. Geological Survey evaluated competing theories for the origin of slaty cleavage that had been posed by University of Wisconsin geology professor Charles Van Hise, and by his friend, the geophysicist George Becker of the U.S. Geological Survey. Peirce concluded that Becker's otherwise brilliant mathematical analysis of the problem did not invalidate the geological observations that were summarized by Van Hise.

My studies of Peirce have been immensely facilitated by the work of Peirce Edition Project in the School of Liberal Arts at Indiana University-Purdue University Indianapolis. Since 1997, when I first visited the Peirce Project, Nathan Houser has graciously facilitated my studies. On April 2, 2004, I was honored by the Peirce Project by being a part of the "Geo-thought Symposium and Peirce Monument Dedication," where I gave a lecture on "Charles S. Peirce: Earth Scientist and Logician." Reflecting upon this title, I think I have made some contributions in regard to the Earth scientist part, and I have also noted various relationships to logical/philosophical issues.

## 2. What do you consider your contribution to the field?

From the foregoing the reader will see that my perspective is not that of conventional Peirce scholars, who generally come to their subject matter as philosophers, logicians, or semioticians. Though I am outsider in regard to philosophical scholarship, I do share with Peirce the experience of having a professional career dealing with the physical aspects of Earth science. Upon receiving my B.S. college degree I was even given the civil service classification of "geophysicist" for a job with the U. S. Geological Survey. This is the same classification that Charles

Peirce would have received if his 19th century work measuring gravity for the U.S. Coastal Survey been under today's civil service classification system in what has now become the National Geodetic Survey.

Today scientists don't generally publish philosophical papers in their field's technical journals. When they do write about philosophy it is most generally in the form of essays and/or books, and often for a general audience. Physicists in particular, especially when they become more senior, do have a tendency to write philosophical articles, commonly purporting to be about science in general, though claiming that generality to be the methodology of physics. There are exceptions, of course, notably the late Stephen Jay Gould, who double majored in geology and philosophy at Antioch College. The physics bias in philosophical discourse emphasizes what scientists have to say about nature. Indeed physics can be defined as that extreme form of science that makes maximal use of mathematics to construct parsimonious theoretical statements that can subsume nature's operations under general principles. Geology, in contrast, emphasizes what nature, in all its complex particulars, has to say to the scientist. The latter, as pointed out by William Whewell, who was a former president of the Geological Society (of London), acts as the interpreter of nature's statements. What nature has to say is conveyed, to use Peirce's terminology, through indexical signs, i.e., via the rock layers, fossils, and landforms of the Earth. Geology then strives for the correct causal interpretation/ understanding of nature's signs (see Baker, 2000).

From my initial readings of Peirce I discovered that a confused understanding of inductive reasoning lay at the core of many philosophical issues in geology. By making reference to Peirce's distinctions between abduction and induction I was able to clarify general issues of how reasoning was accomplished in the Earth sciences. During a 1988 sabbatical at The University of Adelaide in Australia, I collaborated with a former undergraduate professor, C.R. Twidale, on a philosophical paper dealing with the methodologies for the science of geomorphology (see Baker and Twidale, 1991). This paper was partly motivated by questions that had occurred to me in writing earlier articles on methodologies used in hydrology (see Baker, 1982), planetary geology (see Baker, 1985), and geomorphology (see Baker, 1988). I have since continued to write many essays dealing with insights gained from Peirce in regard to methodology in geology and related subject areas (see, for example, Baker, 1993, 1998, 1999, 2000, 2007, 2012).

In tracing the history of writings by geologists about the role of hypotheses in their investigations I began to analyze the classical papers from the late 19th century that were written on the methodology of geology. Especially pertinent were works by Grove Karl Gilbert (see Baker and Pyne, 1978) and Thomas Chrowder Chamberlin, who were two of the most esteemed of American geologists of their day. What I discovered (see my 1996 paper "The Pragmatic Roots of American Quaternary Geology and Geomorphology"), was that these geologists had professional interactions with Charles Peirce, and that it is reasonable to make the abductive inference that these interactions influenced how they portrayed geological reasoning in their papers. Moreover, it is clear that Peirce himself had been influenced by geological modes of thinking through his post-college experience of 6 months under the tutelage of his father's friend, the great naturalist Louis Agassiz.

At a 1996 conference entitled "The Scientific Basis of Geomorphology" I continued with the theme of role of hypotheses as central to the reasoning by geologists. My paper from the meeting was entitled "Hypotheses and geomorphological reasoning," and it emphasized the abductive mode of inference as articulated by Peirce. One Earth scientist reviewer, an advocate of empiricist methodologies, labeled the paper "sophistry." Another reviewer, an analytic philosopher, complained that I misrepresented Galileo's methodology of science because, following Peirce, I claimed that it involved considerations of *il lume naturale*. In his anonymous commentary, this reviewer, who I later discovered was the author of a respected textbook on the philosophy of science, stated:

> I know Galileo's writings fairly well, along with a good bit of the scholarly literature. I cannot think of any place where such a notion appears, let alone plays a prominent role. A review of several relevant texts has not provided me with any evidence that such a notion played an important role in Galileo's understanding of science.

Obviously my philosopher/critic did not know of Charles Peirce's rather intensive inquiry into Galileo's methodology. Thus, I was motivated to look more closely into the issue, though my publication on this matter did not come out until much later (see my 2009 paper "Charles S. Peirce and the Light of Nature"). I found that there were interesting reasons why Galileo's reliance on *il lume naturale* was not familiar to most Galileo scholars and philosophers. The most trivial reason is simply one of bad translation, but a more interesting reason has to do with the "myth of Galileo." In this myth Galileo serves as a kind of folk-hero for modern science, particularly when "science" is equated methodologically to physics. In the myth Galileo is portrayed as the heroic proponent of employing both mathematics and experimentation for the advancement of science against the dogmatic literalists of medieval Aristotelian scholasticism. This methodology of science is commonly held up as an exemplar in introductory college physics courses.

After a long search of the Harvard libraries, to which some of Peirce's personal books were eventually deposited after his death, Jaime Nubiola (2004) apparently located Peirce's long-lost copy of the fifteen-volume edition of *Le Opere di Galileo Galilei* (Firenze edition). In volume XIII, *Dialoghi delle Nuove Scienze*, Nubiola found what seems to be Peirce's underlining of the words *il lume naturale*. Peirce had actually read the key writings of Galileo in their original form. It turns out that portions of those writings were later mistranslated and/or set aside because of the presumption that they were not really Galileo's own thoughts. Because the writings did not conform to "the myth" they were presumed to be merely Galileo's copying of scholastic nonsense.

Building upon my 1996 conference experience and my work on the methodology of geology, I made a bold move to bring the philosophy of Charles Peirce more directly to the attention of geologists. As the President of the Geological Society of America (GSA) I was provided with a unique platform at the 1998 annual meeting of the Society. In addition to making a presidential address on a theme of my choosing, I was allowed to have a short theatrical sketch performed, both to illustrate and to introduce my more formal address. I titled the address "Geosemiosis," and the full paper on the topic was subsequently published in the *Bulletin of the Geological Society of America* (see Baker, 1999). Publication was granted as a privilege to the President of the Society, thereby guaranteeing the acceptance of a philosophical paper that otherwise might have proven very difficult to place in such a prominent outlet for reaching the community of geologists. Creating a new English word for the paper's title put me right in the spirit of Charles Peirce, and the paper allowed me to outline the fundamentals of his philosophy for an audience of geologists.

Local drama students performed the theatrical sketch that I had written. The meeting was in Toronto, Canada, and my sketch magically resurrected two former presidents of The Geological Society of America, the famous Messrs. Gilbert and Chamberlin noted above, who introduced Charles S. Peirce to the audience geologists, as might have happened (in a better world) during the late 19th century. Three bearded actors presented the sketch on October 26, 1998, as follows:

**Grove Karl Gilbert:** Good evening, my fellow geologists. What a delight it is for me to be back here in Toronto. You know I was in this grand city for the very first annual meeting of The Geological Society of America. That was August 28, 1889, and I presented the second paper at that meeting. It was entitled "The Strength of the Earth's Crust". I later served twice as President of the Society, first in 1892 and then in 1909. Those who don't recognize me should think a bit about the glorious heritage of their science. But there is another thing that needs discussion here, and that is the logic, rhetoric, and grammar of your science. For this task, I can think of no better philosopher than Mr. Charles Sanders Peirce, who once corrected a logic mistake that I made in a paper that I published in 1884, but whose work became neglected in later years.

**Thomas Chowder Chamberlin:** Excuse me, Mr. Gilbert, but I believe that I deserve the honor of introducing Charles Peirce. After all, I am guilty of not getting Charles' important 1897 paper on the slaty cleavage controversy into *The Journal of Geology*, which I founded and edited. However, I did do much to show that the method of geology is the method of hypotheses, as I famously explained in my 1890 paper "Method of Multiple Working Hypotheses". This is really the pragmatic philosophy of Charles Peirce, though that work is not credited. Sadly, there have also been philosophical abuses of Mr. Peirce's insights concerning pragmatism.

**Charles Sanders Peirce:** Gentlemen, Mr. Gilbert and Mr. Chamberlin, do not quarrel. I am happy to introduce myself: Charles Sander Peirce. Yes, my work has been neglected and even misrepresented, but some modern philosophers have now come to consider me the most important philosopher of logic and science to have been born in the Western Hemisphere. I will let you in on the secret of my success in this regard. You see, I actually did science, and I did it with an unbridled passion for its objects of study, its practitioners, and its modes of inquiry. Moreover, the science that I did was Earth science, specifically the measurement of Earth's gravity for the U.S. Coast Survey. Why, I even spent 6 months learning to classify fossil brachiopods under the tutelage of the great Louis Agassiz. Now there was a man who knew the spirit of science far better than what gets conveyed by the many who continue to peddle philosophical snake oil!

### 3. What is the proper role of Peirce's work in relation to philosophy and other academic disciplines?

Peirce's work can provide critical insights in regard to the relationship between science and philosophy. The breadth of what Peirce considered to be science offers a means for unifying the process of scientific reasoning while also maintaining a kind of disunity in scientific knowledge that promotes the interdisciplinarity that affords the greatest opportunities to make discoveries. Of course, there has long been a philosophical quest to achieve a unity of all knowledge, reaching perhaps its peak in the Unity of Science program of the logical positivists. A recent resurrection of this quest appeared in E. O. Wilson's 1998 book *Consilience: The Unity of Knowledge*. Besides misrepresenting William Whewell's original concept of "consilience" the title of Wilson's book also misrepresents science in the sense that Peirce understands it. Science is not the "knowledge" that follows etymologically from its name; science is the living attitude of those who passionately inquire toward the truth of things.

Wilson's obvious enthusiasm for the spectacular advances in knowledge that are the by-products of scientific inquiry compels his vision for extending the web of causal explanation achieved in the hard sciences to the social sciences and even to the humanities. It is this ideal alignment of knowledge to which Wilson applies Whewell's term "consilience." Wilson's vision coheres with that of those who would promote a new kind of scientism, one that ultimately views science as knowledge and power. This also is the view of science that is shared by many scholars in the humanities, but it compels them to resist any such unification. One of the few philosophers to engage in debate on this issue is Richard Rorty, who observed, "...it is not clear that our answers to...moral...questions will be improved by better knowledge of how things work..." (Rorty, 1998). Rorty is certainly not the philosopher to appreciate how the insights of Charles Peirce would apply to this issue. The limited work on employing Peirce's insights to relate science and the humanities is encouraging (see Sheriff, 1994), but this has not made much impact on current debates.

The idea of science as the exemplar for all knowledge is closely related to the infatuation of philosophy of science with mathematics and physics, and a hold over from the now discredited idea that all science will ultimately reduce to physics...a view still perpetrated by those physicists who commonly turn their attention to philosophical matters in the later years of their careers. But the infatuation with mathematics and physics by philosophers goes much deeper. Philosophy has classically quested for an image of knowledge that can be universal, necessary, and certain (UNC). By being the science that most employs the methodologies of mathematics, which for Peirce is "the science that draws necessary conclusions," physics achieves the type of science that most conforms to the UNC concept of knowledge. However, this comes at a cost. Mathematics is free to draw conclusions that follow from totally unnatural presumptions, and this makes physics, despite the etymology of its name, the least natural of the natural sciences.

The infatuation with UNC knowledge is something that Peirce recognized as being decidedly contrary to the spirit of science. What can one do scientifically with UNC knowledge? By its blockage of the path of inquiry (we already know the truth, so why investigate any further) any claim of UNC knowledge becomes a violation of Peirce's "First Rule of Reason." Peirce wanted to make all forms of inquiry (including philosophy) scientific in the sense of being an attitude, not a product, but this is something that has been resisted by mainstream philosophers. It was because of attitudes like this that Peirce once observed that, given the etymology of their names, philosophy and science are like two infants who were mixed up at birth, each receiving the name of the other.

**4. What do you consider the most important topics and/or contributions in the field of Peirce studies and 5. What are the most important open problems in this field and what are the prospects/ avenues for progress?**

Peirce studies have obviously been most focused on semiotics (or Peirce's "semeiotics"), pragmatism (or Peirce's "pragmaticism"), phenomenology (or Peirce's "phaneroscopy"), logic, and the modes of inference (abduction, deduction and induction). Peirce's philosophy of science has generally received less attention from philosophers, and philosophers generally have little of the scientific experience that is necessary to understand fully Peirce's approach to philosophy. (In fairness one should add that most scientists have none of the philosophical knowledge needed to even begin to understand Peirce.) Of 250 presentations at the 2014 Charles S. Peirce International Centennial Congress less than a handful were authored by scientists of the types with whom Peirce was most closely aligned and for whom his insights would be most rewarding. Peirce was a scientist who delved more deeply, probably than any other, into questions of philosophy and logic. This in sharp contrast to the legions of philosophers whose acquaintance with science, if deep, generally is limited to physics, supplemented by some recent, limited forays into biology. Philosophy of science (POS) is an area that badly needs a transformation inspired by Peirce studies, but how can a discipline informed mainly by one extreme form of science pretend to be concerned about the fundamental issues that underlie science in general?

Consider the relationships of philosophy to geology, and to the Earth sciences more generally. Philosophical interest in these areas was not always at the low ebb that prevailed in the late 20$^{th}$ century. Moreover, many of the pre-20$^{th}$ century philosophers who gave serious attention to geology (often because they had at least some experience with its actual practice) were commonly engaged in very serious controversies about the nature of science with other philosophers, all of whom seem to have been quite ignorant about geology. Such philosophical disagreements go back at least to Aristotle, a keen observer of nature, who strongly disagreed over the nature of reality with his former mentor Plato, a believer in the mathematical perfection of the forms. Among the prominent past philosophers who produced concepts of relevance to geological thought are Gottfried Wilhelm Leibniz, who had profound disagreements with Isaac Newton; F.W.J. Schelling, whose naturalistic views contrasted sharply with those of his former colleague, G.W.F. Hegel; William Whewell, who had a major dispute over the nature of inductive reasoning with John Stuart Mill; and, of course, Charles Sanders Peirce, whose pragmatist views contrasted sharply with the logical empiricist doctrines of Bertrand Russell and the many others who came to dominate Anglo-American philosophy in the last century.

Philosophical fame at the time of above-mentioned disputes was most often accorded to those philosophers most ignorant in the ways of geology. However, in recent decades there have been major shifts in much of philosophical thinking about science. Philosophy of science has taken a "naturalistic turn" in which philosophy is no longer seen as the ideal perspective from which to view all science. Instead, philosophical naturalism holds philosophy to be a discipline that is continuous with the scientific enterprise. The philosophical infatuation with absolute truth that made for its singular focus on mathematics and physics has given way to a view that recognizes the diversity of the various sciences while trying to deal with philosophical problems in terms of the best current scientific views of the world.

Unfortunately some of the new naturalism has embraced old habits of scientism. There has developed a serious debate in the academy propelled by prominent scientists, science advocates, and naturalistic philosophers, who promote, through very high-profile books, media, and other inroads to public understanding, various metaphysical/ philosophical perspectives as though these are essential ingredients in what it is to be "scientific." This new form of scientism includes agendas that are materialisic, physicalistic, atheistic, etc., and they are commonly justified as necessary responses to the dubious claims of creationists, post-modernists, climate change deniers, and other critics of establishment "science." By claiming to possess a priori various truths attained via scientific reason, these new manifestations of scientism are totally contrary to the scientific attitude that is so ably described by Peirce, and they are likely to be damaging to the spirit of science in the long run.

What of the few attempts to draw out the philosophical problems with this outburst of scientism, notably Thomas Nagel's 2012 book, *Mind and Cosmos: Why the Materialist Neo-Darwinian Conception of Nature is Almost Certainly Wrong*? The storm of righteous criticism heaped upon Nagel's effort is not likely to encourage other voices of moderation to enter the current debate.

It seems to me that philosophy's failure here is a result of compartmentalization. At the large scale American philosophy is divided into two camps, each reflecting broader trends in the academy, rather than contributing to the generation of a common position. One trend mostly operates on the fringes of the established academic philosophy departments, finding its home among sociologists of knowledge and programs of literary criticism. This camp gets associated with the "relativist" position that provoked the much argued, though seldom illuminating "Science Wars" of the 1990s. The other camp, highly disdainful of the first, is that of the establishment, now espousing a kind of naturalism that sees philosophy as an extension of the cognitive science that builds upon materialist, reductionist, and physicalist presumptions.

The views of Peirce, extended to a modern context, would have much to criticize in regard to both these spheres. Peirce's notions of fallibilism (or "anti-cock-sureism"), critical common sensism, and anti-foundationalism hold the promise for defending a rational form of science in the face of relativism, while also avoiding the excesses engaged in by the current proponents of scientism. While some Peirce scholars are indeed pursuing this goal, I suspect that too many remain immersed in the micro-issues of a new kind of scholasticism, seeking a certainty of knowledge about what Peirce meant, when Peirce himself argued so effectively for the fruitfulness of inquiry as opposed to achieving any certainty. They continue to work on what outsiders would view as trivial. It is true that much needs to be done to make better sense of the immense body of Peirce's work, and to put together the great system of philosophy that he envisioned. However, it seems to an outsider that the Peirce scholars are bit like Hegelians in that they sense that the total perspective of Peirce's unfinished system is essential for a proper understanding of any part of the "birth of time" that will arise from the completion of that system. Does one have to wait until "the end of inquiry" to act on what should be done?

In the later twentieth century American philosophy underwent professionalism, but also a fragmentation into spheres that advanced technical rigor in proportion to their societal irrelevance (Kucklick, 2000). Just as our modern condition can be usefully criticized from both postmodern and pre-modern perspectives, current American philosophy needs criticism from considerations that both precede it and advance beyond it. The philosophical insights of Charles S. Peirce were a catalyst for the high point of American philosophy, and they could well be a catalyst for its resurrection.

There is so much to be done. There is the scholarship of Peirce's life and the subsequent legacy of his work. How has this work truly influenced other scholars, some of whom many have inadvertently (or purposefully) neglected to acknowledge that influence? There are insights to be gained from Peirce in regard to economics, morality, and religion. From Peirce it is clear that much of our politics and related policy work is replete with fake and sham reasoning, relying on the methods of authority and tenacity, while eschewing any commitment to authentic scientific reasoning for the fixation of belief. Science itself is being misrepresented as a kind of authority. The meanings of fallibilism and critical common sensism are completely alien to modern culture. Many scientists continue to think of their activity as based in premises derived from the philosophical viewpoints of the 1960s, particularly those of logical empiricism and/or Popperian falsificationism. Very few are aware that these doctrines have been largely discredited by relatively recent philosophical advances, many of which were foreseen and rather strongly expressed by Peirce in an earlier century.

Finally, the insights of Charles S. Peirce need to be made more known to the broad audience of the potentially interested public. How can Peirce scholars be satisfied with the current state of affairs in which the most widely read introduction of Peirce's ideas is the deeply flawed account provided by Henry Menard's Pulitzer-Prize-winning 2001 book *The Metaphysical Club*?

**References**

Brent, J. *Charles Sanders Peirce: A Life*. Bloomington, Indiana University Press, 1993.

Collingwood, R. G. *The Idea of History*. Oxford, The Clarendon Press, 1946.

Delaney, C. F. *Science, Knowledge, and Mind: A Study in the Philosophy of C. S. Peirce*. Notre Dame, University of Notre Dame Press, 1993.

Hauser, N., and C. Kloesel (eds.) *The Essential Peirce: Selected Philosophical Writings, Volume I (1867-1893)*. Bloomington, Indiana University Press, 1992.

Hoopes, J. (ed.) *Peirce on Signs: Writings on Semiotic by Charles Sanders Peirce*. Chapel Hill, University of North Carolina Press, 1991.

Ketner, K. L. (ed.) *Reasoning and the Logic of Things: The Cambridge Conferences Lectures of 1898*. Cambridge, Harvard University Press, 1992.

Kuklick, B. *A History of Philosophy in America: 1720-2000*. Oxford: Oxford University Press, 2000.

Menand, L. *The Metaphysical Club: A Story of Ideas in America*. New York: Farrar, Straus and Giroux, 2001.

Nagel, T., 2013, The core of 'Mind and Cosmos' New York Times Opinion Page The Stone August 18, 2013

Nagel, T. *Mind and Cosmos: Why the Materialist Neo-Darwinian Conception of Nature is Almost Certainly False*. Oxford: Oxford University Press, 2012.

Nubiola, J. "Il lume naturale: Abduction and God." *Semiotiche*. I/2: 91-102.

Rorty, R. "Against Unity." *Wilson Quarterly*. 20: 38.

Sheriff, J. K. *Charles Peirce's Guess at the Riddle: Grounds for Human Significance*. Bloomington, Indiana University Press, 1994.

Von Engelhardt, W., and Zimmermann, J. *Theory of Earth Science*. Cambridge, Cambridge University Press, 1988.

Wilson, E. O. *Consilience: The Unity of Knowledge*. New York: Alfred E. Knopf, 1998.

**Selected Authored Books**

Baker, V.R. *Paleohydrology and Sedimentology of Lake Missoula Flooding in Eastern Washington*. Geological Society of America Special Paper 144, 1973.

Baker, V.R. *The Channels of Mars*. Austin, Texas, University of Texas Press, 1982.

**Selected Edited Books**

Baker, V.R. (ed,) *Catastrophic Flooding: The Origin of the Channeled Scabland*. Stroudsburg, Pennsylvania, Hutchinson Ross, 1981.

Baker, V.R. (ed.) *Rethinking the Fabric of Geology*. Geological Society of America Special Paper 502, 2013.

**Selected Articles**

"Erosion by catastrophic floods on Mars and Earth." (with D. J. Milton) *Icarus*. 23: 27-41, 1974

"The Spokane Flood Controversy and the Martian Outflow Channels." *Science*. 202: 1249-1256, 1978.

"G.K. Gilbert and Modern Geomorphology." (With S. J. Pyne) *American Journal of Science*. 278: 97-123, 1978.

Geology, Determinism, and Risk Assessment." In *Scientific Basis of Water-Resource Management*, 109-117. Washington: National Academy Press, 1982

"Models of Fluvial Activity on Mars." In M. Woldenberg, M. (ed.), *Models in Geomorphology*, 287-312. London: Allen and Unwin, 1985.

"Geological Fluvial Geomorphology." *Geological Society of America Bulletin*. 100 1157- 1167, 1988.

"The Reenchantment of Geomorphology." (with C. R. Twidale) *Geomorphology*. 4: 73-100, 1991.

"Uncertainty and Tolerance in Science and Decision-making." *Arizona Journal of International and Comparative Law*. 9: 253-258, 1992.

"Extraterrestrial Geomorphology: Science and Philosophy of Earthlike Planetary Landscapes." *Geomorphology*. 7: 9-35, 1993.

"The Pragmatic Roots of American Quaternary Geology and Geomorphology." *Geomorphology*. 16: 197-215, 1996.

"Hypotheses and Geomorphological Reasoning." In B. L. Rhoads, and C.E. Thorn (eds.), *The Scientific Nature of Geomorphology*, 57- 85. New York: Wiley, 1996.

"Hydrological understanding and societal action." *Journal of the American Water Resources Association*. 4: 819-825, 1998.

"Catastrophism and Uniformitarianism: Logical Roots and Current Relevance in Geology." In D. J. Blundell, and A. C. Scott (eds) *Lyell: The Past is the Key to the Present*, 171-182. Geological Society of London, Special Publication 143, 1998.

"Geosemiosis." *Geological Society of America Bulletin*.111: 633-646, 1999.

"The Methodological Beliefs of Geologists." *Earth Sciences History*. 18: 321-335, 1999.

"Let Earth Speak!" In J.S. Sneidermann (ed.), *The Earth Around Us: Maintaining a*

*Livable Planet*, 358-367. New York: Freeman, 2000.

"Conversing with the Earth: The Geological Approach to Understanding." In R. Frodeman (ed.), *Earth Matters: The Earth Sciences, Philosophy, and the Claims of Community*, 1-10. New Jersey: Prentice-Hall, 2000.

"Flood Hazard Science, Policy and Values: A Pragmatist Stance." *Technology in Society*. 29: 161-168, 2007.

The Spokane Flood Debates: Historical Background and Philosophical Perspective." In R. Grapes, D. Oldroyd, and A. Grigelis (eds.), *History of Geomorphology and Quaternary Geology*, 33-50. Geological Society of London Special Publication 301, 2008.

"Charles S. Peirce and the Light of Nature." In G. D. Rosenberg (ed.), *Scientific Revolution in Geology from the Renaissance to the Enlightenment*, 259-266. Geological Society of America Special Paper 203, 2009.

"Terrestrial Analogs, Planetary Geology, and the Nature of Geological Reasoning." *Planetary and Space Science*. vhttp://dx.doi.org/10.1016/j.pss.2012.10.008, 2012.

# 4

# Mats Bergman

Research Fellow
Academy of Finland

---

**1. Why were you initially drawn to Peirce?**
Peirce sometimes said that he was drawn to the study of logic because of his lack of natural aptitude for practical reasoning, the idea being that inquisitive minds are bound to be intrigued by such deficiencies in themselves. He may have been only half-serious, but I believe that there is something to this. I have never been a great communicator; yet from a very early stage, my studies gravitated toward questions of communication. And that was the path that led me to Peirce.

Having gone through the usual youthful flirtation with Nietzsche and having pretended to understand fashionable French philosophers in the first year of my philosophy studies, I began to settle for the rationalism of Jürgen Habermas as a reasonable alternative to analytic philosophy (which did not seem to be really interested in my questions) and continental thought (which seemed to have little interest in answers). Unfair to all concerned, of course. Still, it was through Habermas that I was initially exposed to Peirce. The first book on Peirce that I read was Karl-Otto Apel's account of the development of Peirce's pragmaticism. My first Peirce texts must – predictably enough – have been "The Fixation of Belief" and "How to Make Our Ideas Clear". Later, I realised that several prominent Finnish philosophers – Jaakko Hintikka and Ilkka Niiniluoto in particular – held Peirce in high esteem, and that philosophical pragmatism had a Finnish champion in Sami Pihlström, who eventually became the supervisor of my PhD thesis in philosophy.

There was also a quite different source for my interest in Peirce in the early days. After a couple of years of undergraduate studies in philosophy, I decided that I needed something more practical – that is, something that could someday lead to a paying job – and enrolled in the communication studies programme at the University of Helsinki. In those days, semiotics was all the rage (at least in Helsinki); the required reading for the entrance examination was John Fiske's *Introduction to Communication Studies*. Fiske's account of semiotics was partial at best; but again, I stumbled upon that mysterious figure of Peirce, albeit in the form of a rather diluted presentation of icons, indices, and symbols (as far as I can recall). When I later discovered that Fiske had written a scathing dismissal of the relevance of Peircean sign theory, I felt that something needed to be done. This led to my Master's thesis in communication studies, a few years after completing my philosophy thesis – also on Peirce, of course.

Although my initial struggles to understand Peirce were relatively solitary (and frequently misguided) affairs, I did gradually realise that Peirce studies is – or at least should be – a communal enterprise. My bond with Peirce was certainly strengthened in 1997, when I discovered the existence of a group of likeminded scholars at the University of Helsinki, just as they were forming the Helsinki Metaphysical Club. The Helsinki branch of this august institution is still operative, making it the longest-running Metaphysical Club of all time – at least that I know of.

Then there is the question of what it is that still makes me return to his writings, again and again, after all these years. I have certainly tried to resist the lure of Peirce at times, and looked hard for inspiration elsewhere as well. That is only healthy, I suppose. Yet, as soon as I read Peirce there is an enthralment that I do not feel with hardly any other philosophical texts. In part, the charm is aesthetic – which, given Peirce's reputation for generating abstruse jargon and his self-professed lack of literary gift, may seem a bit odd. But at his best, Peirce can be as elegant in expression as in thought. I must confess that the more archival aspect of Peirce research also holds some appeal for me; the notoriously labyrinthine character of Peirce's manuscripts offers some fascinating puzzles, if one is so inclined. Yet, the ultimate attraction of Peirce as a thinker must be the fact that with him one is in the company of a genuine inquirer, more interested in finding things out than in constructing a maximally defensible position. With Peirce, one may set out to craft the optimal definition of logic and along the way discover that that requires a general account of signs. One may end up more puzzled than before, but mostly in a good way. In spite of his many shortcomings – he was only human, after all – there is an intellectual honesty in Peirce's explorations that is truly engaging. At its best, it is almost like being invited into discussion with a great mind - not as an audience, but as a fellow-inquirer.

## 2. What do you consider your contribution to the field?

My modest contributions to Peirce studies have mainly focused on questions of communication from a Peircean perspective. I suppose that I – along with James Liszka, Vincent Colapietro, and a handful of others – have done something for the recovery and development of

Peirce's rhetoric. If nothing else, I have at least tried to draw attention to the significance of the often ignored rhetorical/methodeutic part of Peirce's sign-theoretical project. I hope that I have also been able to contribute something of value to the controversial question of Peirce's intellectual development, in particular with regard to the emergence of his sign theory.

Along the way, I think I have also made some minor discoveries that may provide some missing pieces of the Peircean puzzle. For example, I have recently worked on questions of Peirce's seemingly anomalous anthropomorphism. Peirce scholars tend to gloss over his approval of an anthropomorphic stance, but I genuinely believe that it is a principle on par with fallibilism in Peirce's general scheme of inquiry. At the very least, increased attention to Peirce's defence of anthropomorphism can cast light on some neglected aspects of the early history of pragmatism, which is perhaps more complex than the standard stories lead us to believe. After all, not too many are aware that Peirce considered F. C. S. Schiller to be the pragmatist closest to himself, with the possible exception of Josiah Royce.

On a more concrete level, I think that I have done some archival work that may benefit the broader research community. Also, I might mention the new version of the web site *Commens* (http://www.commens.org), which is set to be launched in the centennial year of 2014 as a "Digital Companion". I hope it will prove to be useful as a research tool and publication platform.

## 3. What is the proper role of Peirce's work in relation to philosophy and other academic disciplines?

This is a very difficult question. Peirce was obviously a pioneer in many fields of philosophy – sign theory, graphical logic, pragmatism, the theory of abduction, phenomenology (phaneroscopy) – as well as in other lines of inquiry. In many cases, we have not caught up with him yet. Yet, Peirce's approach is not easily reducible to the big questions of today. Although I can understand – and partly sympathise with – efforts to relate Peirce to contemporary concerns in epistemology and metaphysics, there is also a risk that we may lose something unique along the way. There are certainly aspects of Peirce that fit our conception of the archetypical analytic philosopher; but there are other sides of him that look more "continental" – to use this rather worn-out division. Perhaps one of the greatest potentials in Peirce's approach lies in the way it transcends many presumed boundaries, and can open up genuinely new perspectives for philosophical study.

So, Peirce's relationship to philosophy and other disciplines is somewhat paradoxical. On the one hand, one often finds many striking affinities between Peirce and later thought; on the other hand, he cuts an almost *sui generis* figure. As an avowed anti-individualist, he would perhaps not have liked the latter assessment; but I think the facts speak for themselves in this case. At the same time, it is prudent to remind ourselves that Peirce saw himself as a part of a broader community of inquiry, in both an ideal and a historical sense. I know of hardly any other major thinker who would have put down as much effort into meticulous reconstructions of scientific reasoning from different epochs. Peirce was well-versed in historical phases of philosophy that most philosophers chose (and still choose) to ignore; and he was certainly more than ready to give credit to his predecessors, sometimes emphasising that the radical originality of some idea was typically an indication that the idea in question was radically false.

So, what could the "proper role" of Peirce's thought be? His accomplishments are innovative, but also deeply connected to earlier, contemporary, and later work in philosophy and the sciences. Self-effacingly, Peirce sometimes characterised himself as a mere backwoodsman, clearing the way for potential future travellers; in a more assertive mood, he occasionally compared his contributions to those of Aristotle. In another self-evaluation, he placed himself on approximately the same footing as Leibniz in the history of thought. This may be a fair assessment as far as it goes; yet, I believe that Peirce is still in many respects undervalued, in both philosophy and other disciplines. He really should be celebrated as one of the foremost truth-seekers of the relatively recent past.

Peirce was an explorer and experimentalist in the best sense of the word. Indeed, some of Peirce's discoveries can look almost inadvertent, things he happened to stumble across in his primary pursuit of logic. It is arguably Peirce's intellectual openness that renders his thought more applicable to diverse disciplines than many other philosophies. But one should of course keep in mind that this is not *always* a strength; there are undeniably many bad applications of Peirce available in the academic marketplace.

### 4. What do you consider the most important topics and/or contributions in the field of Peirce studies?

The only honest answer would be: too many to mention. From a strictly personal point of view, the award for most important areas of research would have to go to Peirce's *Theory of Signs* and pragmati(ci)sm; but obvious contenders include the theory of categories, the existential graphs, and his account of abductive reasoning – among many others. One of the key questions of Peirce scholarship concerns the development of Peirce's philosophical system – and, inevitably, the precise nature of that system. This has been a central topic in the field at least since the 1961 publication of Murray Murphey's *The Development of Peirce's Philosophy*; and I suspect the developmental controversy will be with us for a long time to come. It would also be possible to identify numerous more specific scholarly topics of relevance, such as questions concerning the proper status of the 'New List' in Peirce's oeuvre or the significance of Peirce's varying attempt to prove pragmatism. Although perhaps not a major question for many Peirce scholars, I think that the connection between rhetoric and methodeutic is a significant topic. The way we understand this relationship, and the role of rhetoric/methodeutic in Peirce's sign-theoretical project, will certainly affect our understanding of the character and potential upshots of his endeavour. T. L. Short has challengingly contended that it – or at least the semeiotic bit – is all *for* methodeutic and rhetoric, which in my view boils down to the suggestion that the ultimate reason for doing Peircean philosophy is improvement of habits of inquiry and communication – a claim that, in spite of appearances, does not conflict with Peirce's emphatic rejection of utilitarian validations of science. And the relationship between inquiry and communication is another – perhaps not immediately obviously Peircean – topic on which Peirce's approach casts interesting light.

## 5. What are the most important open problems in this field and what are the prospects/avenues for progress?

Of the topics listed above, most are still in fact open problems. The question of Peirce's development continues to be debated, sometimes quite hotly. The explication of the role of semeiotic within Peirce's system – if we accept that he had one (or several) – is another example of an unresolved issue in Peirce studies, in spite of impressive efforts by some of the best Peirce scholars. Similarly, the systemic role of the existential graphs involves many open questions, not to speak of the numerous issues concerning the precise relationship between Peirce's semiotic philosophy and his most technical work in logic. Some consider the proof of pragmatism to have been satisfactorily established; I have some doubts about the feasibility of providing such a demonstration (admittedly a rather un-Peircean position).

Personally, I find two areas of Peirce studies to be of particular interest at the moment. One is the question of the relationship between rhetoric and methodeutic, referred to above (and related issues concerning the scope of rhetoric/methodeutic and their respective applicability). The other is Peirce's logic of vagueness, on which some solid work is being done, perhaps for the first time since Jarrett Brock's groundbreaking efforts. I feel that there is a connection between Peirce's rhetoric and his logic of vagueness (or, perhaps more accurately, his semiotic of indeterminacy), which has not been fully articulated yet, and which is likely to open up some new tracks of research in the future.

Finally, it is perhaps appropriate to point out one of the biggest problems for the field – one that is surely blocking the path of inquiry and diminishing the prospects of Peirce research. I am of course referring to the availability of the primary materials, that is, Peirce's writings. Scholars need to be given open access to them as soon as possible; for as Peirce once pointed out, nothing is properly speaking scientific unless it is *made* public – by which he meant that it should be concretely available for study, criticism, and further communication. As we are now in the centennial year of his death, it is imperative that his manuscripts, steadily decomposing in the archives, be saved for future generations in print and on line. This is one of the most critical challenges facing the collective Peirce community.

**Selected Publications**

Bergman, M. (2013). Fields of Rhetoric: Inquiry, Communication, and Learning. *Educational Philosophy and Theory*, 45(7), 737-754.

Bergman, M. (2012). Improving Our Habits: Peirce and Meliorism. In C. de Waal & K. P. Skowronski (eds.), *The Normative Thought of Charles S. Peirce* (pp. 125–148). New York: Fordham University Press.

Bergman, M. (2012). Charles S. Peirce: Signs of Inquiry. In J. Hannan (Ed.), *Philosophical Profiles in the Theory of Communication* (pp. 409-436). New York: Peter Lang.

Bergman, M. (2011). Beyond the Interaction Paradigm? Radical Constructivism, Universal Pragmatics, and Peircean Pragmatism. *The Communication Review*, 14(3), 96-122.

Bergman, M. (2010). Serving Two Masters: Peirce on Pure Science, Useless Things, and Practical Applications. In M. Bergman, S. Paavola, A.-V. Pietarinen, & H. Rydenfelt (eds.), *Ideas in Action: Proceedings of the Applying Peirce Conference* (pp. 17-37). Helsinki: Nordic Pragmatism Network.

Bergman, M. (2010). C. S. Peirce on Interpretation and Collateral Experience. *Signs*, 3, 134 -161.

Bergman, M. (2010). Productive Signs: Improving the Prospects of Peirce's Rhetoric. *Signs*, 3, 54-68.

Bergman, M. (2009). *Peirce's Philosophy of Communication: The Rhetorical Underpinnings of the Theory of Signs*. London: Continuum.

Bergman, M. (2009). Experience, Purpose, and the Value of Vagueness: On C. S. Peirce's Contribution to the Philosophy of Communication. *Communication Theory*, 19(3), 248–277.

Bergman, M. (2007). Development, Purpose, and the Spectre of Anthropomorphism. *Transactions of the Charles S. Peirce Society*, 43(4), 601-609.

Bergman, M. (2007). The Secret of Rendering Signs Effective: The Import of C. S. Peirce's Semiotic Rhetoric. *The Public Journal of Semiotics*, 1(2), 2-11.

Bergman, M. (2007). Representationism and Presentationism. *Transactions of the Charles S. Peirce Society*, 43(1), 53-89.

Bergman, M. (2007). Common Grounds and Shared Purposes: On Some Pragmatic Ingredients of Communication. *Cognitio*, 8(1), 23-43.

Bergman, M. (2006). Common Experience, Scientific Intelligence, and the Literary Spirit: Reflections on Charles S. Peirce's Conception of Philosophy. In H. Koskinen et al. (eds.), *Science – A Challenge to Philosophy?* (pp. 15–25). Frankfurt am Main: Peter Lang.

Bergman, M. (2005). C. S. Peirce's Dialogical Conception of Sign Processes. *Studies in Philosophy and Education*, 24, 213–233.

Bergman, M. (2004). *Fields of Signification: Explorations in Charles S. Peirce's Theory of Signs*. Vantaa: Dark.

Bergman, M. (2003). Peirce's Derivations of the Interpretant. *Semiotica*, 144(1/2), 1-17.

Bergman, M. (2000). *Meaning and Mediation: Toward a Communicative Interpretation of Peirce's Theory of Signs*. Helsinki: Department of Communication.

Bergman, M. (2000). Reflections of the Role of the Communicative Sign in Semeiotic. *Transactions of the Charles S. Peirce Society*, XXXVI(2), 225-254.

# 5

# Vincent Colapietro

Professor of Philosophy
Department of Philosophy, The Pennsylvania State University

---

A CLOSE(R) ENCOUNTER OF THE SECOND KIND

### 1. Why were you initially drawn to Peirce?

My "first" encounter with Charles Peirce was in graduate school (in fact, the first semester of my first year of graduate studies). But I had already read at least three essays by him – "The Fixation of Belief," "How to Make Our Ideas Clear," and "Evolutionary Love." Just as it is possible to meet a flesh-and-blood human being without the event being hardly memorable, so it is possible to read an author without having the experience being noteworthy, let alone transformative. Though I was especially struck by Peirce's metaphorical characterization of my mother tongue (English as "a pirate-lingo") and his equally arresting metaphor regarding the cultivation of philosophical ideas,[1] my earliest exposure to his writings was glancing and superficial. The fault was mine, not Peirce's: *I* was not ready to register the force of his arguments or even the salience of his questions to my lines of query. Having been trained in classical Greek thought and being principally preoccupied with contemporary European philosophy (in particular, Husserl, Heidegger, Jaspers, Sartre, de Beauvoir, and Camus), his concerns were mostly not mine and, of greater importance, his manner of addressing those concerns were for the most part quite distant from my own.

In my estimation, at least, William James exaggerates in "On a Certain Blindness in Human Beings" when he asserts: "The occasion and the experience ... are nothing. It all depends on the capacity of the soul to be grasped, to have its life-currents absorbed by what is given." Our experience itself however testifies to the significance of the occasion and whatever happens to be encountered in our experience. What grasps us, we feel, does so partly by *its* presence or power. Even so, the

---

[1] "It is not by dealing out cold justice to the circle of my ideas that I can make hem grow, but by cherishing and tending them as I would the flowers in my garden" (*Essential Peirce*, volume 1, p. 354).

capacity or readiness of the psyche to be grasped by what is encountered cannot be overlooked.

In my own case, my "first" encounter with Peircean texts (the one wherein I began truly to be transformed and reoriented by this singular genius) was strictly speaking not my initial exposure. As a result of this subsequent, genuine encounter, I was drawn to the author of these texts, first and foremost, because he not only championed but also exemplified a communal form of experimental inquiry in which philosophical questions were to be addressed with the painstaking care but also the speculative imagination of an uncompromising experimentalist. Here was a thinker who appeared to me to possess an interior understanding of experimental inquiry, one who grasped the logic of science, but did so precisely because he appreciated the *history* of the sciences.

The revolution wrought by Thomas Kuhn was, I discovered very quickly, one already inaugurated by Charles Peirce. I did not however appreciate initially just how critical or central history was to his exploration of science and indeed other topics, but I did sense that Peirce was a contemporary of mine (at least in part) by virtue of being, among other things, an archivist and student of the past. Only such a student is in a position to comprehend the past as living and life itself as an integral phase in an ongoing history.

## 2. What do you consider your contribution to the field?

It is hard, if not impossible, for me to identify my contribution to the study of Peirce. And the main reason is in fact Peircean or, more accurately, Emersonian (though in this instance the Peircean and the Emersonian sensibility coincide). There is a line from Emerson's poem "The Sphinx" to which Peirce was drawn, time and again: "Of thy eye, I am eyebeam." By this beam of vision, the eye sees what is other than itself and only in unusual circumstances does it catch a glimpse of itself. At least, this is Peirce's assessment.[2] "Each man has," he insists, "an identity which far transcends the mere animal; – an essence, a *meaning* as subtle as it may be. He cannot know his own essential significance; of his eye it is eyebeam" (*CP* 7.591). In my case, this significance is bound up with my contribution: I am in possibly the worst imaginable position to ascertain the one or the other.

Even so, my sense is that my monograph on Peirce[3] has been widely read. Many, perhaps most, scholars would identify this as my main

---

[2] This accords with his tendency to quote approvingly the lines from Shakespeare's *Measure for Measure*: " ... proud man,/Most ignorant of what he is most assured,/His glassy essence" (see, e.g., *Essential Peirce*, volume 1, p. 55).

[3] *Peirce's Approach to the Self: A Semiotic Perspective on Human Subjectivity* (Albany, NY: State University of New York Press, 1989).

contribution to the study of Peirce. But my interest in his account of selfhood or subjectivity, as the subtitle of that work suggests, is of a piece with my preoccupation with Peirce's semeiotic. In turn, I take his general theory of signs to be one of the very best exemplifications of the heuristic function of his categories. In my judgment, at any rate, the function of Peirce's categories is to goad and guide inquiry, not least of all by opening new fields of experimental investigation. This function is nowhere more evident than in Peirce's efforts to map a vast territory and, then, to explore expanses of this terrain. With respect to semeiotic, I am especially interested in the third and culminating branch of Peirce's semeiotic – speculative rhetoric or, as he tended in later years to identify this part of his theory of signs – *methodeutic*.

While Peirce bemoaned "the merciless way that words have to expect when they fall into literary clutches" ("What Pragmatism Is"), I have tried to show the *merciful* way in which his texts might be treated when they fall into my own admittedly literary hands.[4] Just as Peirce devoted himself to the history of science before most philosophers appreciated the relevance of this study to an adequate understanding of the intergenerational work of experimental inquirers, so too he preoccupied himself with the *rhetoric* of science before most theorists, philosophical or otherwise, had any inkling of there even being such a thing. My animating hope is to bring the rhetorical and even poetic dimensions of Peirce's philosophical writings into critical focus without in the least sacrificing their rigorous philosophical character or their avowed experimentalist orientation. I do not know whether anyone would identify *this* as my contribution to the study of Peirce, but I remain hopeful that someday this might come to be seen as one of my accomplishments.

### 3. What is the proper role of Peirce's work in relation to philosophy and other academic disciplines?

It is certainly ironic that such an anti-foundationalist as Peirce has been regarded by so many of his champions as providing a foundation for not only philosophy but also an array of other disciplines. In my judgment, Peirce's writings are nothing more, but also nothing less, than an invaluable resource for responsible inquirers in diverse fields. The relevance of Peirce's semeiotic to a number of disciplines cannot be gainsaid, yet his categoreal framework as a heuristic resource is no less important.

---

[4] I do not mean to imply that I am especially gifted in this regard, only that my formal training has been primarily historical, hermeneutical, and in a broad sense "literary," rather than strictly scientific.

## 4. What do you consider the most important topics and/or contributions in the field of Peirce studies?

Peirce's encompassing vision of philosophical inquiry helps us to identify the most important topics to be addressed by responsible inquirers. These topics range from phenomenology (or phaneroscopy) to ontology, through the distinct domains of normative discourse.

The most important of these topics are best conceived in reference to contemporary thought, without reducing Peirce's writings to being more or less novel answers to *our* customary questions. More often than not, the value of Peirce's philosophy resides in helping us to frame more fruitful and important questions than contemporary fashions invite, *not* in providing ingenious answers to what from a Peircean perspective are frequently suspect questions.

## 5. What are the most important open problems in this field and what are the prospects/avenues for progress?

The most obvious and pressing problem yet to be adequately addressed by contemporary philosophers (not merely interpreters of Peirce) concerns non-reductive naturalism. But to reduce Peirce to a non-reductive naturalist is itself almost certainly an injustice. However much his unabashed commitment to traditional theism might embarrass many of his contemporary admirers, there it is: this commitment cannot be wished away. This disposes me to identify the most important open question not exclusively in terms of naturalism but conjunctively in terms of theism (i.e., to conjoin the two in the very identification or formulation of this question). Given the emergent focus of contemporary debates and the central concerns of Peirce's intellectual life, then, we ought to consider carefully the extent to which forms of traditional theism, poetically interpreted, are compatible with what is even now an unorthodox form of naturalism, rigorously conceived.

Perhaps connected to this, however remotely, there is also the open question of the relationship between experimental intelligence and narrative consciousness. Experimental intelligence can learn from its exertions only insofar as it can gather these, along with their antecedent conditions and various consequences (intended and otherwise, in a frame of a comprehensive narrative. In brief, experimental intelligence seems to be depended on narrative consciousness (as an experimental inquirer, I *did* this and the result was otherwise than expected – or precisely as predicted).

This point can be seen as directing us to one of the central preoccupation of contemporary philosophy – defining the limits, scope, nature, function, and origin of rationality. The pragmatist critique of human rationality (especially the more overweening forms of philosophical reason, e.g., the a priori capacity to obtain apodictic certainty regarding fundamental matters) might be taken to result in the rejection of the classical conception of λόγος or, alternatively, to drive toward a radical reconstruction of this conception. For some, espousing the pragmatist understanding of experimental intelligence entails jettisoning the classical conception of human rationality; while for others this espousal enforces no such abandonment. In any event, Peirce was self-consciously a descendent of Aristotle, for whom the powerful wings of speculative imagination and a painstaking eye for minute detail are equally needed by the responsible inquirer.

In the end (and at every step along the way), λογος needs to be rejoined to μυθος, in various ways. For Peirce, this involved envisioning himself, precisely as a scientist, engaged in a form of worship, also playing a part in the drama of creation. At the very least, scientific knowledge is from a Peircean perspective a moral achievement (cf. John E. Smith 1992, 117); whether or not it is also a religious accomplishment remains an open question. But it is one of countless such questions and, more than anything else, the depth and quality of our questions define the value and vitality of our philosophy.

When Herbert Spencer died on December 8th, 1903, during the course of a series of Peirce's lectures, the lecturer took occasion to mark the loss of this figure. As part of his tribute to Spencer, Peirce suggested: "When philosophy becomes an adult science, as it will before the twentieth century is half over, the first question to be asked in weighing the importance of any philosopher will be what important truths did he *prove*, in the sense in which truths of philosophy can be proved" (MS 470, 38; quoted by Max H. Fisch 1986, 362). But is this so? Is not the very first question to be asked in this connection "What fruitful questions did this theorist pose?" rather than "What important truths did this philosopher prove?"?[5] The force of a thinker's arguments are of great importance, but no greater than the fecundity and timeliness of that inquirer's *questions*. The fruits by which inquirers are known and indeed to be judged are as much the expansive power of their questions as the logical force of their arguments. For example, when Peirce asks how laws, the means by which we can explain phenomena, are themselves to be explained, he explodes the boundaries of traditional inquiry and points in a promising direction.

In conclusion, then, three points especially merit emphasis. *First*, Peirce's categories are goads and guides for inquiry. What he has to

---

[5] I am grateful to Ahti-Veikko Pietarinen for suggesting that philosophical questions (or question-answer sequences) might be taken as "important 'parts' of proofs, widely conceived, kinds of abductive steps in the argument, not necessarily two different things (e-mail correspondence, April 29, 2014). While I am disposed to agree with this point, the continuum stretching from questions as invitations for abductive inferences to ones tightly integrated into a sequence of questions and answers (this sequence itself constituting a "part" of a "proof") seems an expansive one.

teach us, more than anything else, is *how* to ask ever more fruitful questions and, moreover, how to be responsive to the fecund guesses of the largely unlawful art of our heuristic imaginations. The extent to which our imagination might be focused and disciplined, without being stultified or otherwise maimed, is itself an open question. Peirce's elaboration and defense of his categories offers invaluable suggestions for how such a delicate task might be executed.

*Second*, his abiding commitment to systematic philosophy provides an exemplification for how the work of systematic inquiry might escape the snares of a philosophical system. Far too often, a philosophical system stands as a monument to a vainglorious ego aggressively committed to defending the inviolable integrity of an elaborate structure of conceptual architecture. It is one thing to be committed to being a systematic inquirer, quite another being devoted to the construction of a philosophical system (cf. Weissman). To be sure, the systematic philosopher cannot avoid constructing, in some sense, a philosophical system. But such a philosopher, as a philosopher, must be attentive to the extent to which the impulse to be as consistent, comprehensive, and adequate to experience as possible carries within itself a drive toward closure, finality, and insularity. A philosophical system is not a conceptual fortress to be defended but rather a heuristic framework to be deployed and, as the inevitable consequence of its conscientious deployment, a working orientation to be refined, modified, and in some respects rejected.

Charles Peirce was a systematic philosopher who nonetheless was deeply suspicious of those monomaniacal minds enthralled by their own philosophical systems (see, e.g., *CP* 6.7). The architectonic character of his own endeavor is accordingly not more important than his deep doubts about systematicity. Unquestionably, inquiry must be systematic. But when the spirit of system,[6] to use George Santayana's meritorious expression, is divorced from the spirit of inquiry, system becomes an end in itself rather than the form of an open-ended undertaking in which the twists and turns of an unpredictable history inevitably result in radical modifications of what is in essence a living thing. The life of inquiry is one with the growth of inquiry and, in turn, this growth is one with transformation and even abandonment (cf. R. W. Emerson's "Circles").

---

[6] "The spirit of system, though it so often renders the mind fanatical and obdurately blind to some facts, is" Santayana states in *The Realms of Being*, "essentially an effort to give all facts their due, not to forget things once discovered and understood, and not to leave illusions and vices unchallenged" (p. 107). At the very least, this spirit is the drive to be as consistent and comprehensive as humanly possible. As Santayana notes, "consistency is but a form of honour and courage" (ibid.).

*Finally*, the appeal to experience is the appeal by a practitioner to the disclosures resulting from an engagement in some historically defined practice or, at least, a historically emergent form such as organic life itself. The irreducible heterogeneity of human practices however means that the disclosures evident in the context of one practice need to be squared with the disclosures manifest in various other contexts (cf. Bruno Latour). Philosophy does both itself and the cosmos a disservice when it uncritically privileges certain forms of disclosure and, thereby, dismisses or (worse) rejects out of hand other forms.

Nothing is truer than true poetry (*EP* 2, 193). But nothing is more reliable than the painstaking results of experimental investigation. The disclosures of the one bear upon those of the other. At the very least, they do so for the open-minded. We make our task all too simple and indeed all too trivial and trifling if make the differential context of scientific inquiry, especially when conceived exclusively in reference to the physical sciences, the *sole* context of noteworthy disclosures. My initial "encounter" with several of Peirce's philosophical essays did not amount to an actual encounter because I took Peircean pragmatism to be yet another example of scientific reductivism. But I rather soon thereafter came to realize that the scope of his philosophical vision extends beyond the limits of the physical sciences, though it demands an interior understanding of those exceedingly complex undertakings. And ever after I have been surprised by just how expansive and penetrating is that vision, regarding not only the logic of science but also other important domains of human experience.

The power and scope of Peirce's semeiotic have yet to be measured, as have the fecundity and salience of his categoreal scheme deployed precisely as a heuristic framework. The one no less than the other provides us with an invaluable resource for the ongoing work of responsible inquiry. But, then, much else in Peirce's voluminous writings provide us with heuristic aids for the difficult yet exhilarating work of honest inquiry.[7] If I have done anything to enable readers to be in a better position than I was when I first encountered Peirce, then my efforts will have been richly rewarded.

In a sense different than that intended by James, there are times when the experience and occasion are nothing, since they are utterly negligible. But subsequent encounters might prove to be not only memorable but also transformative, because in the time between the initial and the later encounter the psyche has been in effect prepared for an engage-

---

[7] "There is ... nothing more wholesome for us than to find problems that quite transcend our powers, and I must say, too, that it imparts a delicious sense of being cradled in the waters of the deep ..." (*CP* 7.263).

ment with what is other than but continuous with his deepest impulses and aspirations. Chronologically and existentially, these are encounters of a second kind. Their secondness is however linked to their thirdness but also their firstness. What is radically other shows itself to be paradoxically intelligible and *sui generis*. It suggests unfathomed (perhaps unfathomable) intelligibility and, because of this, promises the romance of discovery. Such was my encounter with Peirce when I "first" truly made his acquaintance, a close(r) encounter of the second kind.

**References**

Emerson, R. W. 1982. *Ralph Waldo Emerson: Selected Essays*, edited by Larzer Ziff. NY: Penguin Books.

Fisch, Max H. 1986. *Peirce, Semeiotic, and Pragmatism*. Bloomington, IN: Indiana University Press.

James, Williams. 1989. "On a Certain Blindness in Human Beings." In *On Some of Life's Ideals*. NY: Henry Holt & Co.

Latour, Bruno. 2013. *An Inquiry into Modes of Existence: An Anthropology of the Moderns*. Cambridge, MA: Harvard University Press.

Peirce, C. S. 1958.
  *Collected Papers of Charles Sanders Peirce*, volume 7, edited by Arthur W. Burks. Cambridge, MA: Belknap Press of Harvard University Press.

  *The Essential Peirce*, volume 1, edited by Nathan Houser and Christian Kloesel. Bloomington, IN: Indiana University Press.

  *The Essential Peirce*, volume 2, edited by the Peirce Edition Project.

Santayana, George. 1942. *Realms of Being*. NY: Charles Scribner's Sons.

Smith, John E. 1992. *America's Philosophical Vision*. Chicago: University of Chicago Press.

Weissman, David. 1989. *Hypotheses and the Spiral of Reflection*. Albany, NY: SUNY Press.

# 6

# Marcel Danesi

Full Professor of Linguistic Anthropology
Department of Anthropology, University of Toronto

---

**1. Why were you initially drawn to Peirce?**

Two events drew me initially to Peirce. First, as editor of the now defunct *Monograph Series of the Toronto Semiotic Circle*—an early series in semiotic theory that published works that major publishers would not—I had the unique opportunity to put together and edit a marvelous second edition of *Introduction to Peirce* by David Savan (1976), a leading Peirce scholar in his era. Professor Savan did not type, so he would come to my office at Victoria College at the University of Toronto and dictate to me what he wanted to write.

I thus had a singular opportunity to ask a leading philosopher to clarify for me some of the more obscure concepts and terms (at least at the time for me) that were rarely discussed in the general literature. I would spend hours with him discussing Firstness, Secondness, Thirdness, iconicity, abduction, and the many other ideas that now have become part of my thought processes when I teach or write about sign theory.

The second event was teaching a first-year course in semiotics at Victoria College in the mid-1980s (which I continue to teach to this day) and the need to make Peirce understandable to a group of students who found Peircean theory abstruse to say the least. I would thus prepare practical exercises on detecting iconic, indexical, and symbolic forms in drawings, advertisements, language, popular music, and the like. This not only allowed students to grasp Peircean semiotics concretely, but also influenced me profoundly in how to do semiotics. As a linguist, I became fascinated by the work of the Italian philosopher Giambattista Vico (1688-1744), who made metaphor and what he called *poetic logic* the essence of human cognition and product of imaginative thinking. I began to see many parallels between Vico and Peirce and thus started writing about the parallels between them.

## 2. What do you consider your contribution to the field?

I believe that my work on Vico (Danesi 1993, 1995), in which I use Peircean ideas both explicitly and implicitly, to argue that metaphor and figurative language generally is a basic iconic form of cognition, is probably the work that I am most satisfied intellectually with. I have also contributed indirectly as editor of *Semiotica* and several book series with major publishers to promote semiotics in a Peircean perspective, although I believe that semiotics should be open to all kinds of approaches, especially structuralist (Saussurean). I see the two approaches—Saussurean and Peircean—as complementary, not as antithetical. Thus, my own textbooks in the field (for example, Danesi 2007, 2008) attempt to show general readers and students that Saussure allows us to understand the framework of structural properties, and Peirce their meaning and interpretation, thus connecting them to larger social and cultural frames.

## 3. What is the proper role of Peirce's work in relation to philosophy and other academic disciplines?

Peirce's ideas are being discovered constantly by linguists, anthropologists, and psychologists, who are beginning to use them to develop their particular theoretical frameworks and research agendas. I believe that Peirce's idea of Existential Graphs, studied rather insightfully by Stjernfelt (2007) and Roberts (1973), may be the concept that can link various disciplines, from philosophy and logic to mathematics (Danesi 2013). It is difficult to apply Peirce to various fields if one does not know sign theory profoundly. However, the notion of Existential graphs is understandable by virtually everyone and can thus be put forward as the conduit among the fields.

## 4. What do you consider the most important topics and/or contributions in the field of Peirce studies?

I believe that the study of image schemata in linguistics and psychology and of graphs in mathematics are going to be influenced more and more by Peirce's idea of Existential Graphs. Visual texts of any kind (diagrams, charts, and so on) display not a linear succession of logical structures, but how these cohere into unities, thus conveying information and simultaneously explaining how it is being done (CP4. 619). Needless to say, this line of research raises many deep questions about the nature of reality, the brain's connection to it, semiosis, and the nature of knowledge. But it is in raising these questions that the power of Peircean semiotics and philosophy lies. To use philosopher Susan Langer's (1948) concept of discursive-versus-presentational meaning, a graph tells us much more than a literal paraphrase because it "presents" the vicissitudes and nuances of meaning inherent in a structure in a much more condensed and suggestive way. We do not process a graph as a combination of parts (as we do a literal paraphrase), but *presentationally,* as a totality which encloses the meaning. Describing it in literal language is, instead, a *discursive* process, which presents the same information in bits and pieces but which never can cover the total ground.

The ideas of Peirce will gain a foothold in various domains of scientific investigation, as, more and more, scientists of the mind discover that visual-iconic thinking is at the core of cognition generally. This explains the growth of interest in phenomenology and blending theory in cognitive science (for example, Lakoff and Núñez 2000)—trends that were prefigured by Peirce's notion of "phaneroscopy," which he described as the formal analysis of appearances apart from how they appear to interpreters and of their actual material content. Appearances are keys to discovering broad classes of ideas, along with their intrinsic features.

Diagrams are, at one level, economical iconic forms, compressing information efficiently and allowing for the visual form itself to suggest further meaning not evident in the verbal counterparts. As Radford (2010: 4) puts it, they present information to us by means of "ways of appearance." They constitute a veritable explanatory system of logic of their own. Diagrams are inferences (informed guesses) that translate hunches (raw guesses) visually. These then lead to abductions (insights). The process of cognition is complete after the ideas produced in this way are organized logically (deduction). In fact, this suggests a model of cognition based on Peirce that can be charted as follows:

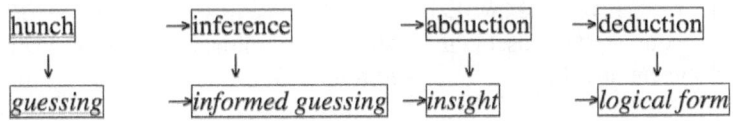

Hunches are the brain's attempts to understand what something means initially. These lead to inferences through a consideration of how the hunches connect us to previous experience or knowledge. So, the Pythagorean triangle leads to the previously-hidden concept of number triples. Eventually, this concept led to an hypothesis, namely that only when n = 2 does the generalized Pythagorean formula hold ($c^n = a^n + b^n$)—called Fermat's Last Theorem. This, in turn, led to many discoveries. It also led to a conclusive proof, which came, of course with the Taylor-Wiles (1995) proof. This seems to happen throughout the domain of mathematical and scientific discovery (Danesi 2013).

## 5. What are the most important open problems in this field and what are the prospects/avenues for progress?

I see two main problems in the field, which have nothing to do with the actual field of Peirce studies, but with its dissemination to the broader scientific community. The first one is the problem of abstruse terminology. No matter what semioticians think, explaining and using Peirce outside of the field meets with resistance because the terms are too confusing and, often, their explications by semioticians even more confusing. Terms such as iconic legisigns, indexical qualisigns essentially make little sense to anyone not conversant with Peirce. Thus, a more general nomenclature must be devised, even if die-hard Peirceans will object to this. This is the claim Sebeok and I made a while back (Sebeok and Danesi 2000), insisting that we would lose nothing but have much to gain by this. Another way to resolve this issue is simply to explicate Peircean terminology in more concrete ways. Thus, a dictionary of Peircean semiotics is a desideratum that I would like to see realized.

The second problem comes from the fact that many Peircean scholars are intolerant of alternative approaches to semiotics. This creates insularity and is ultimately counter-productive. Attending some of the more recent semiotic conferences, I sense that the reverence with which Peirce is used is tantamount to an unconscious fanaticism that can only be destructive. Semiotics needs to move away from being a tool with "Sausurrean," "Peircean," "Greimasean," and other orientations, and just "semiotics." How many times do we read mathematicians' research alluding to "Euclidean," "Pythagorean," "Gödelian" and other names and orientations? Unless there is a historical reason for doing so, mathematicians simply do mathematics, not a partisan form of the discipline.

If we resolve these two problems, I believe that Peirce will become an unconscious mindset in many disciplines influencing their future development and thus allowing us to truly understand the human mind.

## Bibliography

Danesi, M. (1993). *Vico, Metaphor, and the Origin of Language*. Bloomington: Indiana University Press.

Danesi, M. (1995). *Giambattista Vico and the Cognitive Science Enterprise*. New York: Peter Lang.

Danesi, M. (2007). *The Quest for Meaning: A Guide to Semiotic Theory and Practice*. Toronto: University of Toronto Press.

Danesi, M. (2008). *Of Cigarettes, High Heels, and Other Interesting Things: An Introduction to Semiotics*, 2nd ed. New York: Palgrave-Macmillan.

Danesi, M. (2013). *Discovery in Mathematics: An Interdisciplinary Approach*. Munich: Lincom Europa.

Lakoff, G. and Núñez, R. (2000). *Where Mathematics Comes from: How the Embodied Mind Brings Mathematics into Being*. New York: Basic Books.

Langer, S. K. (1948). *Philosophy in a New Key*. New York: Mentor Books.

Radford, L. (2010). Algebraic thinking from a cultural semiotic perspective. *Research in Mathematics Education* vol. 12, 1-19.

Roberts, D. D. (1973). *The Existential Graphs of Charles S. Peirce*. The Hague: Mouton.

Savan, D. (1976). *An Introduction to C. S. Peirce*. Toronto: Monograph Series of the Toronto Semiotic Circle.

Sebeok, T. A. and Danesi, M. (2000). *The Forms of Meaning: Modeling Systems Theory and Semiotics*. Berlin: Mouton de Gruyter.

Stjernfelt, F. (2007). *Diagrammatology: An Investigation on the Borderlines of Phenomenology, Ontology, and Semiotics*. New York: Springer.

# 7

# André De Tienne

Professor of Philosophy
Director & General Editor, Peirce Edition Project
Institute for American Thought, Indiana University at Indianapolis

---

## 1. Why were you initially drawn to Peirce?

I was eighteen when I attended for the first time a public lecture by a professional philosopher at a university in Brussels. Professor Jacques Bouveresse had come from Paris to speak about connections between Peirce and Popper. Attending philosophy students were required to pick some subtopic from the lecture and explore it at greater depth. I thereupon went to the library, serendipitously found Gérard Deledalle's recent translation of Peirce's *Écrits sur le signe* (1978), and got my first exposure to Peirce, in complete innocence and ignorance. The paper I submitted summarized whatever I was able to understand, which could not have been much. But unbeknownst to me, a seed got planted deep into my mind's recesses, and it germinated three or four years later while I was studying at the Catholic University of Louvain. There I was drawn again to Peirce, and one motive was superficially practical: the Higher Institute of Philosophy required that the "mémoire de licence" (equivalent to an M.A. thesis) addressed an "original topic." Through an elective class in communication studies I had been exposed to elements of Peirce's category theory and his semiotics, which was founded on a "phaneroscopy." I had at the same time taken a course on Husserl, whose *Logische Untersuchungen* began with "essential distinctions of signs." I became intrigued in the fact that both authors were developing analyses based on phenomeno-semiotic distinctions in ways worthy of multiple comparisons. One question this raised was whether there were essential distinctions to be made between signs or representations, and phenomena or manifestations. I resolved to investigate such matters in my M.A. thesis, which would compare Peirce and Husserl in those regards. The fact that no philosopher in Belgium was doing any work on Peirce at the time guaranteed that whatever I would do in that humble thesis would be bound to meet the originality criterion. I began by delving again into Peirce's writings, far more seriously than during my initial year. After a few weeks of research I realized the immensity and difficulty, both theoretical and logistical, of studying Peirce, and so I resolved to concentrate exclusively on his writings and to let go of Husserl for sheer lack of space and time. My M.A. thesis then turned into a sort of elaborate introduction to Peirce's phenomenology, and constituted for me a full awakening to the fact that studying Peirce at real depth in order to reach a more robust understanding of the tenets of his philosophy would require years of dedicated and single-minded study. I began planning a course of doctoral research that would allow me to do so. Gérard Deledalle advised me to go to Indianapolis and study at the Peirce Project because that research center had all the necessary resources and especially a cadre of specialists who might be very helpful. I wrote to Max H. Fisch for permission to come for one year, explaining my aims. He and PEP Director Christian Kloesel replied I would be welcome. Thanks to a fellowship granted by the Belgian American Educational Foundation I arrived in Indianapolis on September 10, 1985, coincidentally on Peirce's birthday. Never could I have guessed that I would end up staying there forever as an editor. And why did I stay? For two reasons: one is that this was the most marvelous job I could ever get, at the very center of Peirce scholarship, in the company of dedicated and respected scholars. The other—and here is the real answer to the question above—is because I would continue to be exposed to one particular aspect of Peirce's type of philosophizing that had always been its main appeal for me even when I didn't know it: its radical and genuine fundamentality. By this I mean that I found in Peirce a logical thinker with an especially powerful ability to rephrase the classic questions and answering strategies of philosophy by revisiting the very methods that gave rise to them, pointing out the logical limitations of those methods, and drilling down to their core to identify the sources of such limitations—usually some far more fundamental structure that had been taken for granted in the absence of an adequate method of analysis. This was particularly evident in Peirce's rethinking and overhauling of the very notion of category. The upshot of his criticism of two millennia of tradition in that regard was to show how and why a central mark had been missed, and what steps needed to be taken to remedy the situation: a pragmatist rethinking of the purport of the very concept of a category, a reflection about the logical method to be used in identifying what could count as a category, and the contextualization of the entire search within the search itself as a search, thus within the process of inquiry as inquiry.

## 2. What do you consider your contribution to the field?

Part of my contribution is a collaborative participation in a cross-generational effort to reconstitute, reorganize, date, edit, and publish Peirce's writings. The production of a scholarly critical edition involves multiple kinds of activities, all of which aim at providing a wide diversity of readers and users with a thoroughly researched, sophisticated, and reliable textual resource. Reconstructing the manuscripts, identifying the texts, establishing their genealogy and their compositional order, selecting those that ought to be published according to thoughtful criteria, getting them transcribed following a rigorous protocol of checks and corrections, editing them according to proven principles of textual criticism bound up with applications of Peirce's pragmatic maxim, studying them in minute detail and annotating them in a spirit of collaborative service to the profession, keeping track of all bibliographic references, building a comprehensive chronological catalog of the papers, designing and laying out the book form of the edition, providing it with an extensive critical apparatus recording the editors' every decision, furnishing it with an exacting scholarly index, administering the entire workflow, applying for grants, fundraising, and answering numerous questions about Peirce's manuscripts, all of those activities are part of the Peirce Project's daily contribution to the community of inquiry. But this is not all: in these times of radical technological developments, it also behooves the Project to envision the electronic future of its dissemination strategies, and to build new tools apt to fulfill the ever growing list of expectations in the online world. Designing and programming those new tools and platforms, paying attention to user needs, testing and modifying solutions accordingly, keeping abreast of new techniques, reflecting anew about the concept of an electronic critical edition and the kind of services and facilities it ought to provide to active web-browsing researchers and the public at large, launching or participating in collaborations to achieve such goals and finding the means to support them, and doing and conceiving all of this so that other editions can also benefit, all of this is also part of our contribution to the field.

Besides that, my philosophical interests in Peirce have consistently focused on the development of his theory of categories (beginning with my thesis and book on the genesis of it in Peirce's earliest writings), on his phaneroscopy, and on the connection between phaneroscopy and semiotics. I have a sustained interest in Peirce's semiotics understood in a broad sense, including its ramifications into metaphysics and its deep connection to all the isms Peirce gave birth to, including centrally his synechism and his pragmaticism. I have written about Peirce's semiotic conception of the person, about the connection between time and semiosis, about Peirce's theory of information, and about his "fundamentalism" understood as his penchant for the treatment of fundamental questions in multiple domains of research.

**3) What is the proper role of Peirce's work in relation to philosophy and other academic disciplines?**

Peirce invites his readers to keep questioning and redesigning their methods of investigation. His writings teach us how to detach ourselves from own specializations in order to get a robust grasp of the logic that presides over our habitual inferences, and to appreciate the value of an unrelenting effort to understand their impact, assess their skewing effects, and identify the ways to reevaluate or redefine them for the sake of readjustment and correction. Peirce's fallibilism captures or underlies the optimism inherent in all heuristic activities and provides an objective reason never to be satisfied with distinctions, categorizations, and inferential conclusions. It constitutes a permanent and unshakeable reminder that no matter how deep we may believe our theories go, that depth will perilously shrink back to the surface if methods and tenets are turned into mere unquestioned recipes. To take just a trivial example, the moment we are tempted for practical convenience to reduce iconicity to resemblance, the moment we bounce back from promising depth to uninteresting shallows. Why? Because we fail to grasp the concept's power by reducing it to a familiar one that fails to elucidate anything. Paying attention to the ways and means of Peirce's relentless logical and philosophical experiments (and of course to those of other thinkers of similar caliber) forces us not to let down our guard and never to be satisfied with any answer to any question. Peirce's proper role is to stand as a provocative model or exemplar of a complete logician who nags all of us, whatever may be our discipline, to look harder and revisit our methods, classifications, and inferences multiple times, especially when we sense we might be getting somewhere. More than that, Peirce happens to have left us with a powerful heuristic equipment, fit to guide us surefootedly because its very structure is in phase with the rhythm of the lived continuum of haphazard evolution and noetic experience—I am referring to his three categories, three dynamic concepts of unmatched universality and unusual range of applicability. From them we may derive a large catalog of well-ordered questions, as comprehensive as can be imagined; they teach us how to observe, suggest what to expect should be observable under certain categorial conditions, and help us therefore to formulate questions we would not have otherwise thought of asking and researching. They alert us against the temptation to reduce our comprehension to binary descriptions of measurable actions and reactions, warning us that the danger of reductionism resides in the comfortable but delusive satisfaction provided by its results. They open up the horizon of research by reminding us that no explanation can be merely local.

**4) What do you consider the most important topics and/or contributions in the field of Peirce studies?**
Importance is a subjective criterion, relative to the individual brain that weighs it in light of favorite pursuits and purposes. There are areas of research that have been neglected, barely explored, or downright misunderstood because of a failure to grasp certain fundamental insights that presided over their conception due to the filters imposed by the pedagogical methods of certain philosophical schools. Witness for instance Peirce's phaneroscopy and the vast bafflement of the profession in its regard, blamed usually on the paucity or ambiguity of Peirce's related pronouncements. Scholars have been divided about the nature of its methods and goals, and about its supposed scientificity. And yet today, once century later, we are finally beginning to lay the ground toward a more robust understanding of Peirce's incomplete but genuine insights, thanks in great part to the recent groundbreaking contributions of Richard Atkins published in *The Pluralist*. That is the kind of area where the more "important" contributions can be made, at least as far as studies of Peirce for Peirce's sake are concerned. Shedding light in the neglected corners of his writings requires century-long patience, for it takes time and intellectual effort to shake off traditional baggage in order to grasp more accurately the real purport of Peirce's incompletely expressed suggestions. The younger generation of scholars appears to be well equipped for this kind of task, I am glad to say. This is due in part to the increased diversification of the curriculum in many philosophy departments, and the consequent widening of the range of topical interests and methodological approaches offered to the contemporary generation. This is also due to the rapid internationalization of Peirce studies, the friendly cross-border and transoceanic competition among eager job-seeking Peirce PhDs, and the ever-broadening appeal of Peircean insights across multiple disciplines in the humanities and the sciences.

It is refreshing to see how certain fields that fell under more or less positivistic domination for decades have begun to yield to richer approaches keen to keep reductionistic shortcuts under check. This is becoming apparent for instance in information and communication theory, where facile binary models are cracking under the need for more comprehensive triadic models. The same is taking place in the booming field of biosemiotics, which has revealed a need to rephrase or reinterpret much of the terminology in use in biology in order to achieve a more complete grasp of the logic of biological phenomena. Triadism à la Peirce comes at a price, for the metaphysics that sustains it transcends prevalent nominalistic approaches. It is not that it renders the latter irrelevant. On the contrary, it helps provide a more exact account of their relevance by determining the categorial limitations of their explanatory range, and showing therefore comparatively where their contributions fall within the larger scheme of logics. Consider for instance the main warring parties in proper-name theory, which has pitted denotationalists against connotationalists. Careful study of Peirce's semiotics shows at once where lies the exact relevance of each position according to the range of its premises, while also showing how each position does not contradict, but merely partly complements the others within the far more comprehensive scheme offered by a dynamic Peircean classification of sign processes. When Peirce identified the seven possible systems of metaphysics on the basis of his categories in 1903, that is exactly what he did: showing the categorial range of different systems and thereby illuminating essential differences helping us to appreciate far better the real and non-dismissible value of each of those systems. That Peirce's own system was about the only one that did justice to all three categories at once is of course telling, not of a possibly self-serving move, but of the principal power of his central hypothesis, the keystone to every fundamental inquiry.

What I thus consider the most important *kind* of contributions in Peirce studies are those contributions that seek to unify other fields not in the sense of forcing onto them artificial commonalities, but by providing a wider logical and metaphysical horizon that encompasses a diverse set of equally sensible but sometimes widely diverging approaches, a horizon that manifests the proper place occupied by each while also revealing suggestively the room left for other logically possible approaches not yet explored but worth considering or designing.

**5) What are the most important open problems in this field and what are the prospects/avenues for progress?**

Peirce's ideas are easy to misunderstand, or rather to misconstrue. They are often so suggestive that the temptation is to run away with the first suggestion they elicit without taking the time to explore patiently the wider and deeper background, logical or metaphysical, that gave rise to that suggestion. One consequence, to use what has now become a stock example, has been the proliferation of semiotic essays that limit their Peircean borrowings to the icon-index-symbol triad without suspecting or appreciating the fact that a mere formal use of their superficial structure will fail to tap the much richer vein offered by a genuine semiotic inquiry well imbued with the very motivations that drove Peirce to conceive his tentative semiotic theories.

Speaking of which, it is clear that a field widely open to investigation consists precisely in basic or fundamental research in semiotics within a Peircean framework. After all, semiotics well understood is logic in the broadest and deepest sense, and it formally precedes as such every discipline in the humanities and the social sciences because of its generality or fundamentality. A perusal of Peirce's manuscripts manifests plainly what is obscured in the printed form of any of his semiotic writings: the fact that they were all tentative, though robustly insightful, shots in the dark, animated by an experimental spirit dismayed by its isolation from the indispensable sounding board of a community of inquiry. When Peirce explained in 1907 that his work in semiotics was that of a backwoodsman, he explained that "the doctrine of the essential nature and fundamental varieties of possible semiosis" constituted a "field too vast," a "labor too great, for a first-comer." He only had time to consider a few of the most important questions, and had no time for the *scientific* study of other questions about which he only harbored "impressions," of which he said there were more than four hundred: "they are all delicate and difficult, each requiring much search and much caution" without even being "the most important of the questions of semiotic" (EP2: 413, 1907). Peirce's lament on the unfinished state of semiotics is a direct appeal to future generations for the continued and systematic completion of the science of signs. His call still remains to be answered. There have been several valuable attempts to revisit and redesign his table of sixty-six classes of signs, some of which adopt Peirce's own divisions and others extend or rephrase them, and there have been plenty of discussions, including several well respected books, analyzing, criticizing, and otherwise attempting to make sense of Peirce's theory of signs as he left it. But there has not been yet a full-blown systematic attempt to pursue the work itself at the fundamental level Peirce was mostly concerned with. This is not being said on a regretful tone: clearly such an enterprise could not have been launched before a full century had passed. Time had to be taken for the scholarship to re-clear Peirce's old backwoods. But now that such solid work has been done, even if not fully completed and even if the specialists are not agreeing on many questions, we may now be readier to pick up the axes, shears, and hoes to continue the land clearing Peirce began, and then to wield more refined prescinding instruments to erect a semiotic edifice that can withstand the vicissitudes of a second century of cautious research on hundreds of delicate questions.

What would this take, apart from a community of researchers in fundamental semiotics? Probably much cooperation with a similar cadre of phaneroscopists, skillful at observing the categorial interplay in multitudes of sign reactions and interactions, and assessing to what extent Peirce's famous heuristic rule (a first can only determine a first; a third can only be determined by a third) allows one to sharpen that observation to the point of predicting what should be observable at particular categorial junctures of semiosic experience. That such an activity is possible has been especially well demonstrated in the work of Priscila Borges, who has displayed astounding skills of observation and analysis in modeling the methods needed to apply the 66 sign processes for instance to the minute examination of every single factor that comes into play in the design and use of artistic character fonts. We need many more researchers similarly dedicated and ingenious, with complementary skills of observation, formalization, and generalization, grasping the logical and metaphysical gist of Peirce's insights, modifying or adjusting them when called for, and extending them to distinct realms of investigation, ever ready to show the heuristic advantages of those methods, both theoretical and practical.

## Bibliography

*L'Analytique de la représentation chez Peirce: la genèse de la théorie des catégories*. Publications des Facultés Universitaires Saint-Louis (Brussels, 1996), 410 pp. (Five reviews of the book have been published.)

*The Cambridge School of Pragmatism*, 4 vols., eds. John R. Shook and André De Tienne. Vol. 1: *The Pragmaticism of Charles S. Peirce* with introduction by André De Tienne (xxxvii + 375 pp.), vol. 2: *The Pragmatism of William James* (xxxii + 322 pp.), vol. 3: *The Pragmatic Idealisms of Josiah Royce and John E. Boodin* (xxi + 347 pp.), vol. 4: *The Pragmatic Naturalisms of George Santayana and Clarence I. Lewis* (xxviii + 313 pp.). London & New York: Thoemmes/Continuum International Publishing Group, The Foundations of Pragmatism in American Thought, 2006.

*Writings of Charles S. Peirce: A Chronological Edition*, Volume 8: 1890–1892 (xcvii + 724 pp.). Bloomington: Indiana Univ. Press, 2010. Editor.

"Selecting Alterations for the Apparatus of a Critical Edition." In *TEXT* 9, An Interdisciplinary Annual of Textual Studies, ed. D. C. Greetham & W. Speed Hill. Ann Arbor: The University of Michigan Press, 1996, pp. 33–62. (Applied research.)

"The Peirce Papers: How to Pick Up Manuscripts that Fell to the Floor." In *TEXT* 10, An Interdisciplinary Annual of Textual Studies, ed. W. Speed Hill & Edward M. Burns. Ann Arbor: The University of Michigan Press, 1997, pp. 259–282.

"Quand l'apparence (se) fait signe: la genèse de la représentation chez Peirce." In *RS•SI (Recherches sémiotiques/Semiotic Inquiry)*, vol. 20/1–3 (2000), pp. 95–144.

"Is Phaneroscopy as a Pre-Semiotic Science Possible?" In *Semiotiche* (Torino: Ananke), vol. 2 (2004), pp. 15–30.

"Information in Formation: A Peircean Approach." In *Cognitio*, revista de filosofia (Centro de Estudos do Pragmatismo, PUC, São Paulo), vol. 6, no. 2 (Julho-Dezembro 2005), pp. 149–65.

"La persona come segno." Transl. by G. Maddalena. In *Semiotica e fenomenologia del Sé*. Ed. by R. Calcaterra. Torino: Nino Aragno Editore, 20060, pp. 91–110.

"The 'Flowing Stream' that Carries Pragmatism: James, Peirce, and Royce." In *Cognitio*, vol. 8, no. 1 (Janeiro-Junho 2007), pp. 45–68.

"Time and the Flow of Signs: Semiosis and Chronogony." In *Caderno* (ISSN 1983-3113), Número 15: Ano XV, Centro Internacional de Estudos Peirceanos (CIEP), Pontifícia Universidade Católica de São Paulo (PUC-SP), Brazil, August 2012, pp. 39–57.

"How to Promote Peirce's Realism without Angering Nominalism." Centro de Estudios Filosóficos Eugenio Puciarelli, Grupo de Estudios Peirceanos - Sección Argentina, V Jornadas "Peirce en Argentina," *Ponencias*, August 2012, pp. 91–100.

"Why Semiotics? A Question Requiring a Fundamental Answer for Peirce's Sake." Presidential address, 38th annual meeting of the Semiotic Society of America, forthcoming in the *American Journal of Semiotics*.

# 8
# Cornelis de Waal

Professor of Philosophy

Indiana University – Purdue University Indianapolis

---

**1) Why were you initially drawn to Peirce?**

What attracted me to Peirce was the subjects he discussed and the manner in which he discussed them. My first philosophical love was George Herbert Mead, whom I discovered while I was a graduate student in economics at Erasmus University, the Netherlands. I saw Mead as providing a fertile alternative to my disenchantments with the mathematical models of neoclassical economics and the odd presuppositions on which they rested. I don't remember what made me read Peirce (Mead barely refers to him, and when he does it's only in passing) but once I did, his writings instantly resonated. I shelved my dissertation proposal for the Economics Department and chose to pursue Peirce at the University of Twente, also in the Netherlands, with Doede Nauta. I then moved to the USA to write a dissertation on Peirce with Susan Haack. In general, Peirce provided a much-needed happy medium between the analytic philosophers I had been reading—people like Quine, Putnam, Moore, and Russell—and continental philosophers, such as Levinas, Merleau-Ponty, Gehlen, and Heidegger. For the analytical philosophers I liked the style of philosophizing, but I was much less attracted to what they wrote about; for the continentals this was pretty much the other way around.

**2) What do you consider your contribution to the field?**

I have worked primarily in three areas: making Peirce's writings available, improving secondary literature, and bringing Peirce to new readers—philosophers as well as non-philosophers. After finishing my doctorate, I worked for over a decade as an Editor at the Peirce Edition Project on the *Writings of Charles S. Peirce*, mostly on volumes 6 to 11, and on restoring the order of composition of Peirce's manuscripts, concentrating largely on the 1890s. The amount of work that goes into this kind of enterprise is staggering and, if done right, invisible: the text flows as Peirce had intended and the manuscripts show no sign of their previous disarray, which in Peirce's case is considerable. My latest project in this area is an edition of Peirce's *Illustrations of the Logic of Science,* published by the Open Court, a project Peirce had abandoned himself (albeit not for a lack of trying) and for which I must confess the hand of the editor remains all too visible. A couple years ago I left the Peirce Edition Project to take charge of the *Transactions of the Charles S. Peirce Society,* facilitating publication of first-rate research on Peirce and American philosophy more generally, having formerly been the journal's Peirce editor. I think that a journal dedicated to promoting and disseminating Peirce scholarship has been of crucial importance during the latter part of the twentieth century and, though the venues for publishing Peirce have since increased significantly, I think that there continues to be an important role for the journal. The third area in which I have been active is that of providing a general overview of the work of Peirce, addressing both a philosophical and a non-philosophical audience. Given that he was a polymath with a deep interest in (the logic of) science, Peirce has much to offer the latter. My 2001 *On Peirce* and my 2013 *Charles S. Peirce: A Guide for the Perplexed* both fall in this area, in that they appeal to both groups. In addition to an overview of Peirce's thought, both books also contain new insights not found elsewhere. Whether any of them can be counted a contribution I prefer to let others decide.

### 3) What is the proper role of Peirce's work in relation to philosophy and other academic disciplines?

As said, Peirce was a polymath. In fact, describing him as a philosopher with an interest in science, as is often the case with philosophers of science today, would be a misconstrual. Peirce was an active scientist—where science must be interpreted broadly—who looked upon all he did with a keen philosophical eye and with a strong interest in the logic of inquiry. Peirce's philosophy is not an ivory tower affair. It is conscientiously developed in dialogue with science, not only as Peirce encountered it as a practicing scientist, but also through his reading the work of contemporary scientists and his study of the history of science. I think that when looking at Peirce's philosophy we must not lose sight of this. It also means that Peirce has many interesting things to say about a great variety of disciplines, and especially given his focus on the *logic* of inquiry, much of this is transferable to disciplines that Peirce did not talk about, that developed much after his time, or that were not yet around. Fortunately, we are seeing lately quite a bit of work being done in the history of various disciplines, from economics to geodesy to theatre studies, calling attention to Peirce's contributions in those areas and thereby bringing him into the discourse. More is certainly still called for. Particularly, I would like to see more work done on Peirce within the philosophy of science. It would be good to see him replace Popper as the go-to philosopher that academic non-philosophers harken back to when they want to say something about the logic of their discipline. Perhaps special mention should be made of mathematics, a discipline in which Peirce was very active and which deeply colored his thinking. One only has to think of the central role he carved out for the mathematical concept of continuity within philosophy.

**4) What do you consider the most important topics and/or contributions in the field of Peirce studies?**

Though Peirce published a lot during his lifetime, much of his more interesting work he did not get published. At Harvard alone there exist about a hundred thousand manuscript pages. They were in disarray when they were still in Peirce's hands, and there is good evidence that things got worse after they came to Harvard. Hence, I think that the most important contribution made during this first century of Peirce scholarship is the editorial work done by people like Charles Hartshorne, Paul Weiss, Arthur Burks, Richard Robin, Carolyn Eisele, Ken Ketner, and, starting with Max Fisch, the Peirce Edition Project. And there is still much work to be done here. Also indicative of the first century of Peirce scholarship are the various attempts to introduce systematic overviews of his work into the philosophic community, such as Chris Hookway's *Peirce* and Murray Murphey's *Development of Peirce's Philosophy*. As far as specific topics are concerned, there is a wide variety of them, as is to be expected from a polymath. It is hard to state this early in the game, though, which topics are "important," although it is safe to say that it includes his logic conceived as semiotics, especially insofar as it concerns his theory of inquiry.

**5) What are the most important open problems in this field and what are the prospects/avenues for progress?**

This is a rather dangerous question for the Editor-in-Chief of the principal journal in Peirce studies to answer. In this role, I like to see myself as a pluralist committed to the idea of a community of inquiry, and hence I want to avoid saying anything that might influence future submissions. What the *Transactions* needs is high-quality papers on Peirce that provide valuable insights and do not repeat what is already out there. As far as I can see it, what counts as valuable is impossible to determine beforehand. From a practical perspective it is the community of inquiry, represented (however fallibly) by the journal's referees, that has to make that call, based on actual submissions, their own expertise, and assisted by the experience of the editors. Hopefully this results in a palette of great work that is neither too narrowly focused on so-called hot topics, nor crowds out excellent papers that have only a limited appeal. Hence, rather than answering this question I prefer to lean back and see what others in this volume say in reply to it. As for my own research I'm very much interested in the relationship between mathematics and what Peirce calls the positive sciences, and I'm surely hoping that the prospects for progress in this area are good.

**Five Peirce Publications**

de Waal, Cornelis.

"*Charles S. Peirce: A Guide for the Perplexed*". London: Continuum Press, 2013.

"Who's Afraid of Charles Sanders Peirce: Knocking Some Critical Common Sense into Moral Philosophy," in Cornelis de Waal and Krzysztof Skowroński (eds), *The Normative Thought of Charles S. Peirce* (New York: Fordham University Press, 2012), pp. 83–100.

"Having an *Idea* of Matter: A Peircean Refutation of Berkeleyan Immaterialism." *Journal for the History of Ideas* 67.2 (April 2006): 291–313.

"Peirce's Nominalist–Realist Distinction, an Untenable Dualism." *Transactions of the Charles S. Peirce Society* 34 (1998): 183–202.

de Waal, Cornelis (ed.) *The Illustrations of the Logic of Science by Charles S. Peirce*. Chicago: The Open Court, 2014.

# 9

# Terrence W. Deacon

Professor of Anthropology
University of California, Berkeley

---

**1) Why were you initially drawn to Peirce?**
While an undergraduate student in the 1970s I was deeply engrossed in the study of systems theory and cybernetics and their applications to problems in physics, biology, neuro-psychology, and linguistics. It was the dawn of the computer age and molecular genetics was becoming a hot new topic in organismal biology and evolutionary theory. As a student living on part-time jobs and dwindling saving I spend hours in bookstores reading the latest books on these topics (since they had not yet reached the libraries and I couldn't afford them). A man working to shelve books in one bookstore regularly saw me reading these books and periodically would recommend to me that I should read something by Peirce as well. I resisted and considered his suggestions an irritation since Peirce was a philosopher and I wanted science.

But at one point while reading through Warren McCulloch's book *Embodiments of Mind* I was surprised to find that he had been significantly influenced by Peirce's semiotic theory. So the next time this fellow suggested that I read Peirce I had him make a recommendation. He suggested that I start with a collection of Peirce's papers in *Philosophical Writings of C. S. Peirce*, edited by Justus Buchler. It didn't take long before I realized that Peirce's work offered a paradigm shift that was a century before its time. Peirce had re-conceptualized conundrums that were still problematic in current systems and information theories, and had provided a way of breaking out of the strictures that made them seem insoluble. Peirce was a systems thinker at a much deeper level of analysis. Where contemporary theorizing focused only on the materialistic surface of information processes Peirce had spent his life exploring what was behind this façade and developing a vision of the physical world in which meaning and value could be understood as real and causally efficacious as energy and matter.

That summer I spent what money I could scrape together and I purchased the then definitive collection of Peirce's writings: the 8 volumes of the Hartshorne and Weiss *Collected Papers of Charles Sanders Peirce*, and spent the next year doing nothing more than studying and taking notes about his work. The following year (1976) I completed a 50+ single-spaced summary of my understanding of Peirce's semiotic system—*Semiotics and Cybernetics: The Relevance of C. S. Peirce*—and submitted it for my senior year interdisciplinary thesis.

After teaching for a year I was accepted into a Masters Program at Harvard University where I intended to continue my studies of Peirce's writings that were housed in Harvard's Houghton Library. While at Harvard, both as a graduate student and a young professor, I never gained access to Peirce's unpublished papers and failed to find an adviser for my study of Peirce's work. I went on to study cognitive development, neuroscience, and evolutionary anthropology, but I have remained deeply influenced by Peircean thinking throughout my career.

## 2) What do you consider your contribution to the field?

Though I have never written a book that focused primarily on Peirce's work, and have only produced a handful of academic papers that directly analyze and use Peirce's semiotic theory, his thinking pervades my work in cognitive neuroscience, evolutionary theory, and the study of emergent processes. I consider my two most important contributions to Peirce's legacy to be my extensive use of Peirce's ideas in two books.

In my 1997 book *The Symbolic Species: The Co-evolution of Language and the Brain* I explicitly developed a Peircean semiotic-based theory of human language evolution. Although I consciously avoided importing much of Peirce's terminology and metaphysics into that work, for fear of losing my readers in its unfamiliar and byzantine complexity, my approach was fundamentally grounded in my analysis of Peirce's way of understanding the relationship between icons, indices, and symbols. I argued that the origin and nature of language could be traced to the semiotic complexity of symbolic as compared to indexical and iconic referential relationships.

I argued that the transition to the use of symbolic means (e.g. language) for communication required a significant reorganization of human neurology and brain function to handle the special demands of symbol use. I based this on the recognition that Peirce's semiotic categorical scheme had a distinctive hierarchic constructive logic (implicit in his categories of Firstness, Secondness, and Thirdness). This implied that symbolic reference depends on underlying indexical reference which depends on underlying iconic reference, and therefore that the symbolic cognition that is the basis for language must have emerged from and depends upon these lower-order semiotic relationships. Moreover, this suggested that the cognitive architecture that supports symbolic thought and language is itself constituted by deeper layers of indexical and iconic processes.

So, not only was this a Peircean-inspired approach to human neural and mental evolution, it suggested the first dim outlines of a semiotic cognitive neuroscience.

Perhaps the main challenge that this approach encountered derived from the fact that Peirce's semiotics was far more complex and subtle than corresponding theories of the time. In contrast, contemporary linguistics, cognitive science, and philosophy tends to employ a comparatively impoverished notion of 'symbol.' This derives in part from the influence of the Saussurean conception of a simple arbitrary "signifier" diadically correlated with what it "signifies" in linguistics, in part from the assumption that all thought can be represented in terms of "symbolic logic," and in part from information theoretic conceptions of symbols as arbitrary tokens that can be manipulated irrespective of reference.

Peirce had carefully distinguished between the properties of the sign vehicle (representamen) and the relationship between a sign and its object of reference. The way that the term 'symbol' is most often used today would correspond best with what Peirce termed a Legisign: a conventionally established token such as an alphanumeric character. All symbolic reference requires legisigns but legisigns can also be used for indexical and iconic reference. Because of this collapsed semiotic distinction many linguists, cognitive scientists, and philosophers were unable to think of the complexity of symbolic referential processes as the critical mental threshold separating human mentality from all other species.

In my 2012 book *Incomplete Nature: How Mind Emerged from Matter* the influence of Peirce's metaphysics is central. Its primary goal is to bring two of Peirce's most fundamental ideas into mainstream science: his defense of metaphysical Realism via an updated version of his concept of 'habit' and his claim that final causality (i.e. true teleology) is an effective mode of physical causality and not merely a heuristic fiction. These are considered illegitimate explanatory principles in much of contemporary science and philosophy, as they were in Peirce's time. But whereas the science necessary to support these arguments was unavailable to Peirce, it is available now. By developing an empirically realistic (and testable) model system (autogenesis) that unambiguously demonstrates the transition from non-living to living dynamics, and from extrinsically caused to intrinsically end-directed processes, I provide a physical demonstration of how final causality can emerge from simple mechanism. It also becomes a demonstration of how a general property can be causally efficacious. As Peirce envisioned, the recognition of the efficacy of generals (Realism) and the physical reality of final causes, also entails the reality of semiotic relationships. And so one of the goals of this work has been to demonstrate how reference and significance can be reintroduced into the information sciences. This is necessary if we are ever going to be able to ground semiotic theory on the physical sciences and escape the shifting labyrinth of Cartesian incompatiblism.

**3) What is the proper role of Peirce's work in relation to philosophy and other academic disciplines?**

Peirce's work was so far-reaching and extends over such a range of academic disciplines that it is easy to underestimate its potential to contribute to the further development of knowledge even a century later. Quite clearly its contribution to philosophy is still being felt, as the recent strong resurgence of interest in his work has demonstrated. However, probably the most significant contributions are being felt in fields that are still struggling with issues of how information means and how systemic order comes into being.

The last century saw two vast paradigms rise to unquestionable prominence and then begin to expose their own untenable assumptions. The first is a nominalistically motivated faith in thorough-going reductionism in the sciences; sometimes referred to as eliminative materialism. By the end of the 20$^{th}$ Century studies of complex and chaotic systems began to provide hints that this paradigm was founded on an oversimplified conception of physical causality. Even in fundamental physics there is a serious reconsideration of Peirce's notion of the evolution of physical laws (such as is independently exhibited in the physical theories of Robert Laughlin and Lee Smolin). The second is a logocentric conception of information, thought, and even social organization that treated language-like structure as the paradigm exemplar upon which all other epistemic phenomena should be modeled. Though linguistics-inspired models dominated 20$^{th}$ Century philosophy and social theory, even in linguistics, where an intense nature/nurture battle has continued unabated to the present, there is a dawning of recognition that language is derived from and dependent upon underlying more basic semiotic relations. The consequences of the radical re-grounding of cognitive and social theories that this recognition requires have yet to be appreciated, but will inevitably need to deal with issues that Peirce made the center of his inquiries, and greatly informed. Thus, these newly exposed internal consistencies of these major intellectual paradigms demand to be addressed by the next generation of natural and social scientists, and since Peirce is one of the few thinkers to have addressed these issues directly his insights will surely be relevant.

**4) What do you consider the most important topics and/or contributions in the field of Peirce studies?**

There needs to be:

A concerted effort by the community of Peirce scholars to reconstruct Peirce's semiotic theory in a form that is detailed, complete, widely accepted, and accessible to a wide readership spanning many fields from the arts to biology.

An effort to complete the full transcription of Peirce's unpublished work, organized so that it is searchable both topically and chronologically, and to make this electronically available to all.

**5) What are the most important open problems in this field and what are the prospects/avenues for progress?**

From my perspective I consider the most important challenge to be the re-grounding Peirce's semiotic theory in the natural sciences. By this I explicitly *don't* mean reframing semiotic theory in reductionistic terms, but rather developing a sufficiently rich expansion of physical theory that explains the emergence and the final causal efficacy of semiotic relations. Only this will enable non-metaphoric application of Peirce's semiotic insights to fields other than human semiotics. The attempt to merely redescribe neural and biological processes by analogy to human phenomenal experience will guarantee that Peirce's semiotic insights will fail to find acceptance in these most important scientific fields. In some respects, this will require abandoning certain aspects of Peirce's attraction to Objective Idealism, or what his friend William James promoted as dual aspect theory, and what some modern Peirceans have called pan-semiosis. So I believe that to truly advance this core insight of Peirce's thinking in a way that significantly impacts the future of science, it may not be possible to embrace Peirce's full metaphysical perspective.

**Bibliography**

**Journal publications**

Deacon T. and Koutroufinis, S. (accepted) Complexity as dynamical depth. *Information*.

Deacon T., Srivastava, A. and Bacigalupi, J. A. (accepted) The transition from constraint to regulation at the origin of life. *Frontiers in Bioscience*.

Book symposium: Terrence Deacon's *Incomplete Nature. Religion, Brain & Behavior,* Fall 2013, pp. 1-52.

Deacon, T. (2011) The importance of what's missing. *New Scientist*, November 2011, pp. 36-42.

Sherman, J. and Deacon, T. (2007) Teleology for the perplexed: how matter began to matter. *Zygon* 42: 873-901

Goodenough, U. and Deacon, T. (2003) From biology to consciousness to morality. *Zygon* 38: 801-819.

Deacon, T. (2005) Language as an emergent function: some radical neurological and evolutionary implications. *Theoria* 54: 269-286.

Deacon, T. (1999) Memes as signs. *The Semiotic Review of Books* 10(3): 1-3.

**Books**

Deacon, T. (2012) *Incomplete Nature: How Mind Emerged from Matter*. W. W. Norton & Co., New York, 604 pp.

Deacon, T. (1997) *The Symbolic Species: The Co-evolution of Language and the Brain*. W. W. Norton & Co., New York, 527 pp.

**Chapters in edited volumes**

Deacon, T. and Cashman, T. (2012) Teleology versus Mechanism in Biology: Beyond Self-Organization. In: Henning, B. and Scarfe, A. (eds.). *Beyond Mechanism: Putting Life Back Into Biology*. Lanham, MD: Lexington Books/Rowman & Littlefield.

Deacon, T. (2012) Information. In D. Favareau, P. Cobley and K. Kull (eds.) *A More Developed Sign*. Tartu University Press, pp. 161-164.

Deacon, T. (2012) Beyond The Symbolic Species. In T. Schilhab, F. Stjernfelt, and T. Deacon (eds.) *The Symbolic Species Evolved*, Springer,

Deacon, T. (2012) Darwin's "several powers". In Timo Maran, Kati Lindström, Riin Magnus and Morten Tønnessen (eds.) *Biosemiotics Turning Wild*. Tartu University Press, pp. 71-78.

Deacon, T. (2011) The symbol concept. In M. Tallerman and K. Gibson (eds.) *The Oxford Handbook of Language Evolution*. Oxford University Press.

Deacon, T. and Cashman, T (2011) Eliminativism, Complexity and Emergence. In *The Routledge Companion to Religion and Science,* James Haag, Gregory Peterson and Michael Spezio (eds.), Routledge.

Deacon T., Haag, J. and Ogilvy, J. (2011) The emergence of Self. In J. Wentzel van Huyssteen and Erik P. Wiebe (eds) *In Search of Self: Interdisciplinary Perspectives on Personhood*, Wm. B. Eerdmans Publishing Co.

Deacon, T. (2010) What's missing from theories of information? In Paul Davies and Niels Henrik Gregersen (eds.) *Information and the Nature of*

*Reality: From Physics to Metaphysics.* New York: Cambridge University Press, pp. 146-169.

Hui J., Cashman T. and Deacon T. (2008) Bateson's Method: Double Description. What is it? How does it work? What do we learn? In Jesper Hoffmeyer (ed) *A Legacy for Living Systems.* Springer, pp. 77-92.

Deacon, T. & Sherman, J. (2007) The physical origins of purposive systems. In John Michael Krois, Mats Rosengren, Angela Steidele, Dirk Westerkamp (eds.), *Embodiment in Cognition and Culture.* Amsterdam/ Philadelphia: John Benjamins.

Deacon, T. (2007) Three levels of emergent phenomena. In Nancey Murphy and William Stoeger (eds.) *Evolution & Emergence: Systems, Organisms, Persons.* Oxford University Press, pp. 88-112.

Deacon, T. (2006) Emergence: The hole at the wheel's hub. In P. Clayton & P. Davies (eds.) *The Re-Emergence of Emergence.* MIT Press, pp. 111-150.

Goodenough, U. and Deacon, T. (2006) Emergence, Ethics, and Religious Naturalism. In Clayton, P. and Simpson, Z. (eds) *The Oxford Handbook of Religion and Science.* Oxford University Press.

Deacon, T. (2006) The aesthetic faculty. In M. Turner & S. Zeki (eds.) *The Artful Mind.* Oxford University Press, pp. 21-53.

Deacon T. (2004) Memes as Signs in the Dynamic Logic of Semiosis: Beyond Molecular Science and Computation Theory. In Karl Erich Wolff, Heather D. Pfeiffer and Harry S. Delugach, eds. *Conceptual Structures At Work*, ICCS 2004, Proceedings, Springer-Verlag, Berlin, pp.17-30.

Deacon, T. (2003) Universal grammar and semiotic constraints. In M. Christiansen and S. Kirby (eds.) *Language Evolution.* Oxford University Press. pp. 111-139.

Deacon, T. (1976) Semiotics and cybernetics: The relevance of C. S. Peirce. In: System and Structure Study Group (eds.) *Sanity and Signification: Essays in Communication and Exchange.* Fairhaven College Press.

**Other authors referenced in my responses to the five questions**

Laughlin, Robert B. (2005). *A Different Universe: Reinventing Physics from the Bottom Down.* Basic Books

Smolin, Lee (1997) *The Life of the Cosmos.* Oxford University Press.

Smolin, Lee (2013) *Time Reborn: From the crisis in physics to the future of the universe.* Houghton Mifflin Harcourt.

# 10

# Susan Haack

Distinguished Professor in the Humanities
Cooper Senior Scholar in Arts and Sciences
Professor of Philosophy and Professor of Law
University of Miami

## WHY I'M A PEIRCE PERSON

> Out of a contrite fallibilism, combined with a high faith in the reality of knowledge, and an intense desire to find things out, all my philosophy has always seemed to grow. — C. S. Peirce.[1]

**1. Why were you initially drawn to Peirce?**
It was a long time ago. As best I can recall, I was first prompted to read Peirce seriously by the brisk paragraph near the end of the first chapter of *Word and Object* where Quine criticized his theory of truth. "Peirce," Quine wrote, "was tempted to define truth outright ... as the ideal theory which is approached as a limit when the (supposed) canons of scientific method are used ... on continuing experience." But this, he assured us, is hopeless. "There is a faulty use of analogy in speaking of a limit of theories, since ... 'nearer than' is defined for numbers but not for theories."[2]

Suspecting that this high-handed dismissal may have missed the mark—which of course it did!—I went straight to the library to check out what Peirce himself had to say. Not knowing which of the eight volumes of the *Collected Papers* might be crucial, I dutifully carted the whole lot back to my office, and started reading. I don't remember anything I did for the next several weeks *except* reading Peirce. But I

---

[1] C. S. Peirce, *Collected Papers*, eds. Charles Hartshorne, Paul Weiss, and (vols. 7 and 8) Arthur Burks (Cambridge, MA: Harvard University Press, 1931-58) (hereafter, CP), 1.14 (c.1897).

[2] W. V. Quine, *Word and Object* (New York, Wiley, 1960), 23.

*do* remember, after I came up for air, happily reporting to anyone who would listen: "I just discovered a philosophical gold-mine!"

It was only years later that I discovered that Quine had reviewed volumes 2, 3, and 4 of the *Collected Papers* shortly after they first came out; and that his review revealed that he didn't fully appreciate the importance of Peirce's contributions to logic[3]—with unfortunate consequences, as Putnam would later point out,[4] for our understanding of how modern logic developed. And it was only some years after this, browsing through the collection of John Dewey's correspondence with Arthur Bentley, that I learned that my reaction was exactly like Bentley's, after *he* buried himself in Peirce for weeks. "... I have had one of the excitements of my life reading Peirce the last six weeks or so. ... Everything that Carnap hollered is fully stated by Peirce, with, in addition, the 'vital spark' that Carnap's crew lack—[Peirce] was doing his best to sketch the living behavior of sign-using men in a longtime world."[5]

Anyway, ever since those first weeks of reading, I have thought of Peirce as a philosophical companion—someone whose wisdom I often consult, whose writings never fail to instruct, illuminate, and inspire, whose ideas I often borrow and adapt—even though, as should go without saying, from time to time we disagree.

## 2. What do you consider your contribution to the field?

Assuming that "the field," here, refers both to Peirce scholarship and to philosophical work influenced by Peirce's ideas, I will tackle this question in two parts: beginning with some of my contributions[6] to the interpretation and understanding of Peirce's work, and then moving to the philosophical work of my own in which ideas borrowed or adapted from Peirce play a significant role.

---

[3] W. V. Quine, Review of CP 2, *Isis* 19 (1933): 220-20; of CP 3 and 4, *Isis* 22 (1935): 285-97, 551-53.

[4] Hilary Putnam, "Peirce the Logician" (1982), in Putnam, *Realism with a Human Face* (Cambridge, MA: Harvard University Press, 1990), 252-60.

[5] Arthur Bentley to John Dewey, June 14, 1939, in Sidney Ratner, Jules Altman, and James E. Wheeler, eds., *John Dewey and Arthur Bentley: A Philosophical Correspondence*, 1932-51 (New Brunswick, NJ: Rutgers University Press, 1964), 72-3. As you see, Bentley had noticed that pragmatism is a kind of prope-positivism; but also that it is far richer and deeper than the Logical Positivists' approach.

[6] I have omitted, for example, an early piece, "Two Fallibilists in Search of the Truth" (*Proceedings of the Aristotelian Society*, Supplement, L, no.1 [1977]: 63-83)—not because it was wrong about Peirce, but because I now know it was much too charitable to Popper. See Susan Haack, "Just Say 'No' to Logical Negativism," in Haack, *Putting Philosophy to Work: Inquiry and Its Place in Culture* (Amherst, NY: Prometheus Books, 2008; 2nd ed., 2013), 179-94, 298-305.

My interpretive work includes papers:

a. On Peirce's critique of Descartes: locating Peirce's position between dogmatism and Cartesian skepticism, probing his critique of Descartes's "method of doubt," and exploring the social aspects of his theory of inquiry.[7]

b. On Peirce's philosophy of mathematics: locating Peirce's position vis à vis logicism; and showing that he was aware of the possibility of defining mathematical concepts in logical terms but, unlike Frege, rejected the idea that mathematics is epistemologically secondary to logic.[8]

c. On Peirce's scholastic realism: arguing that pragmatism doesn't preclude metaphysics, and that pragmatist metaphysics doesn't preclude realism; offering an interpretation of Peirce's thesis that there are real generals; exploring his critique of the idea that science is inherently nominalistic; and showing the relevance of all this to more recent (but still too often nominalistic—or nominalistic-Platonist)[9] philosophy of science.[10]

d. On Peirce's account of perception: arguing that (contrary to what many had supposed) there is a coherent account of perception to be found in Peirce's later work, and offering a categorial analysis of what he calls the "percipuum."[11]

e. On Peirce's "First Rule of Reason": offering my interpretation of this principle, and showing its relevance to philosophy today.[12]

f. On Peirce's hope of making philosophy scientific, and his attitude to literature and to literary scholars:[13] showing that Peirce's

---

[7] Susan Haack, "Descartes, Peirce, and the Cognitive Community" (1982), reprinted in Eugene Freeman, ed., *The Relevance of Charles Peirce* (La Salle, IL: The Hegeler Institute, Monist Library of Philosophy, 1983), 238-63.

[8] Susan Haack, "Peirce and Logicism: Notes Towards an Exposition," *Transactions of the Charles S. Peirce Society* 29, no.1 (1993): 333-56.

[9] The phrase is Peirce's. CP 5.503 (c.1905).

[10] Susan Haack, "Extreme Scholastic Realism: Its Relevance to Philosophy of Science Today," *Transactions of the Charles S. Peirce Society* 27, no.1 (1992): 19-50.

[11] Susan Haack, "How the Critical Common-Sensist Sees Things," *Histoire, epistémologie, langage* 16, no.1 (1994): 9-33.

[12] Susan Haack, "The First Rule of Reason," in Jacqueline Brunning and Paul Forster, eds., *The Rule of Reason: The Philosophy of C. S. Peirce* (Toronto: University of Toronto Press, 1997), 241-61.

[13] Susan Haack, "As for that phrase, 'studying in a literary spirit,' ..." (Romanell Lecture, American Philosophical Association, 1996), reprinted in Haack, *Manifesto of a Passionate Moderate: Unfashionable Essays* (Chicago, IL: University of Chicago Press,

objections to "studying in a literary spirit" indicate no hostility to literature, as such, but only to those "dilettanti" who "have so perverted thought to the purposes of pleasure that it seems to vex them to think that the question on which they delight to exercise it may ever get finally settled, and a positive discovery that takes a favorite subject out of the arena of literary debate is met with ill-concealed dislike."[14]

g. On Peirce's conception of "scientific metaphysics": showing how radically this differs from Kant's attempt to put metaphysics on "the secure path of a science,"[15] from the apriorist metaphysics now familiar to us from the work of David Lewis and Saul Kripke, *and* from the scientistic metaphysics we find in Quine.[16]

h. On Peirce's synechism: tracing the shift from synechism as a metaphysical thesis to synechism as a regulative principle, tracking the applications of this principle in Peirce's own philosophy, and suggesting its relevance to our own times.[17]

i. On Peirce's idea that meanings grow as our knowledge grows, that "men and words reciprocally educate each other":[18] showing how this idea relates to the Pragmatic Maxim, illustrating it with reference both to scientific and to legal concepts, and reflecting on its consequences for the analytic paradigm still (more or less) dominant in English-language philosophy.[19]

I should also mention:

j. The "conversation" between Peirce and Richard Rorty that I compiled from their own words;[20] a dialogue which, I hope, showed—what could not, within the limits of polite academic discourse, be

---

1998), 48-68.

[14] CP 5.396 (1878).

[15] Immanuel Kant, *Critique of Pure Reason* (1781/1787), trans. Norman Kemp Smith (London: Macmillan, 1929, corrected ed. 1933), Preface to the B edition.

[16] Susan Haack, "The Legitimacy of Metaphysics: Kant's Legacy to Peirce, and Peirce's to Philosophy Today" (2004), reprinted in *Polish Journal of Philosophy* 1 (2007): 29-43.

[17] Susan Haack, "Not Cynicism but Synechism: Lessons from Classical Pragmatism" (2005), reprinted in Haack, *Putting Philosophy to Work: Inquiry and Its Place in Culture* (Amherst, NY: Prometheus Books, 2008; 2nd ed., 2013), 83-96, 276-77.

[18] CP 7.587 (n.d.).

[19] Susan Haack, "The Growth of Meaning and the Limits of Formalism, in Science and Law," *Analísis filosófico* 29, no.1 (2009): 5-29.

[20] "'We pragmatists ...'; Peirce and Rorty in Conversation" (1997), reprinted in Haack, *Manifesto of a Passionate Moderate* (note 20 above), 31-47.

said—that Peirce's thought was incomparably deeper, broader, and more rigorous than Rorty's Vulgar Pragmatism.[21]

Many of these papers have been reprinted and/or translated, some several times; and that "conversation" has not only been reprinted over and over and translated into Portuguese, Chinese, and Danish, but also performed (at least) twice: once, in English, as after-dinner entertainment at a meeting of the Society for the Advancement of American Philosophy (with me playing the part of Peirce), and once, in Spanish, at the University of Granada, Spain (with me playing myself, as the somewhat-harassed interviewer).

But at least as important as my contribution to Peirce scholarship in these and other papers, I believe, is my contribution to training younger Peirce scholars: Mark Migotti, Cornelis de Waal, Robert Lane, Rosa Mayorga, Cheng Hsi-Heng, and, most recently, Aaron Wilson—all of whom have done excellent work, and some of whom are already known internationally for their contributions.[22] I am proud of them (as I am of the undergraduate, Will McAuliffe, who just last year wrote me a term paper carefully distinguishing Peirce's conception of abduction from the fashionable-but-feeble notion of "inference to the best explanation," and carefully tracked down the sources of the confusion).

\*\*\*

Turning now to the second way of taking this question, I can list only some of the countless ways in which Peirce's ideas have influenced my thinking:[23]

- Early on in my epistemological work, I mulled over Descartes's idea of the "chain of reasons," Peirce's critique, and his preferred analogy, the cable of reasons.[24] For a while I played with the idea of the structure of evidence as like a jigsaw puzzle; but then came up with the crossword analogy—which has proved enormously fruitful. And now, looking back, I see that (just as Peirce always

---

[21] A phrase I introduced in Susan Haack, *Evidence and Inquiry* (1993; 2nd ed., Amherst, NY: Prometheus Books, 2009), chapter 9.

[22] I'm not sure whether Cheryl Misak should be on the list; but I should add here, for the record, that her Oxford D. Phil. dissertation was jointly supervised by David Wiggins and myself.

[23] When I wrote my first two books, *Deviant Logic* (Cambridge: Cambridge University Press, 1974) and *Philosophy of Logics* (Cambridge: Cambridge University Press, 1978), I had no more than the most superficial acquaintance with Peirce. But scholars may observe that, while the first edition of *Deviant Logic* opens with a quotation from Quine, the expanded second edition, published in 1996, opens with a quotation from Peirce.

[24] CP 5.265 (1868).

provides us with congeries of reasons for his theories) my own work often moves, as it were, from a completed crossword entry to another, as-yet-uncompleted, entry where the previous solution has provided a letter or two.

- In *Evidence and Inquiry*[25] you can see the influence of Peirce's awareness of the need for exactitude in philosophical terminology and his *penchant* for neologisms; of his distaste for false dichotomies; and of his direct realism. My epistemological theory ("foundherentism") is intermediate between the traditional rivals, foundationalism and coherentism; and my account of the role of perception is informed by Peirce's defense of a realist view ("it is the external world that we directly observe").[26]

- In *Defending Science—Within Reason*,[27] I adapted Peirce's term "Critical Common-Sensism" for my understanding of science—an understanding that, again, steers a middle course, this time between the logical imperialism of the Old Deferentialists and the sociological imperialism of the New Cynics. And since key theses of this book are that inquiry in the sciences is continuous with everyday empirical inquiry, and that the natural and the social sciences are "the same, only different," *Defending Science* is also, obviously, a thoroughly synechist work.

- In "Preposterism and Its Consequences,"[28] and in some of my more recent work on the differences between inquiry and advocacy,[29] and on what's wrong with litigation-driven science,[30] Peirce's distinction between pseudo-inquiry (a.k.a. "sham reasoning") and the real thing plays a key role—though in my papers it is extrapolated to a threefold distinction: (i) genuine inquiry, (ii) sham reasoning [seeking evidence to bolster a conclusion of the truth of which you are unbudgeably convinced from the outset], and (iii) fake reasoning [seeking evidence to bolster a conclusion to the

---

[25] Note 21 above.

[26] CP 8.144 (1901).

[27] Susan Haack, *Defending Science—Within Reason: Between Scientism and Cynicism* (Amherst, NY: Prometheus Books, 2003/2007).

[28] Susan Haack, "Preposterism and Its Consequences" (1996), reprinted in *Manifesto of a Passionate Moderate* (note 13 above), 189-208.

[29] Susan Haack, "Epistemology Legalized: Or, Truth, Justice, and the American Way" (2004), reprinted in Haack, *Evidence Matters: Science, Proof, and Truth in the Law* (New York: Cambridge University Press, forthcoming 2014), 27-46.

[30] Susan Haack, "What's Wrong with Litigation-Driven Science?" (2008), reprinted in Haack, *Evidence Matters* (note 29 above), 160-207.

truth-value of which you are indifferent, but championing which you believe will be to your advantage].

- My work in ontology, especially "Realisms and Their Rivals"[31] and "Die Welt des unschuldigen Realismus"[32]—though the Innocent Realist picture I develop is in some ways very different from Peirce's—is scientific metaphysics in precisely Peirce's sense; and his scholastic realism, and especially his distinction between existence and reality, also play a significant role here (as they do in chapter 5 of *Defending Science,* where I try to identify the metaphysical underpinnings of the scientific enterprise).

- Similarly, in my meta-philosophical reflections, from "Between the Scylla of Scientism and the Charybdis of Apriorism"[33] to "The Fragmentation of Philosophy,"[34] there is not only an unmistakable synechism, but also—as I try to steer between the apriorism of some recent work and the scientism of much of the rest—a clear affinity with Peirce's conception of philosophy as depending on experience, but requiring, not the recondite experience sought by the special sciences, but close attention to familiar, everyday experience. And Peirce's idea of the growth of meaning plays a significant role in my repudiation of the idea of philosophy as purely a priori conceptual analysis,[35] as it also does in my philosophy of science and my philosophy of law.

- In "The Fragmentation of Philosophy"[36] I documented how the professional-philosophy "mainstream" is breaking up into smaller and smaller rivulets (with epistemology, for example, first distancing itself from philosophy of science, metaphysics, etc., and then itself splitting into reliabilist epistemology, virtue epistemology, social epistemology, feminist epistemology, Bayesian epistemo-

---

[31] Susan Haack, "Realisms and their Rivals: Recovering our Innocence," *Facta Philosofica* 4, no.1 (March 2002): 67-88.

[32] Susan Haack, "Die Welt des unschuldigen Realismus," in Markus Gabriel, ed., *Die Neue Realismus* (Berlin: Suhrkamp, forthcoming 2014).

[33] Susan Haack, "Between the Scylla of Scientism and the Charybdis of Apriorism," in Lewis Hahn, ed., *The Philosophy of Peter Strawson* (La Salle, IL: Open Court, 1998), 50-63.

[34] Susan Haack, "The Fragmentation of Philosophy, the Road to Reintegration," in Julia F. Göhner and Eva-Maria Jung, eds., *Susan Haack: Reintegrating Philosophy* (forthcoming).

[35] See, e.g., Susan Haack, "The Continuum of Inquiry: Response to Christoph Fischer and Eva-Maria Jung," in Göhner and Jung, *Susan Haack: Reintegrating Philosophy* (note 34 above).

[36] Susan Haack, "The Fragmentation of Philosophy" (note 34 above).

logy, etc., etc.). Our profession, I argued, is rapidly becoming a federation of self-referential, self-serving cliques. But this fragmentation is an intellectual disaster; as Peirce said, philosophy should be integrated, "architectonic."[37]

- And all through my work you will see the influence of the "contrite fallibilism, combined with a high faith in the reality of knowledge," of which Peirce speaks in the passage with which I opened. Like Peirce, I have never been able to muster much interest in trying to "refute the skeptic" (what's the point?); like him, I have always been far more concerned to figure out how we can figure things out. And I *hope*—though I can't claim to be the most patient person in the world—that at least *something* of Peirce's peirce-istence and peirce-severance has rubbed off on me.

### 3. What is the proper role of Peirce's work in relation to philosophy and other academic disciplines?

Peirce was a man of many parts: a scientist, a pioneer both of modern logic and of semiotics, *and* a philosopher of extraordinary breadth and depth. So the idea that his work has a unique "proper role" is quite misleading. But if I had to give a general, simple answer to this question, it would be: *we should treat Peirce's work as a valuable intellectual resource*, a treasure-trove of ideas many of which were ahead of our time, as well as of his own.

Cataloging that trove of ideas is well beyond my powers, and far beyond the scope of this short interview; all I can do is mention a few gems.

The editors of the *Collected Papers*, commenting on the vast range of Peirce's interests, mention "geodesy and astronomy, telepathy, criminology, and optics."[38] Peirce's professional scientific work, I recently learned—the subject of the only book he published in his lifetime[39]— was the first to define a unit of measurement (the meter) in terms of a natural phenomenon (the length of the spectral line).[40] This work is now part of the fabric of science, specifically, of metrology. But there are lessons here for philosophers, too: that all the fuss and bother over the "standard meter bar" in Wittgenstein and in Kripke is just that: pointless

---

[37] CP 1.176-79 (c.1896).

[38] Hartshorne and Weiss, "Introduction" to vol. 1 of the *Collected Papers* (note 2 above), iii.

[39] C. S. Peirce, *Photometric Researches* (1878).

[40] I learned this from Laura J. Snyder, "The Perfected Yardstick," *Wall Street Journal*, October 28, 2011, A15 (reviewing Robert P. Crease, *World in the Balance* [New York: W. W. Norton, 2011]), this laid the foundation of what is now called the International System of Units.

apriorist fuss and bother!

Peirce's logical innovations included not only a unified propositional and predicate calculus (a few years after, and independently of, Frege),[41] but also a three-valued logic,[42] and the intensional logic of the gamma graphs.[43] We might find that Peirce's approach to modal logic has advantages over the more recent tradition stemming from the work of Lewis and Langford;[44] that his graphical notation is in some ways more perspicuous than the now-more-familiar algebraic notation; that there's something in his idea that the "soul" of necessary reasoning is diagrammatic (an idea that Frege, too, eventually came to think plausible).[45] And we can certainly still learn from his fascinating pieces on the grounds of validity of the laws of logic[46] (including that remarkable analysis of the Strengthened Liar paradox),[47] and on why logic is worthy of study.[48]

I'm no expert on Peirce's semiotics, having ventured only briefly into this "amazing maze." But I'm sure this work is a valuable resource for all those (whether in philosophy, in linguistics, or in the study of film, photography, animal communication, or ..., etc., etc.) interested in the "labyrinth of signs" Peirce drew so vividly and explored so deeply—all the more so, because the triadic structure of Peirce's approach seems superior to the dualism of Saussure's. And when I think about the extraordinary complexities of modern societies[49] and especially modern

---

[41] See Peirce, "On the Algebra of Logic" (1880), and "The Logic of Relatives" (1883), CP 3.154-251 and 3.328-58; and Peirce's student, O. H. Mitchell, "On a New Algebra of Logic," in *Studies in Logic by Members of the Johns Hopkins University* (Boston, MA: Little, Brown, 1883), 72-106 (a book edited by Peirce, though his name does not appear). Frege, *Begriffsschrift* (1879), reprinted and translated in *Conceptual Notation and Related Articles*, ed. Terrell Ward Bynum (Oxford: Clarendon Press, 1972), 101-203.

[42] Peirce, *Logic Notebook* for 1909; reproduced in facsimile in Max Fisch and Atwell Turquette, "Peirce's Triadic Logic" (1966), in Kenneth Lane Ketner and Christian Kloesel, eds., *Peirce, Semeiotic, and Pragmatism* (Bloomington, IN: Indiana University Press, 1986), 171-83, pp.173-75.

[43] CP 4.510-529 (1903), 4.573-84 (1905).

[44] C. I. Lewis and C. H. Langford, *Symbolic Logic* (1932; New York: Dover, 1959).

[45] According to Bynum, by 1924 Frege had abandoned logicism, and was seeking the foundations of arithmetic in geometry. Terrell Ward Bynum, ed., *Conceptual Notation and Related Articles* (note 41 above), 54.

[46] CP 5.318-57 (1868).

[47] The Liar Paradox is "This statement is false"; the Strengthened Liar Paradox is "This statement is not true." The latter is often thought of as a relatively recent new wrinkle; but it was already to be found in Peirce in 1868.

[48] CP 2.119-202 (1902).

[49] See, e.g., Susan Haack, "Brave New World: On Nature, Culture, and the Limits of Reductionism," in Bartosz Brosek and Jerzy Stelmach, eds., *Explaining the Mind* (Kraków: Copernicus Center Press, forthcoming 2015).

legal systems, this semiotic labyrinth and especially Peirce's talk of interpretations of interpretations of interpretations[50] often comes to mind.

As for Peirce's legacy to philosophy, I will simply say that he contributed so much to so many areas that it's hard to think of any philosophical field—from philosophy of logic and language, metaphysics and theory of inquiry, philosophy of science, philosophy of religion, cosmology, philosophy of mind, even ethics[51] and aesthetics[52]—where we can't still learn something from him. Even in writing about the law[53] (not one of Peirce's strongest suits), I've found him helpful: his critique of the adversarialism of "our [i.e., the U.S.] atrocious legal system,"[54] though not much more than a passing remark, poses questions no less challenging than Jeremy Bentham's critique of exclusionary rules of evidence;[55] and his synechism suggests a fruitful approach to that hoary old question, "what is law?"[56]

**4. What do you consider the most important topics and/or contributions in the field of Peirce studies?**

There are many kinds of contribution to our understanding of Peirce, and to making the resources he left us available.

Murray Murphey's *The Development of Peirce's Philosophy*[57] and Thomas Goudge's *The Thought of C. S. Peirce*[58] helped me find my way around in the early days—though I always resisted Goudge's idea that there were two Peirces, the pragmatist and the metaphysician. (Recently, asked to give the after-dinner speech at a meeting of the Canadian Institute for the Administration of Justice, I was thrilled to find in my audience Justice Stephen Goudge, of the Ontario Court of Appeal—

---

[50] See, e.g., Susan Haack, "Cracks in the Wall, a Bulge Under the Carpet: The Singular Story of Religion, Evolution, and the U.S. Constitution," *Wayne Law Review* 57, no. 4 (2011): 1303-32.

[51] See, e.g., Rosa Mayorga, "Peirce's Moral Realism," in Cornelis de Waal and Krysztof Piotr Skowronski, *The Normative Thought of Charles S. Peirce* (New York: Fordham University Press, 2012), 101-24 (this volume also includes papers by de Waal and James Liszka on Peirce's ethics, but I'm less familiar with these).

[52] See, e.g., Rosa Mayorga, "On the 'Beauty of the Unbeautiful' in Peirce's Esthetics," *Cognitio* 14 (Jan.-Jun. 2013): 85-100.

[53] Haack, "Epistemology Legalized" (note 29 above).

[54] CP 2.635 (1878).

[55] Jeremy Bentham, Treatise on *Judicial Evidence* (1827; New York: Garland, 1978).

[56] See, e.g., Susan Haack, "The Pluralistic Universe of Law: Towards a Neo-Classical Legal Pragmatism," *Ratio Juris* 21, no.4 (2008): 453-80.

[57] Murray Murphey, *The Development of Peirce's Philosophy* (Cambridge, MA: Harvard University Press, 1961).

[58] Thomas Goudge, *The Thought of C. S. Peirce* (Toronto: University of Toronto Press, 1950).

Thomas Goudge's son. What a small world!)

At the other end of the spectrum, I have reason to be grateful to all the cataloguers, editors, etc., who have helped make Peirce's work more accessible, on paper and now online.

But I've always preferred to work with Peirce, rather than read up on secondary literature. So I can't do much to identify the "most important contributions" to Peirce scholarship: in part because I'm aware that there's so much, even in English, with which I'm not familiar; but also because, as I see it, Peirce's legacy belongs, not just to the English-speaking philosophical world, but to the philosophical world — no, to the intellectual world — as a whole. I know there's a good deal of relevant work being done throughout Europe (e.g., in Spain, France, Italy, Germany, Poland, Finland, Slovakia, Greece, Romania), in Latin America (e.g., Brazil, Argentina, Mexico, Uruguay, Colombia) and elsewhere (e.g., Israel, China, Taiwan). But I'm sure I don't know the half of what's out there. And I know that one of the most interesting people writing today about the mind, neurosurgeon Raymond Tallis,[59] is an admirer of Peirce's work; but I'm sure I don't know even one percent of what's being done outside narrowly philosophical circles.

## 5. What are the most important open problems in the field, and what are the prospects/avenues for progress?

Once again that phrase "the most important" makes me uneasy; and once again I stress that I'm in no position to know all the avenues that have been explored, or with what success. I can offer only a list of topics where I'd like to know more, both about exactly what Peirce had in mind, and about how his ideas might be applied, adapted, elaborated, etc., by philosophers working today.

Almost certainly there's much more to be done exploring Peirce's voluminous writings on logic and (as we would say today, though he used "logic" in a broader sense) philosophy of logic; his ideas about mathematics, and his conceptions of continuity and of reduction; his cosmological speculations; his writings on the mind; his theory of inquiry, his account of perception, inner and outer, and (still) the interaction of the individual and the social elements in his account of truth; his "extreme scholastic realism" and its consequences for the sciences; his categories; his thoughts about classification, and specifically his classification of the sciences; his unique (and I believe, uniquely plausible) understanding of metaphysics; his thoughts about precision; his relatively brief, but tantalizing, suggestions about ethics and aesthetics,

---

[59] See e.g., Raymond Tallis, *Aping Mankind: Darwinitis, Neuromania, and the Misrepresentation of Humanity* (Durham: Acumen, 2011).

..., etc., etc.—not to mention his work in semiotics, in mathematics, in metrology, in psychology, on great men in history,[60] ...

Almost certainly, too, there's much more work to be done exploring Peirce's extraordinarily broad knowledge of the history of philosophy, and how this broad knowledge shaped his own views—along the lines of Boler's, and now Mayorga's, work on the influence of Duns Scotus, and of de Waal's, and now Wilson's, work on Peirce's relation to the empiricist tradition, and so on. And I'm sure there's still plenty to learn by exploring Peirce's reflections on the lessons to be learned from history of science, and from his interactions with other scientists of his day.

And perhaps some day someone—maybe it will even be me!—will explore those remarkably vivid and philosophically instructive metaphors and analogies we find in Peirce's writings. Here, I'll just list some of my favorites—first, like Peirce, begging my audience's pardon for "hopping from one branch of my discourse to another and back again with no more apparent purpose than a robin redbreast or a Charles Lamb":[61] the cable of reasons;[62] paper doubts;[63] the genuine inquirer as "drawing the bow upon truth";[64] an unclear idea as like "an obstruction in an artery" in a young man's brain;[65] the "blight of cocksureness";[66] the fallibilist's willingness to "dump the whole cart-load" of his beliefs the moment experience is against them;[67] consciousness as a bottomless lake;[68] the barriers philosophers erect on the road of inquiry;[69] British philosophers as like a man building a house entirely of various forms of paper;[70] the empirical

---

[60] Peirce, in Peirce Edition Project, eds., *Writings of Charles S. Peirce* (Bloomington, IN: Indiana University Press, 1982— ), 5:26-106 (1883-84). See also Susan Haack, "The Differences that Make a Difference: William James on the Importance of Individuals," *European Journal of Pragmatism and American Philosophy* 2, no. 1 (2010): 1-10.

[61] Id., 1.656 (1898).

[62] Note 24 above.

[63] See, e.g., CP 5.514 (c.1905): "a third mark of the Critical Common-sensist is that he has a high esteem for doubt. ... Only [he] is not to be appeased with paper doubts; he must have the heavy and noble metal, or else belief."

[64] Id., 1.235 (1902).

[65] Id., 5.393 (1878).

[66] Id., 1.13 (c.1897).

[67] Id., 1.55 (c.1896).

[68] Id., 7.547 (n.d.): "I think of consciousness as a bottomless lake, whose waters seem transparent, yet into which we can see clearly but a little way."

[69] Id., 1.135 (c.1899.

[70] Id., 6.7 (1891): "English" philosophers, Peirce writes, referring to Hobbes, Hartley, Berkeley, and James Mill, are like a man who goes to work "to build a papier mâché house, with roof of roofing paper, foundations of pasteboard, windows of paraffined paper, bath tubs, locks, etc., all of different forms of paper ..."

basis of science as a swamp;[71] rescuing philosophy from the "lawless rovers of the sea of literature";[72] clearing our logical chimney by burning a straw man;[73] the derelict ship that logical fatalism will eventually bring to shore;[74] the "philosophical soup-shops at every corner," in which Peirce declines to display his intellectual wares;[75] conducting "experiments to ascertain, for example, whether there be any uniformity in nature or no" as like "adding a teaspoonful of saccharine to the ocean in order to sweeten it";[76] natural law without force to carry it out as "a court without a sheriff";[77] and, of course, Peirce's announcement of the birth of the word "pragmaticism," "ugly enough to be safe from kidnappers."[78]

The last example reminds me to add that there will likely still be work to do keeping the pragmatist tradition safe from imperialist colonizers (whether post-modern or neo-analytic, or ...) hoping to annex it to their turf; and that thought, in turn, prompts me to add that, on the other hand, there's likely still much to learn by comparative work on the pragmatist and other traditions.

Looking around me, I see professional philosophy becoming more and more specialized and more and more distanced from its own history. And even in history of philosophy, now, much work seems to be increasingly focused on smaller and smaller points of interpretation or, even more depressingly, on what other scholars of X or Y have had to say about these smaller and smaller points of interpretation.[79] I for one would be *very* sorry if "Peirce studies" were to become yet another philosophical niche, and "Peirce people" yet another clique talking only among themselves.

So if I had to leave readers with just one thought it would be, as I said in response to the third question, that the way to look at Peirce's work is emphatically *not* as yet another subject of specialization, but as a valuable—or maybe I should say an *in*valuable—intellectual resource.[80]

---

[71] Id., 5.589 (1898): science "is still not standing on a bedrock of fact. It is walking upon a bog, and can only say, this ground seems to hold for the present."

[72] Id., 5.449 (1905): writing of "rescu[ing] the good ship Philosophy for the service of Science from the hands of lawless rovers of the sea of literature."

[73] Id., 5.503 (c.1905): "I have found the combustion of a man of straw one of the best means of stopping my logical chimney from smoking."

[74] Id., 7.78 (according to the editors, undated, but referring to results from the census of 1900).

[75] Id., 1.11 (c.1897).

[76] Id., 5.522 (c.1905).

[77] Id., 1.212 (1902).

[78] Id., 5.414 (1905). See also Susan Haack, "The Meaning of Pragmatism: The Ethics of Terminology and the Language of Philosophy," *Teorema* XXX/III, no.3 (2009): 9-29.

[79] See again "The Fragmentation of Philosophy" (note 34 above).

[80] My thanks to Mark Migotti for his helpful comments on a draft.

## Bibliography[81]

### Books

*Deviant Logic* (Cambridge: Cambridge University Press, 1974). [Also in Spanish.] Expanded 2nd edition, *Deviant Logic, Fuzzy Logic: Beyond the Formalism* (Chicago: University of Chicago Press, 1996).

*Philosophy of Logics* (Cambridge: Cambridge University Press, 1978). [Also in Spanish, Italian, Korean, Portuguese, Chinese, and Croatian.]

*Evidence and Inquiry* (1993; expanded 2nd ed., Amherst, NY: Prometheus Books, 2009). [Also in Spanish and Chinese.]

*Manifesto of a Passionate Moderate: Unfashionable Essays* (Chicago: University of Chicago Press, 1998). [Also in Portuguese.]

*Defending Science—Within Reason: Between Scientism and Cynicism* (Amherst, NY: Prometheus Books, 2003). [Also in Chinese.]

*Pragmatism, Old and New* (ed., with associate editor Robert E. Lane) (Amherst, NY: Prometheus Books, 2006). [Also in Chinese.]

*Ciencia, sociedad y cultura: Ensayos elegidos* (ed. Edison Otero) (Santiago de Chile: Diego Portales University Press, 2008).

*Putting Philosophy to Work: Inquiry and Its Place in Culture* (2008; 2nd ed. Amherst, NY: Prometheus Books, 2008).

*Evidence Matters: Science, Proof, and Truth in the Law* (New York: Cambridge University Press, forthcoming 2014).

### Articles

"Descartes, Peirce, and the Cognitive Community" (1982), reprinted in Eugene Freeman, ed., *The Relevance of Charles Peirce* (La Salle, IL: The Hegeler Institute, Monist Library of Philosophy, 1983), 238-63.

"Extreme Scholastic Realism: Its Relevance to Philosophy of Science Today," *Transactions of the Charles S. Peirce Society* 27, no.1 (1992): 19-50.

"Peirce and Logicism: Notes Towards an Exposition," *Transactions of the Charles S. Peirce Society* 29, no.1 (1993): 333-56.

"How the Critical Common-Sensist Sees Things," *Histoire, épistemologie, langage* 16, no.1 (1994): 9-33.

"The First Rule of Reason," in Jacqueline Brunning and Paul Forster, eds., *The Rule of Reason: The Philosophy of C. S. Peirce* (Toronto: University of Toronto Press, 1997), 241-61.

---

[81] I have included only a few of the most relevant of my articles. A complete list is available at http://www.law.miami.edu/faculty-administration/susan-haack.php?op=1

"As for that phrase, 'studying in a literary spirit,' ..." (Romanell Lecture, American Philosophical Association, 1996), reprinted in Haack, *Manifesto of a Passionate Moderate: Unfashionable Essays* (Chicago, IL: University of Chicago Press, 1998), 48-68. [Also in Spanish and Portuguese.]

"'We pragmatists ...'; Peirce and Rorty in Conversation" (1997), reprinted in Haack, *Manifesto of a Passionate Moderate*, 31-47. [Also in Chinese, Portuguese, and Danish.]

"Between the Scylla of Scientism and the Charybdis of Apriorism," in Lewis Hahn, ed., *The Philosophy of P. F. Strawson* (La Salle, IL: Open Court, Library of Living Philosophers, 1998), 50-63. [Also in Spanish and Chinese.]

"Realisms and Their Rivals: Recovering our Innocence," *Facta Philosophica* 4, no.1 (2002): 67-88. [Also in Spanish and Chinese.]

"The Legitimacy of Metaphysics: Kant's Legacy to Perce, and Peirce's to Philosophy Today" (2004), reprinted in *Polish Journal of Philosophy* 1 (2007): 29-43, and in *Philosophical Topics* 36, no.1 (2008): 97-110. [Also in Spanish.]

"Epistemology Legalized: Or, Truth, Justice, and the American Way," *American Journal of Jurisprudence* 49 (2004): 43-61; reprinted in Haack, *Evidence and Inquiry*, 2$^{nd}$ ed., 361-81, and in *Evidence Matters*, 27-46. [Also forthcoming in Spanish.]

"Not Cynicism but Synechism: Lessons from Classical Pragmatism" (2005), reprinted in Haack, *Putting Philosophy to Work: Inquiry and Its Place in Culture* (Amherst, NY: Prometheus Books, 2008; 2$^{nd}$ ed., 2013), 83-96, 276-77.

"On Legal Pragmatism: Where does 'The Path of the Law" Lead Us?" *American Journal of Jurisprudence* 50 (2005): 71-105. [Also in press in Spanish, and forthcoming in Polish.]

"The Pluralistic Universe of Law: Towards a Neo-Classical Legal Pragmatism," *Ratio Juris* 21, no.4 (2008): 453-80. [Also in Portuguese and German.]

"What's Wrong with Litigation-Driven Science? An Essay in Legal Epistemology," *Seton Hall Law Review* 38, no.3 (2008): 1053-83; reprinted in Haack, *Evidence Matters*, 160-207.

"The Growth of Meaning and the Limits of Formalism, in Science and Law,"*Analísis filosófico* 29, no.1 (2009): 5-29. [Also in Portuguese.]

"The Meaning of Pragmatism: The Ethics of Terminology and the Language of Philosophy," *Teorema* XXX/III, no.3 (2009): 9-29. [Also forthcoming in Polish.]

"Out of Step: Academic Ethics in a Preposterous Environment" (2010), in Haack, *Putting Philosophy to Work*, 2$^{nd}$ ed., 251-67 and 313-37. [Also in Chinese, Portuguese, and Spanish.]

"Pragmatism, Then and Now" (SH interviewed by Sun yong), *Pragmatism Today* (2010). [Also in Chinese.]

"Die Welt des unschuldigen Realismus," in Markus Gabriel, ed., *Der Neue Realismus* (Berlin: Suhrkamp, forthcoming).

"The Fragmentation of Philosophy, the Road to Reintegration," in Julia Fredericke Göhner and Eva-Maria Jung, eds., *Susan Haack: Reintegrating Philosophy*.

"Brave New World: On Nature, Culture, and the Limits of Reductionism," in Bartosz Brozek and Jerzy Stelmach, eds., *Explaining the Mind* (Kraków: Copernicus Center Press, forthcoming 2015).

# 11

# Leila Haaparanta

Professor of Philosophy
School of Social Sciences and Humanities/Philosophy,
University of Tampere, Finland

---

**1. Why were you initially drawn to Peirce?**
I think the very first influences came from my Finnish teachers and senior colleagues, Risto Hilpinen, Jaakko Hintikka, Ilkka Niiniluoto, and Veikko Rantala, who all worked on Peirce's thought and its relevance to contemporary philosophy. One source of inspiration was the externalist view of the relations between thought and language, as I first started to write my thesis on Wilfrid Sellars's analogy theory of thinking and found the externalist, anti-Cartesian tradition, to which Peirce also belonged. Moreover, I was influenced by Simo Knuuttila, who as an expert of medieval philosophy made me interested in Peirce's medieval roots.

I wrote my doctoral thesis in the early eighties on Frege's doctrine of being. My intention was to dig into the epistemological and metaphysical background of Frege's "formula language of pure thought." That project brought me to a wider problem. I asked how modern logic was discovered, and more specifically, how Frege and Peirce made their great discoveries at the end of the nineteenth century. Primarily I sought the possible philosophical origins of their discoveries, and naturally came up with Immanuel Kant, who was part of their common philosophical background. I also came up with studying Edmund Husserl and thereby making comparisons between Frege, Peirce, and Husserl. I also wished to show the importance of geometry in the three philosophers' thought. It was thus Frege, Peirce, and Husserl and their background in Kant and geometry that became my research topic at the end of the 80's.

**2. What do you consider your contribution to the field?**
My interests have focused on two themes. First, I have made an attempt to reconstruct Peirce's as well as Frege's discoveries of the structure of a new logical language. The two logicians discovered quantification theory. Frege's achievement was published in his *Begriffsschrift* (1879), while Peirce's important articles appeared in the early 1880's.

Frege and Peirce both rejected the Aristotelian and the Boolean view of the structure of propositions, in which a proposition was seen as a combination of subject and predicate. I have shown that whether Frege and Peirce made any conscious choice, they used the method of analysis when they discovered their logical languages. I have also argued that the method of analysis used by Frege and Peirce had its philosophical origin in Kant's method of analysis. To support my thesis, I have developed an interpretational model which relies on the basic ideas of geometrical problem-solving; the geometrical way of thinking is Frege's guide in reconstructing the conceptual notation and Peirce's guide in the discovery of the general algebra of logic. I have also stressed the role of Peirce's students, particularly, Christine Ladd-Franklin and O.H. Mitchell. I have mainly focused on the first half of Peirce's philosophy. However – and this brings me to the other interest I have had – I have sought to show that Peirce's phenomenology and his view according to which all reasoning is diagrammatic have something to do with his logical discovery in the 1880's. I have argued that there is phenomenology and the emphasis on diagrams at the time when Peirce discovered his new algebra of logic. The model of geometrical drawing activities helps us to understand Peirce's view of judgments as drawings and the analysis of those drawings, and it was this new understanding of the role of judgments that was largely responsible for the rise of the new formula language in late nineteenth century logic. I have also studied Peirce's views of thinking, including philosophical thinking, understanding, and the mind more generally, and sought to show the emphasis of the role of diagrams in whatever part of Peirce's philosophy we wish to look at.

## 3. What is the proper role of Peirce's work in relation to philosophy and other academic disciplines?

As I have limited my studies to specific problems, I tend to see Peirce as a logician, as a philosopher of mind, and as a representative of Kantian philosophy. However, what is peculiar in his philosophy is that he is definitely not a thinker who specializes in certain subfields. That attitude, openness to all fields, I think, made it also possible for him to contribute to formal developments. He searches for a comprehensive system, which is all the time in the state of becoming, and that is obviously visible also in his style and in the variety of texts that a scholar must face. But what is a demanding task for Peirce scholarship has become a special source of inspiration for philosophy and several academic disciplines; if his philosophy works in many directions, let it be that way.

## 4. What do you consider the most important topics and/or contributions in the field of Peirce studies?

It is not easy to give a list of the most important topics or contributions. What I pick up from my point of view are the following: Peirce's theory of signs and his contribution to views of human understanding, reconstructions of his views of scientific research and the influence of those views on contemporary philosophy of science and science studies, and the studies of Peirce's philosophical sources, such as medieval philosophy, Kant, and Hegel. Now that metaphysics has become an important field after the antimetaphysical period of twentieth century philosophy, it is interesting to pay attention to Peirce as a philosopher who assented to both science and metaphysics.

## 5. What are the most important open problems in this field and what are the prospects/avenues for progress?

There are still many open questions for one who focuses on Peirce's philosophical background and his logical discoveries. Peirce's role in the history of logic still needs more attention. What I also find important is to consider the ways Peirce understands the relations between logic and metaphysics. I find the interfaces between philosophical traditions particularly interesting; in that respect, much can still be said about Peirce and Husserl, or Peirce and the analytic tradition. One avenue for progress is certainly co-operation between various subfields of philosophy, and also co-operation between the humanities and the formal sciences.

### Bibliography

**Leila Haaparanta, articles on Peirce and Peircean themes:**

"The Analogy Theory of Thinking," *Dialectica* 46, 1992, pp. 169-183.

"Charles Peirce and the Logic of Logical Discovery," in E. Moore (ed.), *Charles S. Peirce and the Philosophy of Science*, Proceedings of Charles Sanders Peirce Sesquicentennial International Congress, Harvard University, 5-10 September 1989, The University of Alabama Press, Tuscaloosa, Alabama, 1993, pp. 158-179.

"Logiikka ja ajattelun ikonisuus" (Logic and the Iconicity of Thinking), in L. Haaparanta et al. (eds.), *Malli, metodi, merkitys*, Filosofisia tutkimuksia Tampereen yliopistosta, Vol. 49, 1993, pp. 39-51.

"Charles Peirce and the Drawings of the Mind," *Histoire, Epistémologie, Langage* 16, 1994, pp. 37-52.

"Älykäsitykset ja moderni logiikka" (Concepts of Intelligence and

Modern Logic), in L. Haaparanta et al. (eds.), *Älyn ulottuvuudet ja oppihistoria*, Suomen Tekoälyseuran julkaisuja, No. 13, 1995, pp. 39 - 46.

"Peirce's Theory of Signs and the Method of Analysis," in P. Weingartner et al. (eds.), *The Role of Pragmatics in Contemporary Philosophy*, Volume 1, Contributions of the Austrian Ludwig Wittgenstein Society, Kirchberg am Wechsel, 1997, pp. 351 - 355.

"Perspectives on Peirce's Logic," *Semiotica* 133, 2001, pp. 157 - 167.

"On Peirce's Methodology of Logic and Philosophy," *Cognitio* 3, 2002, pp. 32 – 45.

"Peircen merkkiteorian filosofinen tausta" (The Philosophical Background of Peirce's Theory of Signs), in E. Kilpinen et al. (eds.), *Pragmatismi filosofiassa ja yhteiskuntatieteissä* (Pragmatism in Philosophy and the Social Sciences), Gaudeamus, Helsinki, 2008, pp. 52 - 60.

"The Relations between Logic and Philosophy 1874 – 1931," in L. Haaparanta (ed.), *The Development of Modern Logic*, Oxford University Press, New York, 2009, pp. 222 – 262.

"Kuva ja oikeutus" (Image and Justification), in L. Haaparanta et al.(eds.), *Kuva, Acta Philosophica Tamperensia, Vol. 5*, 2009, pp. 121 - 131.

# 12

# Jaakko Hintikka

Helsinki Collegium for Advanced Studies, University of Helsinki
& Department of Philosophy, Boston University

---

**1. Why were you initially drawn to Peirce?**

My attention was initially drawn to Peirce by the similarities and dissimilarities between his ideas and those of other important philosophers. The first such relationship was probably that of Peirce's emphasis on the iconic aspect of meaning and Wittgenstein's picture theory. Why did Peirce use it prominently to understand inference while for Wittgenstein picture relations were the gist of permanent meaning relations?

**2. What do you consider your contribution to the field?**

In general terms my contribution to Peirce studies has been to come to understand his ideas by understanding their topical significance. Typically, this is made possible by deepening our grasp of those topical ideas themselves. Dramatically, I have repeatedly found that my own ideas had been discovered and discussed by Peirce. They include the following, in a rough chronological order:

i) Peirce's innovation in extended modal logic. In this he was far ahead of his time. Formal logics of modality were cultivated first prominently by Peirce's follower C. I. Lewis and became a subject of philosophers' serious interest only after 1950.

ii) Peirce's "first real discovery" of the difference between theorematic and corollarial reasoning was a logical distinction concerning the individuals (real or "arbitrary") involved in reasoning (Hintikka 1980). I had discussed those issues extensively in Hintikka (1973).

iii) As Hilpinen was the first to point out, Peirce had discovered all the leading ideas of the game-theoretical interpretation of quantifier logic explicitly. In Peirce game-theoretical ideas nevertheless remained semantical rather than strictly logical – in his logic of graphs, Peirce in effect used game-theoretical semantics more widely than in the traditional first-order logic.

iv) Peirce noticed specific examples where traditional first-order logic goes wrong. They include the alleged equivalence of:

Someone is such that if he fails in business, he commits suicide; and Someone is such that if everyone fails in business, he commits suicide.

What is needed is to make the conditional "if" informationally independent of the quantifier "someone". See here Hintikka (2012b).

v) Peirce exemplified one horn in the important overall contrast between visions of language and its logic as a universal medium and language as a re-interpretable calculus. In this respect Peirce differed from most of his major contemporaries, which helps to understand the relative neglect of his ideas about logic, reasoning and meaning.

vi) Peirce's ideas about the scientific method including the interpretation of the notions of abduction and induction are best discussed by reference to an interrogative approach to inquiry. This holds especially of Peirce's notion of abduction (see Hintikka 1998).

## 3. What is the proper role of Peirce's work in relation to philosophy and other academic disciplines?

As a consequence of these discoveries, the place of Peirce in the history of philosophy and more generally in philosophical discussion has to be reconsidered and revisited.

Peirce's work in logic has to be seen in the perspective of the logization of mathematics that is usually referred to as an increase of the "rigor" of mathematical reasoning and concept formation. The use of logic was at first unformalized, but according to the prevailing view that logic was formalized by Gottlob Frege who thereby became the founder of modern logic. Peirce's contribution is viewed as a partial and independent co-discovery.

This picture has turned out to be radically wrong (see Hintikka 2012a). Frege failed to capture by his logic all the principles of reasoning that mathematicians of his time were using. Frege thereby left serious flaws in the logic he formalized, including the traditional first-order logic and set theory.

Peirce in contrast mastered the working logic of mathematicians. He did not formalize it the same sense as Frege formalized his, but his graphical method could easily be extended so as to fill gaps. Hence Peirce has a much more solid claim to be the real founder of modern logic.

This can be generalized. Peirce's ideas are far too often discussed by reference to standard 20th century issues and developments, often as a partial anticipation of later "discoveries". This is a misleading perspective that does not do justice to Peirce. It should be acknowledged that many of Peirce's ideas still are in fact ahead of those of the majority of contemporary philosophers. An example is offered by a recent collection of studies of Peirce's philosophy of mathematics (Moore 2010). In it, those ideas of Peirce that still have not been carried out are conspicuous by their absence.

**4. What do you consider the most important topics and/or contributions in the field of Peirce studies?**

What one considers important in Peirce depends on one's own philosophical orientation. A metaphysician like Robert Neville or a historian of American philosophy is impressed by different ideas than a semiotician or a philosopher of science. From my own perspective, the developments described above could scarcely be more important.

It is also important to realize that attempts to enroll Peirce as a precursor of the likes of Richard Rorty are a gross distortion of historical reality.

**5. What are the most important open problems in this field and what are the prospects/avenues for progress?**

The developments reported in (2) leave many historical and/or systematic questions open. Why did Peirce not systematize explicitly his game-theoretical semantics? The primary topical reason is that he did not have the game-theoretical concept of (complete) strategy that was introduced by John von Neumann (1928). Peirce comes nearest to it in his notion of habit, whose epistemological and logical properties deserve further study.

In logic, the crucial notion that Frege missed is the concept of informational independence which again is explicated in game theory. One cannot but wonder to what extent Peirce was aware of the need for such a notion and why he did not realize its full role in the logic of mathematical reasoning – wonder especially because Peirce was aware of such reasoning in practice.

Again the notion of abduction needs more attention both systematical and as used by Peirce. Abduction is still often mistakenly identified with inference to the best explanation. The most promising idea seems to be to realize that in an interrogative inquiry educated guesses can be thought of epistemologically as a species of possible answers.

Peirce presented examples for ordinary language in which the received first-order logic leads to plainly wrong formalizations. Such examples show the need of revising our familiar first-order logic in yet a new way that can only be captured by game-theoretical semantics. Philosophers and logicians are mostly unaware of the need of this revision. It needs to be spelled out systematically.

The prospects of Peirce studies depend essentially on progress in dealing with the systematic issues he was struggling with. To study him as a merely historical figure misses what is most interesting in his writings.

## References

Hilpinen, Risto, 1982, "On C. S. Peirce's theory of the proposition: Peirce as a precursor of game- theoretical semantics". *The Monist*, vol. 65. 182–188.

Hintikka, Jaakko, 1973, *Logic, Language-Games and Information*. Oxford University Press, Oxford.

Hintikka, Jaakko, 1980, "C. S. Peirce's 'first real discover' and its contemporary relevance". *The Monist*, vol. 63. 304–315.

Hintikka, Jaakko, 1996, "The place of C. S. Peirce in the history of logical theory" in Jacqueline Brunning and Paul Forster, editors, *The Rule of Reason: Philosophy of Charles Sanders Peirce*. University of Toronto Press, Toronto. 140–160.

Hintikka, Jaakko, 1998, "What is abduction? The fundamental problem of contemporary epistemology". *Transactions of the Charles Peirce Society*, vol. 34. 503–533.

Hintikka, Jaakko, 2012a, "Which mathematical logic is the logic of mathematics?" *Logica Universalis*, vol. 6. 459–475.

Hintikka, Jaakko, 2012b, "IF logic and linguistic theory" in *Philosophy, Mathematics, Linguistics: Aspects of Interaction*. The Institute of the Russian Academy of Sciences - Steklov Mathematical Institute - The Euler International Mathematical Institute, St. Petersburg. 70–77.

Moore, Mathew E. (editor), 2010, *New Essays on Peirce's Mathematical Philosophy*. Open Court, Chicago.

von Neumann, John, 1928, "Zur Theorie der Gesellschaftsspiele". *Mathematische Annalen*, vol. 100. 295–320.

# 13

# Michael H. G. Hoffmann

School of Public Policy, Philosophy Program
Georgia Institute of Technology, USA

---

**1. Why were you initially drawn to Peirce?**

My current interest in Peirce is driven by the question of how learning is possible—learning not only in education, but also in public deliberation and in processes that contribute to the solution of conflicts. With regard to this question, I focus in particular on Peirce's ideas on "abductive," "theoric," and "theorematic" reasoning, and on the role that working with external representations—that is: "diagrammatic reasoning"—can play to explain the creativity that Peirce envisioned for these three kinds of reasoning. Initially, however, I got drawn into Peirce in the context of a research project on his philosophy of mathematics. Michael Otte, one of the directors of the interdisciplinary Institute for Mathematics Education (IDM) at the University of Bielefeld (Germany), invited me to join a project on Peirce's concept of "continuity" and its implications for a philosophy of mathematics that stands in the tradition of Immanuel Kant. Peirce developed his philosophy of mathematics before the field moved into the now famous "Grundlagenstreit," the Foundational Debate, with its distinction of "Platonism," "Intuitionism," and "Formalism." Peirce, as it turns out, is less interested in questions such as those on the ontological status of mathematical "objects" or how we can have knowledge of those "objects," but in the question of how the development of mathematical knowledge can be possible if mathematics—as everybody seems to agree, at least at Peirce's time—allows only deductive reasoning. How can there be any creativity in mathematics if every mathematical result can be derived from some prior propositions by means of deduction?

Part of Peirce's answer to this question is rooted in Kant's idea that mathematics is not an analytical science—as the primacy of deduction would suggest—but based on "synthetic a priori judgments." While "*philosophical* cognition," according to Kant, "is *rational cognition from concepts*, mathematical cognition that from the *construction* of concepts" (Kant, CPR B 741; Kant's emphasis).[1] For Peirce this meant in particular that we gain new mathematical knowledge mainly through what he called "diagrammatic reasoning." He defines diagrammatic reasoning by a five-step process: constructing diagrams, experimenting with these diagrams, discovering regularities in our experiments, testing these regularities to see whether they represent generality, and finally, formulating these generalities as new knowledge (Peirce, NEM IV 47-48).

Since I consider my work on diagrammatic reasoning as one of my main contributions to the field, I will say more about this in my answer to the next question. But it should be important, with regard to motivations that "drew" me to Peirce, to mention another problem that is crucial when it comes to learning mathematics, but also a major stumbling block in any discipline that deals with "abstract objects": How can it be possible to communicate mathematical facts that do not have any material manifestation, that cannot be "seen" in the way apples and chairs can be seen—like the fact that the lengths of side and diagonal in a square are "incommensurable"? It is quite easy to train children to manipulate symbols such as $\sqrt{2}$ that represents this fact, but how is it possible to foster the sort of comprehension that is necessary to go from there to even more abstract facts?

## 2. What do you consider your contribution to the field?

After a few years all these questions converged in a research program that focused on the role of diagrammatic representations for cognitive processes that seem to be essential in learning, creativity, deliberation, and conflict management. Peirce's concept of "diagrammatic reasoning" turns out to be key for understanding not only the development of knowledge in mathematics—because abstract facts are only accessible and communicable by means of diagrammatic representations—but in any endeavor that depends on working with representations. Overall, I see my main contribution to both the Peirce literature and a general theory of "knowledge development"[2] in the elaboration of two theses:

---

[1] I published a piece about the historical context in a book chapter that is available only in German. Its English title would be: "Contrasting a synthetic-pragmatic and an analytic conception of mathematics in the history of philosophy of mathematics" (Hoffmann, 2001).

[2] "Knowledge development" is the core concept that I used in the title of my book "Erkenntnisentwicklung. Ein semiotisch-pragmatischer Ansatz (Knowledge Development. A Semiotic and Pragmatic Approach)." Since it has been written in German, I will not say much about it here (Hoffmann, 2005a). The book has been published in 2005 but it was completed, for the most parts, in 2002. Many of its ideas were either previously or afterward (or both) discussed in articles and chapters that I mention below.

1. The creativity which is characteristic for learning and the development of knowledge, and that Peirce describes with the newly coined concepts of "abductive," "theoric," and "theorematic" reasoning, can be explained if we go beyond what Peirce himself achieved in this area and use another concept he developed: diagrammatic reasoning. By "going beyond Peirce" I mean connecting ideas that he himself discussed separately as belonging to different disciplines. Whereas he discusses "theorematic deduction" and "theoric steps" only, as far as I can see, in relation to mathematics and "diagrammatic reasoning" only in relation to logic and mathematics, "abduction," for him, is primarily a form of scientific reasoning.

2. The potential of diagrammatic reasoning for the explanation of learning and creativity depends fundamentally on the normativity of the representational system that we need to choose for any form of diagrammatic reasoning. This second thesis also goes "beyond" Peirce. Even though Peirce mentions at one time that a diagram "should be carried out upon a perfectly consistent system of representation, founded upon a simple and easily intelligible basic idea" (Peirce CP 4.418), and even though he points out that the respective system defines those transformations of a diagram that are "permissible" (NEM IV 318), he does not develop any more detailed analysis of what he means by a "system of representation."[3] But it is clear from the context of both quotes (and others) that his prime example of a representational system or "diagrammatic syntax" (NEM III 162) is the logical notation of his Existential Graphs. If we consider the Existential Graphs as a system of representation, we can conclude that representational systems in general can be characterized by (a) a certain ontology that specifies what can be represented, (b) rules that determine permissible transformations of diagrams, and (c) certain conventions.

In the following, I would like to provide a rough outline of the arguments that I developed in several publications to justify both these theses. The purpose, though, of these considerations is rather to point out where the arguments can be found, not to repeat them in detail. In closing, I will hint at a few more contributions developed along the route: first, a new classification of 15 forms of abduction; and second a distinction of four different functions signs can fulfill which goes beyond Peirce's focus on the representational function of signs.

---

[3] References that should be studied with regard to this notion include CP 2.599 (1901-2/²1911), NEM III 1120 (1903), NEM IV 318 (1906), CP 4.530, 534 (1906), NEM III 162 (1911).

## 13. Michael H. G. Hoffmann

The first thesis that the possibility of learning and creativity can be explained by diagrammatic reasoning resulted from a certain frustration about the fact that Peirce's life-long attempts to explain just this possibility by his concept of abduction do not succeed. As I showed in "Problems with Peirce's Concept of Abduction" (Hoffmann, 1999), abductive reasoning takes place, according to Peirce, when we form hypotheses to explain surprising or hitherto unexplained facts. Even though his distinction between induction and abduction constitutes a crucial contribution to scientific methodology, and even though Peirce defines the "logical form" of both inferences clearly enough, the logical form of abduction cannot explain the genuine creative act of coming up with an explanatory hypothesis. In this paper, I developed a distinction between the logical form of abduction—in which the conclusion states that there is reason to assume that an explanatory hypothesis is true if it can explain an observation—and the genesis of this hypothesis in an act of perception. However, since Peirce defined perception itself as an abductive inference, his attempt to explain the creative side of abduction by perception runs inevitably in an infinite regress or circle. No less problematic seem Peirce's attempts to explain the possibility of abductive creativity by some sort of "instinct."

However, Peirce's concept of "diagrammatic reasoning" can be used in this situation as a way forward. By liberating it from its mathematical context—where it refers exclusively to necessary, i.e., deductive reasoning—I developed the notion of diagrammatic reasoning to a general method that is used in all sciences. In order to better understand how exactly diagrammatic reasoning can contribute to the development of knowledge I focused, on the one hand, on specific activities that can happen in working with diagrams and, on the other, on the cognitive role of external representations in general.

Specific activities are described in "Signs as Means for Discoveries. Peirce and His Concepts of 'Diagrammatic Reasoning,' 'Theorematic Deduction,' 'Hypostatic Abstraction,' and 'Theoric Transformation'" (Hoffmann, 2005c). In this paper I show that in the process of diagrammatic reasoning each of the other concepts mentioned in this title can play a crucial role in a three-step process. First, looking at diagrams "from a novel point of view" in what Peirce calls a "theoric step" offers opportunities to synthesize elements of these diagrams which have never been perceived as connected before. Second, by forming those observed syntheses to "new objects" of thinking, and by signifying these objects through new signs in "hypostatic abstractions," new means of thinking and acting are created that then can be used for "theorematic deductions." And finally, by applying these new means—in proofs, for instance—the "intelligibility" of new discoveries and their power to explain problematic facts can be tested.

Maybe the most interesting of these Peircean concepts is that of a "theoric step" or "transformation." To my knowledge, its significance for explaining the possibility of knowledge development is so far not yet recognized in Peirce scholarship or elsewhere. In "'Theoric Transformations' and a New Classification of Abductive Inferences" (Hoffmann, 2011d), I analyzed in some detail Peirce's main example for a theoric transformation—the proof of Desargues's theorem—to demonstrate its potential for explaining important scientific discoveries. This switch of perspective that Peirce called "theoric transformation" has much later been conceptualized—in research on conflicts—as "reframing" (Donohue, Rogan, & Kaufman, 2011; Hoffmann, 2011a; Lakoff, 2004; Lewicki, Gray, & Elliott, 2003; Schön & Rein, 1994). According to this literature we always "frame" situations from a specific point of view and based on given background knowledge, beliefs, and values. In so-called "intractable" conflicts the main issue is that problems and possible solutions are "framed" in incommensurable ways so that mutual understanding is impossible. In these situations the crucial question is whether "reframing" is possible. The epistemological significance of "theoric transformation," "framing," "frame reflection," and "reframing" has yet to find its way into the philosophical literature.

The cognitive role of external representations is first discussed in "Learning from people, things, and signs" (Hoffmann, 2007). Empirical research shows that small children demonstrate a more reliable command of the number sequence when they count objects in front of them than when they just count the numbers. Also, obviously all children start to learn calculating with the help of their fingers. In this article I discussed phenomena like these in the context of cognitive science literature on "distributed cognition" (e.g. Hutchins, 1995). I proposed a terminological distinction between "knowledge" and "cognitive abilities" where cognitive abilities are defined as parts of "cognitive systems" in which a certain environment and social setting are constitutive parts. Whereas knowledge is "at our disposal," independently from any specific environment, cognitive abilities are always dependent on certain things, signs, or persons that are present in a specific situation. It is one cognitive ability to count a specific set of wood blocks and another to count certain apples. It is only in the process of learning that we gradually transform specific abilities into general knowledge.

In the context of these considerations, the cognitive role of external representations is to "scaffold" the growth of cognitive abilities. As Edwin Hutchins showed, the apprentice on a ship learns by repeated observation of how the map of a sea route into a harbor, in connection with the changing landscape and its landmarks that are noted on the map, regulates the captain's navigation (Hutchins, 1995, pp. 292-293).

From this point of view, signs and representations are crucial for the self-control of reasoning. They are part of a cognitive system because they organize, structure, constrain, and guide our cognitive activities. For Peirce, "reasoning is essentially thought that is under self-control" (Peirce, EP II 249). Logic is a "normative science" because it defines standards of good reasoning that we should use for this self-control (EP II 250; and CP 1.606, 1903). This means that in working with diagrams that are constructed by means of a certain representational system—which, as the Existential Graphs, incorporates such a standard—the norms of this representational system regulate our reasoning just as the sea map regulates the captain's navigation.

These considerations lead to the second thesis mentioned above, that diagrammatic reasoning can only support creativity and foster learning if the learner knows the norms of the representational system (and its ontology and conventions) that she chooses for diagrammatic reasoning. In "Cognitive conditions of diagrammatic reasoning" (Hoffmann, 2011c), I analyze the first-ever recorded (or imagined) lesson in mathematics that we can find in Plato's *Meno* as a case of diagrammatic reasoning in which learning happens in the form of distributed cognition. In contrast to Plato's own interpretation I show that the geometrical figures Socrates draws in the sand, and the experiments that he and the boy perform with these figures, are crucial for this example of successful learning. But more importantly, reasoning with these diagrams works only because of the normative power that is given in the rules of geometry as the chosen system of representation. The boy learns only because he understands that—based on these rules as they become visible in experiments with the diagram—doubling the sides of a square leads necessarily to a square that is four times the size of the original square, not double, as he first hypothesizes.

As I show with this example, a necessary condition for learning something by means of diagrammatic reasoning is knowing and accepting the rules, conventions, and ontology of a chosen system of representation; a system by means of which diagrams can be constructed, and that determines the results of experimenting with diagrams. Such a system, which has to be well-defined, constrains reasoning in a way that our cognitive energy gets focused on points that are crucial for creativity—just like a fireman's jet of water will be the more focused the more it is constrained. Without any constraints there would be no direction for our reasoning. This way, the possibility of learning and creativity depends fundamentally on the normativity of the representational system that we need to choose for any act of diagrammatic reasoning. (I developed a slightly different argument for the cognitive power of the rules of representational systems also in "Diagrams as Scaffolds for Creativity"

[Hoffmann, 2010], in the section "Representational Systems as a Scaffold for Abductive Insights," p. 48).

While the normativity of representational systems seems, thus, to be crucial for creativity, learning, and reframing—because the rules of these systems make that a diagram, as Kathleen Hull put it, "stands up against our consciousness" (Hull, 1994)—there is one essential point that needs to be taken into account in addition to that. In "How to Get It. Diagrammatic Reasoning as a Tool of Knowledge Development and its Pragmatic Dimension" (Hoffmann, 2004), I argued that any conceptualization of diagrammatic reasoning should include certain elements of Peirce's pragmatism, in particular its underlying realism. Since, unfortunately, the overall structure of this argument misses some clarity, I would like to summarize here what I think the argument should have been.

In the first part of this argument I showed that determining the meaning of concepts by means of the Pragmatic Maxim works only if there is a real connection between a concept and its conceivable practical consequences or applications. "If, for instance, everybody would interpret and apply the words of our languages completely at will, the meaning of these words could indeed never be clarified by the Pragmatic Maxim" (pp. 289-290). This means that Peirce's pragmatism presupposes what he called an "extreme scholastic realism." This form of realism claims "the reality of some possibilities" (CP 5.435, 8.208, both 1905). "In order to have a chance to determine the meaning of a concept by determining its *conceivable* or possible applications, we have to presuppose that there is a "real, 'lawlike relation' between this concept and its—in principle—*infinite* set of possible consequences" (p. 290).

But what can it mean to presuppose the reality of possibilities? What kind of realism can do that? In the second part of this argument I showed—by developing three strategies that could be used to justify such a "possibilia realism"—that the decisive point of such a realism would be that assuming the reality of one thing is required to guarantee the possibility of something else. This is as far away from Platonism with its assumption of the eternal existence of "pure forms" as it gets. Something is assumed to be "real" only in so far as it "sustains" the possibility of something that we take for granted. For example, we take it for granted that we will find our way home tonight from work, but in order to find this belief justifiable we need to assume that the city is still structured as always, that our eyes and memory are working as they did in the past, and so on—and all this without being necessary able to describe the structure of the city and the working of eyes and memory. Kant called this a "*pragmatic* belief" because even if we do not know whether a certain belief is true or not, we can use as if it were true (CPR B 852). It works for a certain purpose and as long as no serious doubt challenges us to reconsider.

Similarly, we might question whether so-called "laws of nature" are real or not, or that any regularities are real that we use to predict events. But it seems to be clear that we would not invest any resources into science if there would not be some hope that there will be some useful outcome. The possibility of science can only be "sustained" if we assume some sort of reality for regularities that allow predictions. If not, the entire endeavor would not make any sense. I called this very peculiar form of realism "sustainability realism" because it assumes as real what sustains and enables something else that we take for granted. This reality is defined mainly by its pragmatic purpose. If we want to know more about what is claimed to be real here, we will study it and, thus, subject it to the normal, evolutionary process of knowledge creation.

The concluding third part of my argument uses the enabling relation between sustainability realism and pragmatism—that is the thesis that pragmatism is only possible if this form of realism is presupposed—as an analogy to argue that the normativity that is given in the rules of representational systems should be conceived in a similar way. This analogy has two dimensions. First, just as the assumption of a "real" relation between a concept and its conceivable practical consequences is a precondition for applying the Pragmatic Maxim, so the normativity of representational systems needs to be presupposed to learn something in diagrammatic reasoning. Secondly, just as what is assumed to be real to sustain a pragmatic relation always needs to be open to refinement and development, so should the normativity of representational systems be understood as evolving. In "How to get it" I illustrate the far-reaching implications of taking the evolution of systems of representation into account by describing the historic development of non-Euclidean geometries out of Euclidean geometry. What all this means is that not only the normativity of representational systems is important, but also the continuous development of these system.

After summarizing my work on the two theses mentioned above—that Peirce's notion of diagrammatic reasoning can be used to explain the creativity involved in "abductive," "theoric," and "theorematic" reasoning, and that this creativity depends on the normativity of the chosen representational system—I would like to point out a few further contributions to the Peirce literature.

In "'Theoric Transformations' and a New Classification of Abductive Inferences (Hoffmann, 2011d), I do not only clarify the first notion, but also bring back my insights about diagrammatic reasoning to the problem of abduction. Starting from a definition of "abductive insight" that specifies success conditions for abductive reasoning, and based on a critical discussion of G. Schurz's distinction of eleven "patterns of abduction" that he organizes in four groups (Schurz, 2008), I propose here an even more comprehensive classification that distinguishes 15 forms in an alternative structure. These forms are organized, on the one hand, with regard to what is abductively inferred—singular facts, types, laws, theoretical models, or representational systems—and, on the other, with regard to the question whether the abductive procedure is selective or creative (including a distinction between "psychologically creative," as in school learning, or "historically creative"). Moreover, I argue that theoretical-model abduction—which seems to be the most important form of abduction—depends on two preconditions: first on the availability of an adequate system of representation, and second on finding a new "perspective" on a given problem, as Peirce described it with the notion of a "theoric transformation." Going beyond what has so far been discussed about abduction in the literature, I develop in this paper additionally the idea that diagrammatic reasoning cannot only explain the creativity in abduction, but that—*vice versa*—the potential of diagrammatic reasoning increases substantially any time the underlying representational systems are improved or extended by means of a form of abduction that I dubbed "meta-diagrammatic abduction." This form of abduction refers to what I described earlier in "How to get it" with the example of the development of Euclidean to non-Euclidean geometries (Hoffmann, 2004, p. 297-303).

Another contribution is "Four Functions of Signs in Learning and Interdisciplinary Collaboration" (Hoffmann & Roth, 2010). It is well known that Peirce struggled for the largest part of his life to develop a comprehensive theory of signs and representations ("semiotic," or "semeiotic"). There are some indications that he himself perceived his efforts at the end as a failure. This paper argues that a fundamental problem of Peirce's approach to semiotics is that he did not realize that signs can fulfill a set of very different functions. Depending on these functions, our understanding of what signs are will vary. In this paper we distinguish a "representational," "epistemic," "volitional," and "formal" function of signs. As far as I can see, Peirce focused exclusively on the representational function, for example when he defines a sign as follows:

> "A sign, or *representamen*, is something which stands to somebody for some-thing in some respect or capacity. It addresses somebody, that is, creates in the mind of that person an equivalent sign, or perhaps a more developed sign. That sign which it

creates I call the *interpretant* of the first sign. The sign stands for something, its *object*." (Peirce, CP 2.228, 1897)

But signs do not only represent something for an interpretant, they are also instrumental for purposes that are related to the creation of knowledge. They have what we call an "epistemic function." We are using signs to *refer* to certain objects, be it indexically or symbolically, to *structure* certain aspects of reality, for example by tables and diagrams, or even to *constitute* objects—as in mathematics—that would not be accessible otherwise. The fact, for instance, that the side and diagonal of a square are incommensurable is accessible only by means of a proof, that is, by a chain of signs that we interpret as proof. Other abstract objects in mathematics—including the imaginary number $i$ and the intersection of parallel lines at infinity—are established by convention and would not exist without signs referring to them. Similarly, signs constitute non-observables in empirical sciences, be it DNA or the Higgs boson.

The "volitional function" of signs, again, becomes visible when an agent uses a sign in a certain context to achieve a certain purpose, for example to manipulate either a social environment or his or her own thinking. And the formal function, finally, refers to those operations with signs in which the meaning of these signs is irrelevant. An example would be the transformation of symbols according to certain transformation rules in a computer.

One of the results of this extension of semiotic functions is that Peirce's famous "triadicity" that he assigned to everything he touched really becomes an inacceptable and hardly convincing Procrustean bed. As we showed with diagrams that depict how signs are embedded in triadic or tetradic relationships, only the formal and the epistemic function are triadic because they alone can work when only three elements are connected: sign, transformation rule, and response in the case of the formal function, and sign user, sign, and object in the case of an epistemic relation. The representational function, however, requires a tetradic relation. Even though Peirce always claimed that, as "a medium, the Sign is essentially in a triadic relation, to its Object which determines it, and to its Interpretant which it determines" (EP II 544, c.1906), we argue that such a determination is only possible when a fourth element is present: collateral knowledge about the sign's meaning. Peirce himself argued, very late in his life, that "no sign can be understood . . . unless the interpreter has 'collateral acquaintance' with every object of it" (Peirce, EP II 496). But he did not draw the necessary conclusion that this requires collateral knowledge as the fourth element in a tetradic sign relation.

## 3. What is the proper role of Peirce's work in relation to philosophy and other academic disciplines?

Peirce once wrote about the "creation of the universe" as a still ongoing process that realizes itself as the "development of Reason." "Under this conception, the ideal of conduct will be to execute our little function in the operation of the creation by giving a hand toward rendering the world more reasonable whenever, as the slang is, it is 'up to us' to do so" (EP II 255 = CP 1.615, 1903). I think that "giving a hand toward rendering the world more reasonable" is exactly how Peirce himself would have liked to see his role. It is "up to us," however, to make this happen because it is often not easy to see what exactly Peirce's contributions could be. In my own work I tried to show the tremendous potential that lies in his work on diagrammatic reasoning in applications that range from reflections on framing in conflict research to the development of AGORA-net, a software-based systems for the representation of arguments (Hoffmann, 2005b, 2011a, 2011b, 2013; Hoffmann & Borenstein, 2014).

## 4. What do you consider the most important topics and/or contributions in the field of Peirce studies?

Any attempt to answer this question would force me to assume a position in relation to the Peirce literature that is kind of un-Peircean. For Peirce we are all—as thinkers—embedded in the growth and "development of Reason" in the universe (EP II 255 = CP 1.615, 1903). There is no point outside of this process from which we could talk about the process itself. It seems to me more appropriate to perceive myself as an interlocutor in an ongoing conversation about the questions I am personally interested in. In this conversation, I very much appreciate the input from Frederik Stjernfelt that he provided in particular with his book *Diagrammatology* (Stjernfelt, 2007) and the work by Sun-Joo Shin, especially her book *The Iconic Logic of Peirce's Graphs* (Shin, 2002). But there are many more, and this is just in my narrow field.

## 5. What are the most important open problems in this field and what are the prospects/avenues for progress?

For me, Peirce is important as a thinker because he raised so many questions and developed so many new approaches to problems nobody had thought of before him. But he is certainly not someone who would claim that he answered these questions in a definite and conclusive way, or that he would have elaborated these approaches to a degree of certainty and completeness that would allow us to simply take and use his results as ready-made tools. Everything in his writing is in flux and ongoing development. This, however, means that everything in Peirce's philosophy is a problem. Whatever he wrote should be seen as an invitation to think on our own and to continue the work of thinking that he began.

If this observation is adequate, however, then the question of what "the most important problems" in the field of Peirce studies are depends entirely on the problems one brings to Peirce. Why do we read Peirce? What do we think he can contribute to the questions we have?

**References**

Donohue, W. A., Rogan, R. G., & Kaufman, S. (eds.). (2011). *Framing Matters: Perspectives on Negotiation Research and Practice in Communication*. New York, NY: Peter Lang.

Hoffmann, M. H. G. (1999). Problems with Peirce's Concept of Abduction. *Foundations of Science, 4*(3), 271–305.

Hoffmann, M. H. G. (2001). Die synthetisch-pragmatische Mathematikauffassung im Gegensatz zur analytischen – ein Blick auf die Geschichte der Philosophie der Mathematik. In K. Lengnink, S. Prediger & F. Siebel (eds.), *Mathematik und Mensch. Sichtweisen der Allgemeinen Mathematik* (pp. 127-140). Mühltal: Verlag Allgemeine Wissenschaft.

Hoffmann, M. H. G. (2004). How to Get It. Diagrammatic Reasoning as a Tool of Knowledge Development and its Pragmatic Dimension. *Foundations of Science, 9*(3), 285-305.

Hoffmann, M. H. G. (2005a). *Erkenntnisentwicklung. Ein semiotisch-pragmatischer Ansatz (Knowledge Development. A Semiotic and Pragmatic Approach)*. Frankfurt am Main: Klostermann.

Hoffmann, M. H. G. (2005b). Logical argument mapping: A method for overcoming cognitive problems of conflict management. *International Journal of Conflict Management, 16*(4), 304-334.

Hoffmann, M. H. G. (2005c). Signs as Means for Discoveries. Peirce and His Concepts of 'Diagrammatic Reasoning,' 'Theorematic Deduction,' 'Hypostatic Abstraction,' and 'Theoric Transformation'. In M. H. G. Hoffmann, J. Lenhard & F. Seeger (eds.), *Activity and Sign – Grounding Mathematics Education* (pp. 45-56). New York: Springer.

Hoffmann, M. H. G. (2007). Learning from people, things, and signs. *Studies in Philosophy and Education, 26*(3), 185-204.

Hoffmann, M. H. G. (2010). Diagrams as Scaffolds for Creativity. *AAAI Workshops, North America*. Retrieved from http://aaai.org/ocs/index.php/WS/AAAIW10/paper/view/2027

Hoffmann, M. H. G. (2011a). Analyzing Framing Processes in Conflicts and Communication by Means of Logical Argument Mapping. In W. A. Donohue, R. G. Rogan & S. Kaufman (eds.), *Framing Matters: Perspectives on Negotiation Research and Practice in Communication* (pp. 136-164). New York, NY: Peter Lang.

Hoffmann, M. H. G. (2011b). Climate Ethics: Structuring Deliberation by means of Logical Argument Mapping. *Journal of Speculative Philosophy, 25*(1), 64-97.

Hoffmann, M. H. G. (2011c). Cognitive conditions of diagrammatic reasoning. *Semiotica, 186*(1/4), 189-212.

Hoffmann, M. H. G. (2011d). "Theoric Transformations" and a New Classification of Abductive Inferences. *Transactions of the Charles S Peirce Society, 46*(4), 570-590.

Hoffmann, M. H. G. (2013). Changing Philosophy through Technology: Complexity and Computer-Supported Collaborative Argument Mapping. *Philosophy & Technology (pre-print version available at http://works.bepress.com/michael_hoffmann/41/)* online first. Retrieved from http://link.springer.com/article/10.1007/s13347-013-0143-6 doi:10.1007/s13347-013-0143-6

Hoffmann, M. H. G., & Borenstein, J. (2014). Understanding Ill-Structured Engineering Ethics Problems Through a Collaborative Learning and Argument Visualization Approach. *Science and Engineering Ethics, 20*(1), 261-276. doi: 10.1007/s11948-013-9430-y

Hoffmann, M. H. G., & Roth, W.-M. (2010). Four Functions of Signs in Learning and Interdisciplinary Collaboration. In I. Semetsky (Ed.), *Semiotics - Education - Experience* (pp. 131-150). Rotterdam, NL: Sense Publishers.

Hull, K. (1994). Why Hanker After Logic? Mathematical Imagination, Creativity and Perception in Peirce's Systematic Philosophy. *Transactions of the Charles S. Peirce Society, 30*, 271–295.

Hutchins, E. (1995). *Cognition in the wild*. Cambridge, MA: MIT Press.

Kant, I. (CPR). *Critique of pure reason* (P. Guyer & A. W. Wood, Trans.). Cambridge 1998: Cambridge Univ. Pr. (quoted according to the first edition—A: 1781—or the second—B: 1787).

Lakoff, G. (2004). *Don't Think of an Elephant: Know Your Values and Frame the Debate—The Essential Guide for Progressives*: Chelsea Green Publishing Company.

Lewicki, R. J., Gray, B., & Elliott, M. (eds.). (2003). *Making Sense of Intractable Environmental Conflicts. Concepts and Cases*. Washington - Covelo - London: Island Press.

Peirce. (CP). *Collected Papers of Charles Sanders Peirce*. Cambridge, Mass.: Harvard UP.

Peirce. (EP). *The Essential Peirce. Selected Philosophical Writings. Vol. 1 (1867–1893), Vol. 2 (1893–1913)*. Bloomington and Indianapolis 1992 +1998: Indiana University Press.

Peirce. (NEM). *The New Elements of Mathematics by Charles S. Peirce* (Vol. I-IV). The Hague-Paris/Atlantic Highlands, N.J., 1976: Mouton/ Humanities Press.

Schön, D. A., & Rein, M. (1994). *Frame reflection. Toward the resolution of intractable policy controversies*. New York: BasicBooks.

Schurz, G. (2008). Patterns of abduction. *Synthese, 164*(2), 201-234. doi: 10.1007/s11229-007-9223-4

Shin, S.-J. (2002). *The Iconic Logic of Peirce's Graphs*. Cambridge, MA: MIT Bradford Books.

Stjernfelt, F. (2007). *Diagrammatology: An Investigation on the Borderlines of Phenomenology, Ontology, and Semiotics*. Dordrecht, NL: Springer.

# 14

# Christopher Hookway

Professor of Philosophy
University of Sheffield

---

**1. Why were you initially drawn to Peirce?**

My interests in pragmatism and, in particular, Charles Sanders Peirce first emerged in the 1970s when I was an MA student at the University of East Anglia in Norwich. One of my teachers was Martin Hollis, and he set me to read C. I. Lewis's book *Mind and The World Order*. Hollis's teaching and Lewis's book had an enormous effect on my understanding of how Philosophy should be done. The philosophy I was exposed to when I was undergraduate had been most influenced by Wittgenstein and the ways of dealing philosophy most common in Oxford. Oxford was still in the grip of 'ordinary language philosophy', and my reading of Lewis's work helped me to see that philosophy could be systematic yet rigorous and I found it rewarding and exciting

I first became aware of Peirce some from remarks in Lewis's book. Especially by his discussions of Peirce's pragmatic maxim: and by reading some reading some writings by the followers of Wilfrid Sellars such as Bruce Aune. Most import here was finding a second hand copy of Bryce Gallie's Penguin, *Peirce and Pragmatism* in the market in Norwich. This elegant little book helped me to see that I wanted to know more about Peirce and Pragmatism. It led me to read Peirce's own work. While I was a junior research fellow in Peterhouse Cambridge, I extended my exploration of his work, even if I was mostly working in philosophy of mind and philosophy of language. It was a pleasure and source of encouragement in Cambridge that Gallie was in Peterhouse. Once I accepted a lectureship in the Philosophy of Birmingham I had more time for work on Peirce and Pragmatism. I obtained a contract to write a Peirce for the 'Arguments of the Philosophers' Series, and then obtained a grant from Fulbright and ACLS to spend a year working on Peirce's Manuscripts in the Houghton Library at Harvard University. By the end of my year in Cambridge MA, I had a complete draft of the book, and it was published in 1985.

## 2. What do you consider your contribution to the field?

My interests in Peirce have been wide, and I have written on a number of topics, most of which arise out of issues about the problems that Peirce raises and about how we should understand his views. My first book on Peirce, (*Peirce: The Arguments of the Philosophers* 1985) was largely concerned with understanding the overall shape of his work; I recall being concerned especially with trying to understand Peirce's views of mathematics and perceptions, but the character of the book meant that I could not address these issues in detail.

The papers in my second book 2001, *Truth, Rationality and Pragmatism* were concerned with truth, especially with idea of *convergence* and *reference*, but also about the role of affective states in rational self-control and related topics about *doubt*.

The papers in my third book, *The Pragmatic Maxim* (2013) contain a wider range of material. A major topic concerns the proper formulation of Peirce's pragmatic maxim and, in the longest chapter, questions about why the pragmatic maxim should be accepted; this involves engagement with debates about 'the proof of pragmatism'. I was also pleased with a paper called 'The form of a relation' which defended the view that Peirce's philosophy of mathematics was a form of structuralism. Other chapters were concerned with Peirce's views about inquiry, considering the aim of inquiry, and the form of abductive inferences.

## 3. What is the proper role of Peirce's work in relation to philosophy and other academic disciplines?

I may not have a short answer this question. His greatest achievement lies in defending a distinctive character to inquiry: he shows why philosophers should be able to avoid scepticism on the grounds that we have no genuine doubts that force us to address these issues. Furthermore, how showed us how to recognize the importance of fallibilism.

Another set of areas in which Peirce's work makes a contribution is semiotics and logic. There are many areas in which Peirce's semeiotic can make contributions. These include areas from philosophy of language to the description and analysis of a variety of contexts, and Peirce's contributions to logic continue to be important.

We can also find insights in research in metaphysics: Peirce has distinctive approaches to metaphysics, and these can also offer new ways of alternatives to the most common approaches to metaphysics and cosmology.

## 4. What do you consider the most important topics and/or contributions in the field of Peirce studies?

1) Peirce's theories of truth and their application, as developed, for example, by Cheryl Misak.

2) Also important are contributions by a number of people to the understanding of the structure of inquiry and of the strategies that should be employed in inquiry that should be applied. These issues involve the proper use of the pragmatic maxim and a number of other epistemic standards.

3) Pragmatistic understanding of how to formulate issues of realism.

4) Contributes to the understanding of diagrammatic reasoning.

5) Identifying issues about the theory of signs and its applications

## 5. What are the most important open problems in this field and what are the prospects/avenues for progress?

There are no particular gaps in our knowledge that need to be filled. We probably need a better understanding of normative reasoning and the metaphysics of norms within a Peircean framework. We may also work towards a better Peircean understanding of ethical inquiries.

### Five publications by Christopher Hookway

*Peirce (The Arguments of the Philosophers)* London: Routledge and Kegan Paul, 1985

'Modest Transcendental Arguments and sceptical doubts', in *Transcendental Arguments*, edited by Robert Stern, Oxford: Oxford University Press, 1999: 173-188

*Truth Rationality, and Pragmatism*. Oxford: Oxford University Press, 2000 (A collection of twelve papers, of which eight had been previously published.)

'Ramsey and Pragmatism: the influence of Peirce', in *F.P. Ramsey: Critical reassessments*, London: continuum, 2005

*The Pragmatic Maxim: Essays on Peirce and Pragmatism*. Oxford: Oxford University Press, 2013 (A collection of eleven papers of which nine had been previously published)

# 15

# Nathan Houser

Professor Emeritus of Philosophy
Indiana University, Indianapolis
Senior Fellow at The Institute for American Thought, IUPUI.

---

**1. Why were you initially drawn to Peirce?**

I first learned about Peirce in the mid-70's in a course on modern philosophy that I was taking at the University of Waterloo, where I studied philosophy. The course was taught by Prof. Don D. Roberts who, as was not then typical, included a segment on Thomas Reid, focusing particularly on Reid's common sense philosophy, which I found attractive. Prof. Roberts explained that the 19th century American philosopher, Charles Peirce, had incorporated key ideas from Reid in his post-Darwinian pragmatic philosophy. My choice for a final essay topic for that course was Reid's theory of signs, my first excursion into that field of thought, and that further stimulated my interest in Peirce, who Prof. Roberts told us had developed an extensive semiotic philosophy.[1] I remember, although now quite vaguely, that in that course I learned enough about Peirce to consider him a leading candidate for serious further study. I was especially attracted to Peirce because of his considerable knowledge of logic and science but, at the same time, by his

---

[1] Our text for the Reid segment of Roberts' course was Reid's 1764 *An inquiry into the Human Mind* (ed. Timothy Duggan [Chicago: University of Chicago: 1970, based on the 1813 Charlestown edition]), and I noted the following quotation from p. 218 as a useful summation of Reid's semiotic theory:

> [T]here are two things necessary to our knowing things by means of signs. First, that a real connection between the sign and thing signified be established, either by the course of nature, or by the will and appointment of men. When they are connected by the course of nature, it is a natural sign; when by human appointment, it is an artificial sign. . . . Another requisite to our knowing things by signs is, that the appearance of the sign to the mind, be followed by the conception and belief of the thing signified. . . . Now, there are three ways in which the mind passes from the appearance of a natural sign to the conception and belief of the thing signified; by original principles of our constitution, by custom, and by reasoning.

willingness to consider metaphysical questions. I was also attracted by the breadth and power of Peirce's mind.

The philosophers at the University of Waterloo were generally supportive of the analytic tradition featuring the British Empiricists, Kant, and the Vienna Circle philosophers and European Émigrés to the US. The American philosopher who seemed to be held in the highest regard was Quine. Logic was still of central importance for the Waterloo curriculum although meta-ethics was almost of equal weight. The philosophy of mind, due largely to the rapidly increasing interest in artificial intelligence, was quickly gaining ground. I discovered that Peirce's philosophy was relevant, but more than that, illuminating, for key problems in all of these areas. I took several more courses with Prof. Roberts, including two logic courses based on Peirce's Existential Graphs and an advanced course on pragmatism for which I remember writing a paper on Peirce's proof of pragmatism. I was a grader for some of Prof. Roberts' courses and was the teaching assistant for his correspondence logic course based on Peirce's graphical syntax. Probably around 1976 or 1977, Prof. Roberts, who was an Associate Editor for the newly established Peirce Edition Project, brought to Waterloo a complete copy of the set of Harvard Peirce Papers that had been prepared by the Institute for Studies in Pragmaticism at Texas Tech University for the Indianapolis critical edition. At this time it was a rare privilege to be able to work freely with Peirce's unpublished manuscripts and I took the opportunity to write a master's thesis under Prof. Roberts' supervision on Peirce's taxonomy of consciousness. After spending a semester in Bristol, England, on a Fulbright Fellowship, I returned to Waterloo to take my Ph.D. and to work under Prof. Roberts at the Waterloo branch of the Peirce Edition Project. In early 1983, I was recruited by Edward C. Moore to join the Peirce Project in Indianapolis, where I was given one day a week to finish writing my dissertation which was based on a reconstructed logic manuscript of Peirce's. Peirce had become the focal point for my research and my academic career.

## 2. What do you consider your contribution to the field?

Just as we must ultimately yield to our peers for our own meaning as persons, so I believe it must ultimately be left up to the ongoing community of Peirceans to determine the contribution of any one of us to the field of Peirce studies. But not knowing how my contribution will ultimately be assessed, and putting aside hope for what might yet be found to be of intellectual value in my writings, I believe it will be my work for the Indianapolis Chronological Edition and my leadership of the Peirce Edition Project (PEP) from 1993 to 2008 that will constitute my most important contribution to the field.

When I arrived in Indianapolis in 1983, the first volume of the *Writings* (W1) had already appeared and first proofs of W2 were being examined. Not long after I arrived, Christian J. W. Kloesel was named director, following the founding director, Edward C. Moore, and my main responsibility quickly became manuscript organization (returning Peirce's manuscripts, as far as possible, to their original order of composition and determining dates of composition). A preliminary manuscript arrangement had already been established, but it was approximate at best and not adequate for our editing mission, so a great deal of effort went into recovering the correct manuscript organization for upcoming volumes and determining which writings to include in the critical edition. It became part of my responsibility, starting with W4, to consult with contributing editors (and sometimes with visiting graduate students such as André De Tienne) to meet these objectives and to assemble annotations for the selected writings (final decisions fell to the project director). This important work, although for many years effectively under my care, was really part of a joint undertaking, beginning with Josiah Royce when Peirce's manuscripts were first brought to Harvard, and continuing with a great many dedicated Peirce scholars before and after me. Because of this fact, it is difficult to sort out the unambiguous contributions of individuals but I am satisfied in knowing that many of Peirce's manuscripts were reassembled under my care, perhaps for the first time since they were first unpacked at Harvard and piled in Royce's office. Reflecting back on this work, certain manuscript 'messes' stand out as ones that occupied many hours and days of effort, for example, R 575, described in Robin's *Catalogue* as notes on logical algebra, turned out to be a draft of Peirce's important 1880 "On the Algebra of Logic" (W4: Selection 19) and, once reassembled, appeared to be significant both for Peirce's intellectual development and for the history of logic—and it also revealed that Peirce had in fact proved a theorem he was later suspected of only pretending to have proved (see W4: Selection 6 and the note to 184.3 on pp. 572–73). Other examples of manuscript 'messes' I was able to help sort out were the puzzling "Guess of the Riddle" set that had been subjected to the infamous 'Harvard manuscript give-away' (and which André De Tienne helped organize) and the indispensable "Letter to the *Nation*" (R 318), parts of which were included in EP 2: 398–433. But these are only three examples from many years spent doing forensic work (almost always teamwork) on Peirce's manuscripts.

Another part of my assignment was to write historical introductions. Already at the University of Waterloo, at the suggestion of Prof. Roberts, I had begun to assemble material for an introduction to W4 with the intention or turning it over to Max H. Fisch to help him prepare his introduction. When I arrived in Indianapolis, he was working on the W3 introduction and I was able to make some minor contributions toward its completion. After examining the materials I had prepared toward an introduction for W4, Max decided to pass the baton to me and to consult with me as needed as long as he continued with the Peirce Project. Of course the extensive research materials he had collected over his many years of leadership in Peirce studies were a crucial resource for my introductions. Because of the scope and complexity of Peirce's work and the inscrutability of his life, writing satisfactory introductions proved to be a difficult part of my work but I tried diligently to put Peirce's writings in the context of his life and times as well as to express to some extent the historical and scholarly significance of each selection. More specifically, I tried to write introductions that would connect the varied selections together and with Peirce's life story and thus help bring unity to each volume of the Indianapolis edition.

Funding long-term critical editing projects is problematic even for editions of writers whose texts are well organized to begin with and have mostly already been edited for non-critical editions. But PEP faced the unusual difficulty of dealing with a mass of manuscripts often in a perplexing state of disorder and then, to make matters worse, discovering that the Harvard Peirce Papers, while the most important set of Peirce manuscripts, could not serve as the exclusive base for the critical edition. So unlike many other editorial projects, PEP needed not only critical editors and supporting staff, but scholars familiar with Peirce's life and work who could investigate archival holdings for additional Peirce writings, study the manuscripts to establish correct compositional order, and based on an examination of Peirce's script, watermarks, correspondence, and other historical factors, index the pages to the calendar of Peirce's life. And because of the scope of Peirce's thought and the many fields to which he contributed, PEP needed more intensive scholarly interdisciplinary collaborations than usual. All of these factors combined to cause PEP to be quite an expensive edition which frequently, in fact usually, was short of staff and suffering budgetary shortfalls. The Peirce community owes a huge debt of appreciation to the discerning administrators at IUPUI[2] who found ways to keep the Peirce Project operating even during the leanest times but when external funding was weak or absent the Project's work suffered greatly.

This happened in 1993, when PEP lost its funding from the National Endowment for the Humanities (NEH) resulting in a major reduction in

---

[2] Indiana University Purdue University at Indianapolis. The Peirce Edition Project is a unit of the Indiana University School of Liberal Arts on the IUPUI campus. Since 2003 the Peirce Project has been aligned with the School of Liberal Art's Institute for American Thought.

staffing. It was at this time when Kloesel left the Project and I was made director. In the absence of a grant-related work plan and knowing that it would take considerable effort and time to reestablish funding through NEH, I refocused the staff we had left on the preparation of a second volume of the *Essential Peirce*. Kloesel and I had edited the first volume together and had planned to produce a second volume, but because of the disorganized state of the later manuscripts we had not been able to make final selections or begin any editing work. It seemed to me that if the effort of the Peirce Project could be turned to reconstructing a core manuscript path through to the end of Peirce's life and then to selecting and editing (suitable for a non-critical edition) key writings, and to use the production of EP 2 as a learning exercise in the production of camera-ready text in-house, we would be far better prepared to proceed apace with the critical edition once new external funding was acquired. This is what we did and I regard the production of EP 2 as a significant achievement of the Peirce Project and an important contribution to Peirce studies and to philosophy in general.

During the lapse in NEH support, US federal funding agencies embraced a new funding model which tied new funding to the requirement that matching funds be raised from external supporters. PEP had operated for years without building or nurturing a constituent base so toward that end I started a Peirce Project newsletter to establish regular communications with Peirceans around the world and hired a graduate student to comb subscriber lists, humanities faculty catalogs, bibliographies, etc., to build a base of names and addresses for our newsletter. Over time this effort helped establish a broad base of moral and financial support which helped convince NEH to refund the critical edition in 1997. Some years later, with the support and encouragement of Herman J. Saatkamp, then Dean of the School of Liberal Arts, the Peirce Project, along with other editing projects at IUPUI, were brought together as part of the newly established Institute for American Thought allowing for some fund raising and public relations needs to be managed by the Institute staff and for some technical editing and research staff to be shared across editions. Since its inception, PEP has been a research destination for students of Peirce and for Peirce scholars from around the world. Before the wide dissemination of Peirce resources across the web, PEP was almost unique as a comprehensive center for undertaking research on Peirce's thought (only the Institute for Studies in Pragmaticism matched PEP in this regard). I think it is not too much to say that PEP played a significant role as a catalyst for the organization and development of the now active international community of Peirceans. Even now, with so many resources available online at important virtual Peirce research centers and through archival websites, PEP remains an important destination for Peirce scholarship and the Institute for American Thought enables PEP to continue to function as center for Peirce studies.

So it is my collaborative work for the critical edition and my leadership from 1993 until 2008 in bringing about the changes described above, that I believe will constitute my most important contribution to the field of Peirce studies. But I believe the work I did to make Peirce's logic more accessible by organizing the three-day logic symposium for the 1989 Peirce Sesquicentennial International Congress at Harvard and editing, with Don D. Roberts and James Van Evra, *Studies in the Logic of Charles Sanders Peirce* (Indiana University, 1997), was a noteworthy contribution to Peirce studies. And for quite a few years I also worked closely with Peter Hare to keep the Peirce Society functioning during some slow periods and to create a more vigorous Peircean contingent within the Society for the Advancement of American Philosophy. I also helped Peter move the *Transactions* to Indiana University Press. And after Peter's death, I helped form a committee to ensure the continuation of the *Transactions* under new leadership dedicated to the journal's established mission. In these and other ways I have contributed to Peirce studies, largely in collaborative or behind-the-scenes efforts.

## 3. What is the proper role of Peirce's work in relation to philosophy and other academic disciplines?

This is a difficult question given Peirce's polymathic scope and his surprisingly modern outlook. Also, his architectonic approach to philosophy brings the various areas of philosophy, along with many other disciplines, into continuous relation. So I believe that Peirce's work is well suited to illustrate, as well as encourage, points of contact between the various areas of philosophy and between philosophy and other disciplines. But it is important to bear in mind that even though Peirce contributed far more to the historical development of philosophy (and many other disciplines) than is generally known, his work is by no means only, or even mainly, of historical interest but is of continuing relevance in many fields of research. In my answer to the next question I list examples of areas where Peirce's work is important, in some cases even central, for current research. So the proper role of Peirce's work in those cases is no different than it would be if he were alive today and on the faculty of a major university.

## 4. What do you consider the most important topics and/or contributions in the field of Peirce studies?

Limited as I am by my own history, and knowing that Peirce's intellectual scope extended to areas I can only view from the outside, my answer to this question should not be taken to mean that contributions I fail to mention are ones I believe are of little importance. I don't doubt that others will presciently find topics or contributions I fail to mention to be of exceptional importance and promise. With that caveat, and considering this question from the standpoint of current importance (from the standpoint of historical importance Peirce contributed a surprising number of influential theories and results), I believe the following contributions of Peirce and those who have developed and extended his work in the areas mentioned, rank very high in importance: theory of reasoning and inquiry and, in particular, Peirce's addition of abduction as a distinctive form of inference that is crucial for inquiry; Peirce's graphical notation for logic (his Existential Graphs) and its development as a system for analysis and, also, as a model for cognition (thought in action); Peirce's pragmatism (pragmaticism); Peirce's semiotic, perhaps ultimately his most important contribution; and, finally, I would add his contrite fallibilism, which requires a very sober assessment of one's own importance and a constant recognition that truth is an elusive goal that must be sought in cooperation with one's fellow searchers by the application of self-correcting methods for however long it will take.

## 5. What are the most important open problems in this field and what are the prospects/avenues for progress?

Because of the breadth and originality of Peirce's probing mind, he opened new pathways into many areas of thought and left much for serious followers to build on and carry forward. Peirce understood this very clearly and wanted nothing more than for followers to improve on his work and correct his errors. As I indicated in my response to the fourth question, I'm inclined to think that Peirce's semiotic may prove to be his most important contribution, really the creation of a new science, and he recognized that, as "a first-comer" to such a vast new field of study, he could do little more than clear the way, and to some extent set the agenda, for subsequent research. Among the important open problems for Peircean semioticians, one that stands out for me is the problem of working out a full analysis of sign characteristics (involving the sign trichotomies, of which there are usually supposed to be ten, but there is some disagreement about that) and sign classes (of which there are usually supposed to be sixty-six). Another important open problem is that of relating the sign classes to types of semiosis and, therefore, types of inference, since all semiosis is inferential. The upshot of Peirce's classification of signs if his classification is, at the same time, a classification of the sixty-six (or more, in case Peirce's classification is found to be incomplete) types of inference, would seem to amount to a sort of mapping of types of possible mental activity (since all thought is in signs). A third open problem for Peircean semioticians who are also formal logicians is one I only vaguely comprehend but believe to be important, namely, the working out of a formal semantics based on Peirce's semiotic. Can this be achieved? Another important open question involving Peircean sign theory but which involves science more generally is how to explain the teleological nature of semiosis (or semiotic causation) and the role of semiosis in cosmology.

Other important open problems in or connected with the field of Peirce studies are: how to explain Peirce's law of love and how it functions in agapastic evolution; in Peirce's theory of perception, what is the fine-tuned explanation for how the intellectual component is attached to a percept to form a perceptual judgment (and thus enter the logical space of reasons); what are Peirce's proofs of pragmatism and to what extent did Peirce's attempts to construct different proofs help unify (or improve the integrity of) his system of thought; and how to resolve the tension in Peirce's thought between the individual and society for the advancement of knowledge (on the one hand, the role of the individual is held to be crucial for the advancement of knowledge while, on the other hand, it is the research community that is supposed to be crucial and the individual of rather minor importance).

Finally, I will mention one additional open problem that seems to me to be of special importance. It is the problem of how to understand Peirce's distinction between natural beliefs, which concern matters of vital importance, and theoretical beliefs, which serve as stepping stones on a path toward knowledge and truth. Peirce's early doubt/belief theory seems rather more explanatory of natural belief (what we might think of as programming for survival) than of theoretical belief. Working out these differences has relevance for Peirce's pragmatism and epistemology but may also have important ramifications for understanding Peirce's views on religion and the function of religion in human culture. I suspect that in the evolutionary struggle for species survival, living organisms have acquired social sensibilities that have led to the development of institutions that program them for behaviors that give their species an evolutionary advantage. In human society, religion is the natural institution that has emerged to inculcate and sustain attitudes and beliefs that enhance life and stabilize culture while science is the non-natural institution that has emerged in the human pursuit of truth. To regard religion as fulfilling this natural function may help explain the ubiquity of religion within human cultures and to highlight crucial differences between religion and science.

As regards the prospects or avenues for progress toward the solution of these important problems, I must point out that several of them have been addressed by contemporary Peirce scholars of note and others, although not all of them, are being worked on currently. But to my way of thinking, a problem remains open as long as its solution is not generally agreed on, so the resolution of these problems requires not only finding the right explanations or answers but building a convincing case that wins general approval. That, of course, is a lot to ask.

## Bibliography

### Papers

"Peirce's General Taxonomy of Consciousness." *Transactions of the Charles S. Peirce Society* 19 (1983): 331–59. Revised and expanded version translated into German by Alexander Roesler: "Das semiotische Bewußtsein nach Peirce." In *Die Welt als Zeichen und Hypothese. Perspektiven des semiotischen Pragmatismus von Charles S. Peirce,* ed. Uwe Wirth (Frankfurt am Main: Suhrkamp, Suhrkamp Taschenbuch Wissenschaft 1479, 2000), pp. 44–67.

"Peirce's Early Work on the Algebra of Logic: Remarks on Zeman's Account." *Transactions of the Charles S. Peirce Society* 23 (1987): 425–440.

"The Significance of Logic as Semiotic." *Semiotics 1987,* ed. John Deely. University Press, 1987, pp. 404–13.

"Toward a Peircean Semiotic Theory of Learning." *The American Journal of Semiotics* 5 (1987): 249–74.

Introduction to *Writings of Charles S. Peirce: A Chronological Edition,* Volume 4: 1879–1884, Bloomington: Indiana University Press (1989), pp. xix–lxx. Introduction to Volume 5: 1884–1886 (1993), pp. xix–xlviii. Introduction to Volume 6: 1887–1890 (2000), pp. xxv–lxxxiv. Introduction to Volume 8: 1890–1892 (2010), pp. xxv–xcvii (unabridged version: www.iupui.edu/~peirce/houserintro.html).

"Peirce's Pre–Phenomenological Categories." *Semiotics 1988,* eds. Terry Prewitt, John Deely, and Karen Haworth. University Press, 1989, pp. 103–108.

"La Structure formelle de l'expérience selon Peirce" ("Peirce on the Formal Structure of Experience"). *Etudes Phénoménologiques,* Nos. 9–10 (1989): 77–111.

"The Fortunes and Misfortunes of the Peirce Papers." In *Signs of Humanity*, vol. 3. eds. Michel Balat and Janice Deledalle–Rhodes; Gen. Ed. Gérard Deledalle. Berlin: Mouton de Gruyter, 1992, pp. 1259–1268.

"The Scope of Peirce's Semiotics." In *Signs of Humanity*, vol. 3. eds. Michel Balat and Janice Deledalle–Rhodes; Gen. Ed. Gérard Deledalle. Berlin: Mouton de Greuter, 1992, pp. 1283–1290. Published in Portuguese in *FACE* 3 (1990): 207–215.

"The Schröder–Peirce Correspondence." *Modern Logic*, 1 (1990/91): 206–36.

"Peirce and the Law of Distribution." In *Perspectives on the History of Mathematical Logic*, ed. T. L. Drucker. Boston: Birkhäuser, 1991, pp. 10–32.

"A Peircean Classification of Models." In *On Semiotic Modeling*, eds. Myrdene Anderson and Floyd Merrell. Berlin: Mouton de Gruyter, 1991, pp. 431–439.

"Charles S. Peirce: American Backwoodsman." In *Frontiers in American Philosophy*, Volume 1. eds. Robert W. Burch and Herman J. Saatkamp, Jr. College Station: Texas A & M University Press, 1992, pp. 285–293.

Introduction to *Essential Peirce; Selected Philosophical Writings*, Vol. 1. Bloomington: Indiana University Press (1992), pp. xix–xli; Introduction to Vol. 2 (1998), pp. xvii–xxxviii.

"On Peirce's Theory of Propositions: A Response to Hilpinen." *Transactions of the Charles S. Peirce Society* 28 (1992): 489–504.

"Competing Icons." *Semiotics 1991*, eds. Terry Prewitt and John Deely. University Press, 1992, pp. 20–26.

"On 'Peirce and Logicism': A Response to Haack." *Transactions of the Charles S. Peirce Society* 29 (1993): 57–67.

"Algebraic Logic from Boole to Schröder, 1840–1900." In *Companion Encyclopedia of the History and Philosophy of the Mathematical Sciences*, ed. I. Grattan–Guinness. London: Routeledge, 1994, pp. 600–616.

"Semiotic as Cognitive Science." *Cruzeiro Semiotico*, nos. 22/25 (1995): 139–149.

"The Case of the Peirce Biography." *Semiotics 1993*, eds. Terry Prewitt and John Deely. Peter Lang, 1995, pp. 595–598.

"The Semiotics of Critical Editing: Is There a Future for Critical Editions?" *Semiotics around the World: Synthesis in Diversity. Proceedings of the Fifth Congress of the International Association for Semiotic Studies, Berkeley 1994*. Berlin: Mouton de Gruyter, 1997, 1073–76.

"Peirce as Logician." In *Studies in the Logic of Charles S. Peirce*, (eds. N. Houser, D. Roberts and J. Van Evra). Bloomington: Bloomington: Indiana University Press, 1997, pp. 1–22.

"Peirce's Pragmatism and Analytic Philosophy; Some Continuities."*Ágora; Papeles de Filosofía* 21 (2002): 11–32.

"Pragmatism and the Loss of Innocence." *Cognitio; Revista de Filosofia* 4 (2003): 197–210.

"The Scent of Truth." *Semiotica* 153–1/4 (2005): 455–466,

"Peirce in the 21st Century." *Transactions of the Charles S. Peirce Society* 41–4 (2005): 729–39.

"Peirce's Contrite Fallibilism," *Semiotics and Philosophy in C. S. Peirce*, eds. R. Fabbrichesi Leo and S. Marietti (2006), Cambridge Scholars Press, Cambridge, England, pp. 1–14.

"Too Many Signs." *Semiotics 2004/2005, eds.* Stacy Monahan, Benjamin Smith, and Terry J. Prewitt. Legas (Ottawa, ON), 2007.

"Peirce as a Sign to Himself." *Semiotics 2008*, eds. John Deely and Leonard Sbrocchi. Legas Publishing, 2009, pp. 387–95.

"Action and Representation in Peirce's Pragmatism." In *New Perspectives on Pragmatism and Analytic Philosophy*, ed. Rosa M. Calcaterra (2010), Rodopi Press, New York and Amsterdam, pp. 61–70.

"Pragmachism." *Semiotics 2006*, ed. Terry Prewitt. University Press, forthcoming in 2009. Published in revised form as "The Church of Pragmatism" (*Semiotica* 178–1/4 (2010): 105–114).

"Reconsidering Peirce's Relevance." In *Ideas in Action; Proceedings of the Applying Peirce Conference*, eds. Henrik Rydenfelt and Mats Bergman (2010), Nordic Pragmatism Network, Helsinki, pp. 1–15.

"The Increasing Attractiveness of Classical Pragmatism." *Cognitio; Revista de Filosofia* 11.2 (2010): 224–240.

"Peirce, Phenomenology, and Semiotics." *The Routledge Companion to Semiotics*, ed. Paul Cobley (Routledge, 2010), pp. 89–100.

"Imagination and the Form of Life to Come." *Balkan Journal of Philosophy* 2.2 (2010): 107–114.

"Peirce's Post-Jamesian Pragmatism." *New Perspectives on Pragmatism and Analytic Philosophy,* ed. Rosa M. Calcaterra (Rodopi, 2011), pp. 61–69.

"Peirce on the Growth of Values." *Philosophical Alternatives* 22.2 (2011): 5–14.

"Signs and Survival." *The American Journal of Semiotics* 29 (2013): 1–16.

"Peirce's Neglected Views on the Importance of the Individual for the Advancement of Civilization." *Cognitio; Revista de Filosofia* 14.2 (2013): 163–177.

"The Intelligible Universe." *Peirce and Biosemiotics: A Guess at the Riddle of Life,* eds. Vinicius Romanini and Eliseo Fernández (Springer, 2014), pp. 9–32.

"Bohemians Like Me." *Charles S. Peirce in his own Words: 100 years of Semiotics, Communication and Cognition* eds. Torkild Thellefsen & Bent Sorensen. Forthcoming: Mouton de Gruyter, 2014.

"Peirce on Practical Reasoning." Festschrift for Ivan Mladenov, eds. Traykova, Cobley, Yanakieva, Kuncheva, and Tashev. Forthcoming: Bulgarian Academy of Sciences, 2014.

**Editions**

*Writings of Charles S. Peirce: A Chronological Edition*, Volume 3: 1872–1878. Bloomington: Indiana University Press (1986), Assistant Editor; Volume 4: 1879–1884 (1989), Associate Editor; Volume 5: 1884–1886 (1993), Associate Editor; Volume 6: 1887–1890 (2000), General Editor; Volume 8: 1890–1892 (2010), General Editor. (Substantial progress was made on several forthcoming volumes during my tenure as General Editor.)

*Essential Peirce; Selected Philosophical Writings*, Vol. 1, eds. Nathan Houser and Christian Kloesel. Bloomington: Indiana University Press, 1992; Vol. 2, eds. Peirce Edition Project (N. Houser, General Editor), 1998.

*Studies in the Logic of Charles S. Peirce*, (edited with Don D. Roberts and James Van Evra). Bloomington: Indiana University Press, 1997.

*Selected Writings of Charles Sanders Peirce.* Selected with introduction by N. Houser. Translated into Basque by Ibon Uribarri. Klasikoa, 2005.

# 16
# Masato Ishida

Department of Philosophy, University of Hawai'i at Mānoa

---

**1. Why were you initially drawn to Peirce?**
The obscurity of his thought, with a clear mark of genius, attracted me. As a graduate student, I was studying classical American philosophy in Tokyo, Japan. I started to read Peirce and quickly became a resolute pragmatist. Peirce says "I suppose I was born a Pragmatist" (MS 313: 22), but perhaps I felt that way too. The genius of Peirce was obvious in the *Collected Papers* and other published works, but I wanted to see more. Since I did not have access to the microfilm edition of the Peirce papers in Japan, I traveled to North America.

The 80,000+ pages of the Peirce papers certainly blew my mind. Numerous fascinating ideas were revealed in incomplete fragments, alternative drafts, and unsent letters; sheets after sheets of graphs, computations, diagrams, formulas, tables, reading logs, and cartoons. It was a new world for me. Given my background, I also found Peirce's notes on East Asia interesting such as his observations of the Chinese and Japanese languages (MS 1226: 3, 1248: 4), the Japanese weight units and currency (MS 1078: 4-5), and so on. In the latter, Peirce's handwriting reads "Tokio 1877," telling us something about the time he lived.

I enjoyed reading Peirce but soon saw that he was a highly unpredictable writer. There is no way to anticipate which direction his thought might flow, let alone how he would approach a problem. He frequently drifts away from the issue at hand and moves on to completely different topics. If not like the writings of the late Nietzsche, I think there is almost constantly a blind move in Peirce's thinking. Great brilliance and blind moves—I often interpret Peirce's phrase "blind to our own blindness"(W6: 381) positively when I read him.

**2. What do you consider your contribution to the field?**
My contribution to the field is small yet, but I consider my efforts worthwhile in two directions. The first direction has to do with Peirce's logic and mathematics. One of my recent papers calls the reader's attention to Peirce's 1897 statement: "There is, I confess, a paradoxical

aspect in the proposition that a collection may be so great that its individuals lose their separate identities. But the key of that paradox will probably ultimately be discovered to lie in some unnoticed condition in the general hypothesis of a collection which requires this mergency of individuals" (NEM 3: 100). The "mergency of individuals" in this passage is an attractive idea, but it is dangerous to immediately jump to his metaphysics of continuity. From the perspective of modern mathematics, the "unnoticed condition in the general hypothesis of a collection" would correspond to a *separation axiom* that characterizes the degree of separability of elements in a topological space. An insight of this sort was not commonly shared by mathematicians until the 1920s.

In the same paper, I also attend to the following words of Peirce: "Mathematical thought advances chiefly by generalization; and the generalized conclusions are made rigorously logical by the device of correspondingly generalizing the premises" (N 2: 85). The second part of the sentence is quite remarkable since Peirce seeks for the generalization of the conclusion first and then suggests that we consider what premises, or again *axioms* in our language today, would imply them. The idea of *reverse mathematics* introduced by Harvey Friedman in the 1970s might be seen as a modern development of such a perspective. Today we know that there is a strong connection between the axioms we adopt and what conclusions – or *theorems* – are provable in corresponding systems, but I don't think logicians in Peirce's days were sensitive to such a connection. I am not overstating Peirce's foresight by saying this. Instead I am trying to observe how easy it is to underestimate his astute and far-reaching vision.

The second direction in which I make efforts has a lot to do with textual research. If we wish to know Peirce's view, not ours, the clues must be sought for in his writings. To pick a well-known example, Peirce's use of the term *representamen* appears to decline after 1905, a helpful survey provided by George Benedict in the 1980s. But on a closer look, it is probably better to say that Peirce's use of *representamen* increased only toward the Harvard Lectures in 1903. Otherwise I do not see drastic change. We know that Peirce used *representamen* as late as 1911, but I would rather take greater notice of the fact that he uses the word in alternative drafts of one and the same paper (MS 675 40-41; 75-76; 77-78). That is, looking at Peirce's revisions from one page to another, it does not appear to be a slip of the pen. Candidly speaking, I prefer *sign* to *representamen*, but I cannot change textual facts. Nor am I in a position to correct Peirce when I am talking about *his* view, not mine. Therefore, my contribution, if any, derives form the kind of attention I pay to the history of logic, mathematics, and to Peirce's own writings including the unpublished texts.

## 3. What is the proper role of Peirce's work in relation to philosophy and other academic disciplines?

In relation to philosophy, Peirce's work offers a great treasure chest of ideas. For instance, his theory of propositions is very comprehensive and thought-provoking. One way to suggest this is to observe that in Peirce's view every sign must arise in a proposition – or in his own words, "non-propositional signs [whatever they are] can only exist as constituents of propositions" (CP 4.583). Of course we don't usually think that a term, a name, or something like a visual symbol is a *proposition*, but that is only because we abstract them from propositions that are constitutive of the greater moving reality. A proposition, linguistic or otherwise, produces a snapshot of reality with varying degrees of factuality. "A fact is," Peirce writes, "something separated out from the rest of the real, being so much as is expressible in a proposition" (MS 492B: 114). In this way a multi-layered context principle of signs is considered by Peirce such that the Fregean 'context principle' can be seen as a special case of the more general idea. Of course this is just a small indication. I think there are many ways in which Peirce's work can contribute to specific topics in contemporary philosophy.

Taking 'academic disciplines' broadly, footprints of Peirce's ideas are found nearly everywhere—from music, anthropology, linguistics, to religious studies – but the 'proper role' of his work in relation to various disciplines is perhaps a little harder to define. A short answer would be that his work continues to inspire researchers across diverse fields, but given Peirce's classification of the sciences – that is, according to the kind of phenomena to be observed, degree of generality of the discipline, purpose of study, and so forth—each disciplinary branch shall have its own set of principles and standards that Peirce's work does not intend to offer. Nor would Peirce consider that the empirical data he consulted with a century ago remains of great value to researchers in the 21st century. From this I consider that it would be the *a priori* side of his general *semeiotic* that benefits disciplines outside philosophy, or what Peirce in 1909 called "General Semeiotic, the *a priori* theory of signs"(MS 634: 16, original emphasis). What I have in mind is something like a detailed study of *interpretants*—for example, their variety and how they are generated. This seems to accord with Peirce's view since he contemplates such a work as a group endeavor: "A great desideratum is a general theory of all possible kinds of signs, their modes of signification, of denotation, and of information; and their whole behaviour and properties, so far as these are not accidental. The task of supplying this need should be undertaken by some group of investigators" (MS 634: 15).

## 4. What do you consider the most important topics and/or contributions in the field of Peirce studies?

Although much of what I have done so far gives weight to the history and philosophy of logic and mathematics, I do not consider them to be the most important subjects in themselves. The reason for this is that formal logic and mathematics are branches of science—they make progress at any given moment such that there is, generally speaking, more to learn from contemporary research than from Peirce's more or less outdated results. However, I still consider them relevant because Peirce's thinking is very often that of a mathematician. If we are not attentive enough, it is always easy to overlook what and how he thinks, two examples of which I mentioned above in my reply to the second question.

But here is another example. It is sometimes thought that Peirce's logic in "On a New List of Categories," published in 1867, was still that of traditional syllogistic logic and that this imposed limitations on his theory of categories. However, even the first few propositions that Peirce brings up in §4 of the *New List* point in the direction of quantificational logic, such as the universal proposition "A griffin *is* a winged quadruped" (W 2: 50) and the existential proposition "There is a beautiful ellipse" (*ibid.*). Nor does Peirce forget to mention that the predicate of a proposition is "the verb which is copula in one of its senses" (*ibid.*), to which we may add that 'griffins' and 'chimeras' are most commonly used in Peirce's writings on quantificational logic. In fact Peirce gives a more explicit example in §15 of the *New List*: "Whatever is the half of anything is less than that of which it is the half" (W 2: 58). From the viewpoint of a working mathematician, the proposition Peirce has in mind is clearly

$$\forall x \forall y \left( (x > 0 \land y > 0 \land x + x = y) \rightarrow \exists z (z > 0 \land z + x = y) \right)$$

which is true in any subset of the set of real numbers. It is worth remarking that nothing like this can be effectively handled within the limitation of Kant's traditional or Aristotelian logic. This is one of the main reasons why the *New List* was declared 'new' by Peirce. But there is nothing surprising about a proposition like the above since Peirce's formal treatment of relations and functions—if not as elaborate as in his later works—predate the *New List*. The progress he made toward the *New List* was that 'is the half of', 'less than', and 'murder' in §9 of the paper (W 2: 53) are now considered instances of two-place predicates in general, though we should be careful that a *predicate* in Peirce's sense is not merely formal—it is a sign that is an active constituent of a developing proposition. This shows how important it is to pay attention to the variety of propositions Peirce considers in the *New List*, not just "This stove is black" (W 2: 52) and "The stove is black" (W 2: 50, 52) commonly discussed in the literature.

Since revealing Peirce's thought in precise terms is always challenging, I regard any work that scratches beneath the surface of his text as a valuable contribution to the field. In terms of topic, the study of the *New List* does not strike me as obsolete. I do not intend to intensify debates over its worth or significance, but there remains a fascinating mystery about Peirce's anticipatory sentiment: "the gift I make to the world. [. . .] In it I shall live when oblivion has me—my body" (W 2: 1). The contrast Peirce later drew between how much he changed as a person and how little the change was for the leading features of the *New List* also deserves notice: "There is mighty little in the C. S. Peirce of 1905 of identity with the C. S. Peirce of 1867. I feel entitled to speak of him as quite another person. But my opinion is that the paper On A New List of Categories is one of the most perfect gems of all philosophy" (MS L 224: 73).

## 5. What are the most important open problems in this field and what are the prospects/avenues for progress?

One important area in which we may find a cluster of open problems is Peirce's philosophy of time. The present – the 'now' — must distinguish itself from the rest of time as a unique moment, but if the present is considered an absolute instant cut off from the rest of time, it would be a radical discontinuity breaking into the otherwise continuous flow of time. In 1902, Peirce remarks that "nothing is more occult than the absolute present" (CP 2.85). Time as a particular irreplaceable moment and time as a general continuous flow – these two aspects of temporality seem to give an 'occult' appearance to the absolute now.

Peirce's 1892 paper "The Law of Mind" takes an interesting approach to time by considering an "infinitesimal interval of time" or "an infinitesimal duration" (EP 1: 315, 322, 331). Such an interval or duration has a temporal breadth that is strictly greater than zero yet smaller than any *measurable* quantity. What backed up this view was the mathematical concept of the *infinitesimal*, which Peirce interpreted not in the classical sense but in the modern sense of what comes close to non-standard real numbers. With this in mind, Peirce argued toward the end of the 1890s:

> If time flows, no instant has an absolutely independent identity. It is [however] so far independent that an instantaneous state of things may be supposed to exist absolutely at that instant alone. But [in that

case] a duration which begins or ends at that instant cannot properly be said absolutely to contain or absolutely to exclude that instant. (NEM 3/1: 747)

To this Peirce adds that "No contradiction is involved in this hypothesis" (*ibid.*). Yet we should note that a system without internal contradiction does not grant that it is the correct model to work with. Nor does the hypothesis solve the secret of the arrow of time—why time flows in one direction, irreversibly and irrevocably, a question Peirce did not pursue further.

The reason I bring these things up is that time is a problem that Peirce himself left wide open. "It may indeed very likely be that there is some minimum space of time within which in some sense only an indivisible thought can exist," he once remarked in 1873, adumbrating something like atomic temporality, but he then turned away from it saying "as we know nothing of such a fact at present we may content ourselves with the simpler conception of an indefinite continuity in consciousness" (W 3: 74). In 1905, Peirce recognized the significance of the subject but decided to back off from detailed inquiry:

> A good question, for the purpose of illustrating the nature of Pragmaticism, is, What is Time? It is not proposed to attack those most difficult problems connected with the psychology, the epistemology, or the metaphysics of Time, although it will be taken for granted [. . .] that Time is real. The reader is only invited to the humbler question of what we mean by Time, and not of every kind of meaning attached to Past, Present, and Future either. (EP 2: 357)

The entire paper ends with a disclaimer that time is "unique and *sui generis*"; "can only be identified by brute compulsion"; and that "we must not go further" (EP 2: 359). Nevertheless—or perhaps all the more—time constitutes an intriguing question since it is eventually where Peirce's three categories must work together. For suppose we consider the *present* from the perspectives of temporal continuity and discontinuity. Then the question becomes: How do *thirdness* and *secondness* operate together in the present?

Furthermore, Peirce in the early 1890s considered that the present "can contain no time" (CP 1.38), a view echoed in his 1898 interpretation of the present: "the past and the future are utterly absent in the sense in which I am conscious of the *now*" (CP 6.231). "So I might express my truth by saying," he continues, "The Now is one, and but one" (*ibid*.), which Peirce identified as the unique locus of quale-consciousness revealed in the pure form of *firstness*. Taken together with *secondness* and *thirdness*, therefore, we are lead to the view that the present is structured in terms of Peirce's all three categories. Since we have a wealth of material on the philosophy of time that can be compared with Peirce's view, I think there are many avenues for progress in this area.

**Bibliography**

1. "A Peircean Reply to Quine's Two Problems," *Transactions of the Charles S. Peirce Society*, Vol. 49, No. 3, pp. 322-347, 2013.

2. "C. S. Peirce's Convergence Theory of Truth: A Survey of Interpretations," *Philosophy of Science: Journal of the Philosophy of Science Society, Japan*, Vol. 45, No. 1, pp. 60-77, 2012.

3. "C. S. Peirce's Definition of Symbol in §14 of the *New List*," *The Public Journal of Semiotics*, Vol. 2, No. 2, pp. 52-72, 2008.

4. "C. S. Peirce and the Early Phases of Model-theoretic Logic," *Philosophy of Science: Journal of the Philosophy of Science Society, Japan*, Vol. 41, No.1, pp. 29-44, 2008.

5. "The Emergence of Peirce's Quantificational Logic," *Philosophy of Science: Journal of the Philosophy of Science Society, Japan*, Vol. 34, No.2, pp. 59-74, 2001.

# 17

# Jiang Yi

Professor of Philosophy
Beijing Normal University

---

**1. Why were you initially drawn to Peirce?**
I heard the name of Charles Sanders Peirce for the first time more than thirty years ago when I was a freshman in college. In the States he has been considered as one of forefathers of pragmatism, which was criticized ideologically as a kind of imperialist philosophy and philistinism in China. In China, John Dewey and William James had gained more notorious fame than Peirce, because their thoughts were severely criticized by Mao Zedong and other politicians on high level. Peirce was mentioned only as the forefather of pragmatism and was well known only by intellectuals. But I began to study Peirce's philosophy as one of the origins of contemporary analytic philosophy of language when I was a graduate student in 1982. What impressed me were Peirce's maxim of pragmaticism and his two famous articles on the clearness of ideas. I learned that Peirce intended to clarify meanings of words by his maxim and that his articles were intended to present pragmaticism as a theory of meaning. I appreciate very much his maxim, according to which we should 'consider what effects, that might conceivably have practical bearings, we conceive the object of our conception to have. Then, our conception of these effects is the whole of our conception of the object.' (Peirce, 1955, 31) I compared this maxim to the Vienna Circle's principle of verification, arguing that the principle has something in common with Peirce's maxim of pragmaticism.

Pragmatism has rehabilitated its reputation as the native American philosophy and one of contemporary Western philosophy in China since 1979, and its philosophy is considered as a theory of meaning rather than a theory of praxis or a philistinism. The name of Charles S. Peirce, pronounced and spelled mistakenly once as Peirce, has been mentioned increasingly not only in academic circles but by the general public. I noticed that Peirce is studied in many fields such as mathematics, logic, language, library, semiotics, communication theory, computer science, ethics as well as philosophy. So I always think of him as a twentieth century encyclopedic thinker, though it was not his ambition to set up a system of philosophy.

## 2. What do you consider your contribution to the field?

As mentioned above, I was initially drawn to Peirce by his maxim of pragmaticism and by his two famous articles. I considered his philosophy as the origin of modern philosophy and focused on its similarities to the Vienna Circle's philosophy. And I also think of his philosophy as the signal of originality of pragmaticism, which is different from the pragmatism of James and Dewey. Thus I took part in the rehabilitation of its reputation in China in the 1980s. I participated in the national conference on pragmatism in 1988, in which the pragmatist philosophy was re-evaluated for the first time since the Cultural Revolution. I have also been engaged in the development of Peirce's logic and philosophy in China by organizing an international conference on Peirce in 2005 and by translating the *Essential Peirce* volumes into Chinese. Many Peirce Scholars attended the conference on Value and Symbol, such as Charles Pearson (Director of Research, the American Semiotics Research Institute), Cornelis de Waal (Editor of Peirce Edition Project and Professor at Indiana University Purdue University at Indianapolis), James Liszka (Vice President of the University of Alaska at Anchorage), Ken Ketner (Texas Tech University), Lu Deping (China Young Political College then, Beijing Normal University now), Zhang Liuhua (CCP School of Pudong, Shanghai then, East China Normal University now), Liu Xinwen (Institute of Philosophy, Chinese Academy of Social Sciences), Wang Chengbing and Lin Jianwu (Beijing Normal University), Peng Zhan (Graduate School, Chinese Academy of Social Sciences), Hu Ruina (Shan'xi University), Tian Ping (Beijing Normal University), Wang Yin (Shanghai Jiaotong University). The conference covered many topics on Peirce's philosophy and logic. After the conference I was elected in the list of international consultant committee of the *Charles S. Peirce Society* in 2009. In 2013 I had Chinese Peirce scholars translate *Essential Peirce* into Chinese, which is part of the larger project of translating the 8 volumes of the *Collected Papers*. The two volumes of *Essential Peirce* are reaching completion.

I have also published some essays on Peirce, and there is a chapter on Peirce's pragmaticism in my book, *Contemporary Anglo-American Analytic Philosophy*, published in 2005. In the book I contributed to the history of analytic philosophy with an explicit interpretation of Peirce's philosophy as a dominant source of analytic philosophy in America. In the paper of 1994, "The Pragmatic and Pragmatism", I clarified some confusions about pragmatism. In 2000 I published three articles on contemporary American philosophy, in which I argued that there is a tendency of marginalization of philosophy in American society at the turn of the century. I attended an international conference on pragmatism at Buffalo and presented a paper on a new approach to realism in terms of pragmatism at the conference in 2000. In 2002 I was supported by the Ford Foundation to visit Harvard and learned more about the similarities between American pragmatism and traditional Chinese philosophy.

## 3. What is the proper role of Peirce's work in relation to philosophy and other academic disciplines?

As I said, Peirce is an encyclopedic thinker in the twentieth century, in the States as well as in the world. So his work made many contributions to many fields, not only in philosophy but in other academic disciplines. First of all, Peirce established the fundamental principles of pragmatism and coined a new word, "pragmaticism", which was intended to be distinguished from the pragmatism of William James and John Dewey. Peirce's philosophy is dominated by a theory of science, a systematic explanation of sciences. By science he meant of course all knowledge. It is no doubt that he did not provide any theory of knowledge itself but an approach to explore all of knowledge. In this sense Peirce is a methodological, not a theoretical philosopher. He provided some instruments to investigate evidences and sensations. In his *Philosophy and the Sciences: A Classification*, he distinguished the sciences of discovery, those of review and the practical sciences. Philosophy was divided, for him, into phenomenology, normative sciences, and metaphysics. What he emphasized here is the role of logic in all sciences. He claimed that 'logic may be regarded as the science of the general laws of signs. It has three branches: 1, speculative grammar, or the general theory of the nature and meanings of signs, whether they be icons, indices, or symbols; 2, critic, which classifies arguments and determines the validity and degree of force of each kind; 3, methodeutic, which studies the methods that ought to be pursued in the investigation, in the exposition, and in the application of truth. Each division depends on that which precedes it.' (Peirce, 1955, 62) This passage shows the originality of Peirce's semiotic terminology.

Secondly, Peirce's work contains criticisms of past philosophies such as metaphysics, fundamentalism, and Cartesian dualism. The influence of his philosophy has been recognized by many successors. Morris's semiotics, Bridgman's operationism, even phenomenology in the Continental tradition, all are confident for their inspiration from Peirce's philosophy. It is most significant that Peirce's thought is viewed as the beginning of contemporary philosophy evidently distinct from the modern philosophy since Descartes. Wittgenstein claimed that he learned about Peirce's thought by Ramsey. Many great philosophers at present times recognize Peirce's philosophy as one of the sources of their thought, as Karl Popper, Jürgen Habermas, Noam Chomsky. Their recognition of Peirce's philosophy illuminates the role of his thought in the development of contemporary philosophy.

## 4. What do you consider the most important topics and/or contributions in the field of Peirce studies?

Peirce opened many new fields of investigation in his life, so that there remain several open issues and puzzles in those fields a century after his death. I think that the following are the most important topics in the field of Peirce studies:

### 1) Trichotomy of signs in semiotics

As we know the trichotomy of signs is the basic element of Peirce's semiotics. In *Trichotomic*, Peirce defined trichotomic as an art of making three-fold divisions. He said, 'expression is a kind of representation or signification. A sign is a third mediating between the mind addressed and the object represented. If the thirdness is undegenerate, the relation of the sign to the thing signified is one which only subsists by virtue of the relation of the sign to the mind addressed; that is to say, the sign is related to its object by virtue of a mental association.' (*The Essential Peirce*, vol.1, 281). On the one hand, the trichotomic relation of sign, mind and object is evident, but on the other hand, Peirce's conception of sign is much complicated, so that there has been much debate concerning the understanding of his trichotomy of signs in semiotic studies. Thus we need to explore more on this understanding.

### 2) The relation of signs to value

What is the value of signs? How does a sign get its value in an expression? Does value have some intrinsic relation to signs? All these questions are relative to Peirce's idea of sign, though he did not refer to the value of signs itself in his writings. But in his many articles in which he discussed validity, fallibilism, and uniformity, the problem of value is involved in different ways. And, more importantly, the relation of signs to value has been vague since his death. So we need to understand what the relation is and whether Peirce contributed somehow to the theory of value.

### 3) The Peircean conception of logic

Peirce is of course one of pioneers in modern logic. But, as we know, his conception of logic is different from that of Frege, Russell and other pioneers. He considered logic as a theory of signs. He said, 'logic, in its general sense, is, as I believe I have shown, only another name for semiotic, the quasi-necessary, or formal, doctrine of signs.' (Peirce, 1955, 98) This conception of logic shows indeed the significance of semiotics in modern logic but modern logic bifurcated in different ways. So we need to clarify this bifurcation in the making of modern logic at the beginning of the last century.

## 5. What are the most important open problems in this field and what are the prospects/avenues for progress?

The study of Peirce's philosophy has increasingly flourished in recent years all around the world. While his known and unknown writings are now known to the public, more and more scholars in this field focus on Peirce's original and innovative thoughts which are inspirations to contemporaries who are challenged by the development of science and language in our ordinary life and trying to find out solutions to those problems raised in that development. And also in China there are many scholars who are interested in Peirce's thoughts, not only in philosophy and logic but in mathematics and other fields such as economics, natural sciences, library studies, and anthropology. Of course Peirce is well-known firstly as one of pioneers of American pragmatism for the public as well as for the intellectuals. There are, however, some confusions and misunderstandings concerning his philosophy both in academic and ideological ways. For example, few could make clear the distinction between James' and Dewey's pragmatism and Peirce's pragmaticism. Another example of such misunderstanding is that Peirce has been considered as a humanistic philosopher rather than a scientific philosopher or logician. By the former I mean that pragmatism has been seen as one of the humanistic philosophies in China, rejected as a kind of philistinism. By the latter I mean that Peirce's pragmaticism should be viewed as a scientific approach to the theory of meaning. So for Chinese intellectuals the first task is to re-evaluate the significance of Peirce's philosophy by rehabilitating his reputation as a logician and philosopher of science.

### References

Peirce, C. S., 1955, *Philosophical Writings of Peirce*, selected and edited with an introduction by Justus Buchler, New York: Dover Publications, Inc.

Peirce, C.S., 1992, *The Essential Peirce*, Vol. 1, edited by Nathan Houser and Christian Kloesel, Bloomington and Indianapolis: Indiana University Press

### Bibliography

Translations of Peirce's writings and others in Chinese

Brent, Joseph, *Peirce*, trans. Shao, Qiangjin, Shanghai: Shanghai People' Press, 2008

De Waal, Cornelis, *On Peirce*, trans. Hao, Changci, Beijing: Zhonghua Book Company, 2003

Peirce, C. S., *Selection of Peirce*, ed. & trans. Tu, Jiliang & Zhou, Zhaoping, Beijing: China Social Science Documentary Press, 2006

Haack, Susan, ed., *Meaning, Truth and Action*, trans. Chen, Bo, Beijing: the Oriental Press, 2007

**Books by others in Chinese**

Chen, Yajun, 1999, *Pragmatism from Peirce to Putnam*, Changsha: Hunan Education Press

Tu, Jiliang, 2006, *From Classic Pragmatism to the Neo-Pragmatism*, Beijing: People's Press

Tu, Jiliang, 2009, *Pragmatism, Logical Positivism and Others*, Wuhan: Wuhan University Press

Wang, Yuanming, 1998, *Action and Consequence: A Study of Pragmatism*, Beijing: Chinese Social Science Press

Wang, Shouchang & Su, Yukun, 1990, *Contemporary American Philosophy,* Beijing: People's Press

Wang, Yin, 2011, *Essence and Origin: A Hermeneutic Interpretation of Peirce's* Issues of Pragmaticism(1905), Hangzhou: Zhejiang University Press

Zhang, Liuhua, 2012, *The Logic Aspect of Peirce's Philosophy*, Shanghai: Shanghai People's Press

**Publications of edited books and Journal articles by Jiang Yi related to Peirce and pragmatist philosophy**

1994, Pragmatic and Pragmatism, in *Encyclopedic Knowledge,* vol. 1

1995, Naturalist Turn in Current American Philosophy, in *Social Sciences Abroad*, vol.7

2005, ed., *Contemporary Anglo-American Analytic Philosophy*, Nanjing: Jiangsu People's Press

2007, Pragmatic Tradition in Contemporary American Philosophy, *Learning Daily,* May 7,

2009, ed., *A History of Contemporary Western Philosophy,* Beijing: People's Press

2013, Pragmatism as a method, *China Social Sciences Daily*, Jan. 15

# 18

# Isaac Levi

John Dewey Professor of Philosophy Emeritus
Columbia University

---

## MY INTEREST IN PEIRCE'S PHILOSOPHY

Graduate students at Columbia University in the postwar era could not avoid having an opinion on the pragmatist philosophers. When I began graduate work at Columbia in 1951, I was an enthusiastic admirer of the logical positivists to begin with. However when I received my PhD in 1957 for a dissertation on Moritz Schlick, I favored the realism he elaborated in his work on relativity and his *Allgemeine Erkenntnislehre* over the positivism he defended in his later work.

In the 1960's, I became interested in the idea of modeling inductive reasoning decision theoretically in order to clarify the relations between scientific inquiry and ethics and politics. My interest in the latter topic had been aroused by the well known exchange between Richard Rudner and Richard Jeffrey. I wrote several articles on this topic in the 1960's culminating in a book *Gambling with Truth* published in 1967 and a paper "Information and Inference" published in the same year that modified some of the views expressed in that book.

I took for granted that inductive reasoning sought to justify adding new beliefs to the stock of information already taken for granted. Adding new information was "accepting" new propositions (sentences, or beliefs). While writing and publishing *Gambling with Truth* and "Information and Inference," I was unsettled as to what acceptance in the context of induction amounted to. According to Kyburg (whose astuteness and learning I admired highly), accepting h amounted to judging h highly probable. Kyburg recognized the need to address the lottery paradox. He opted for abandoning the requirement of deductive closure in order to save the high probability rule. I have never understood his stance even though many others stand by him. Nor was I enthusiastic about R.C. Jeffrey's "radical probabilism" that denied that scientists should accept propositions at all.

During the 1970's, what I had called "acceptance as evidence" in *Gambling with Truth* morphed into "knowledge" and then "full belief". I argued for the need to acknowledge a conception of full belief as a standard for serious possibility. That is to say, inquirer X cannot coherently recognize that X's full beliefs are false in contexts where X fully believes them. X is rationally committed to judging X's full beliefs to be infallibly true. Yet, X is also committed to judging X's full beliefs to be subject to revision. While fully believing that h X is absolutely certain that h is true. Yet X should acknowledge that it is seriously possible that X will have good reason in future inquiry to come to doubt that h and assign it some degree of credal probability.

I thought that full belief so conceived captured what the Peircean inquirer judged free of doubt. At least I thought this is what ought to be free of doubt according to Peirce even though Peirce had embraced fallibilism according to which all beliefs might be false and, hence, subject to doubt. In *The Enterprise of Knowledge* of 1980 I explicitly took note of this and suggested that Peirce was confusing fallibilism (all beliefs might be false) with corrigibilism (all full beliefs might be subject to revision.)

In the same year, I published an essay in a *Festschrift* honoring Richard Braithewaite defending the view that Peirce's conception of the self – correction property of induction is to be understood in terms of his anticipation of the Neyman Pearson account of statistical estimation.

Even though Peirce and Dewey confused fallibilism and corrigibilism, they both rejected the demand that all beliefs and all actions require a justification. They replaced this foundationalist demand with the requirement that *changes* in belief (and other attitudes) call for justification. Justifying changes in belief and value calls for giving an account of inquiry understood along the lines of the models of inquiry elaborated by Peirce and then Dewey. As early as the 1860's Peirce recognized the importance of avoidance of error and informational value as two primary desiderata to be balanced in scientific inquiry. These aspects of his work have influenced my own efforts to develop these ideas in *The Fixation of Belief and Its Undoing* and *Mild Contraction*. I have collected many of my views on the work of the pragmatists in general and Peirce in particular in *Pragmatism and Inquiry*.

My preoccupation with Peirce has been primarily with his contributions to epistemology, the structure of inquiry and statistical reasoning. However, Peirce's interests and contributions range well beyond these topics. He made major contributions to modern deductive logic, he was an accomplished physicist and had interests ranging throughout the natural sciences.

In my judgment, more can be done to integrate the ideas of the classical Pragmatists and, in particular extend pragmatic models of problem solving inquiry to cover not only natural but social science, morals and political theory. Dewey, of course, is the pioneer in attempting this project. But Peirce might also be exploited for this purpose in the hope of finding a good conception of the relevance of truth as an aim in inquiry.

**List of Publications by Isaac Levi relevant to Peirce**

*Gambling with Truth*, Cambridge, Mass. MIT Press (1971)

*Enterprise of Knowledge*, Cambridge, Mass. MIT Press (1980)

"Induction as Self-Correcting According to Peirce," *Science, Belief and Behaviour: Essays in Honour of R.B.Braithwaite,* ed. D.H. Mellor, Cambridge: Cambridge University Press, 127-140. (1980)

*The Fixation of Belief and Its Undoing*, Cambridge: Cambridge University Press (1991)

*Pragmatism and Inquiry*, Oxford: Oxford University Press (2012)

# 19

# Giovanni Maddalena

University of Molise (PhD. University of Roma Tre)

---

**1. Why were you initially drawn to Peirce?**

Chance is very important in a living organism, Peirce said. So, at the beginning it was the chance, τύχη, that brought me to Peirce.

In Italy you have to win a public contest in order to be admitted into a PhD program. I won the public contest in the Department of Philosophy at the University of Roma Tre but I was coming from Turin where the interest of the department was continental philosophy, especially studies on nihilism. At the first meeting with the professors in charge of the program, I proposed to develop a project about the history of nihilism in American culture. It was a topic of my original philosophical school and I had first wrote a master dissertation on A. MacIntyre and communitarians (then published as *La lotta delle tradizioni*, 2000), so that I had some background in American culture. However, the Department of Roma Tre was a strong analytic department and one of the professors said: "Well, among the people in your project the only serious one is Peirce, who was a great logician, a founder of analytic philosophy in a way. You will do the rest of it when you grow older".

I was not so happy that night, but studies on Peirce caught my attention afterward. What I found in Peirce was the third way between analytic and continental philosophy. Peirce disclosed the possibility to have both precision of thought and freedom of interpretation, strict logic and broad imagination. As Peirce himself would have said, it was like an encounter with a contemporary Aristotle or Plato or Duns Scotus. Peirce provided fresh and sharp tools in order to explore eternal questions that are at the heart of the fascination of philosophy to me.

Among the tools, I discovered the power of signs and the novelty of the abductive pattern of reasoning first. Logic understood as semiotics, in particular according to the version given by the late Peirce, (1908-1914) became the topic of my PhD dissertation (then published as *Istinto razionale*, 2003) and the focus of my intellectual interest. Studying those late years of Peirce's life and work I discovered that at the end of his life Peirce was striving for a unity encompassing what he had done, a unity that went beyond pragmatism itself. This unity – the complexity of the design – had to involve all the tools he had forged and many philosophical views that were original in many ways. He was looking for a comprehensive understanding of knowledge and he was sure that the secret of this unity had to be found in the mathematical concept of continuity. This is why I dedicated several years to look at the different parts of Peirce's philosophy from this perspective, and according to the changes to which Peirce's conception of continuity underwent over the years.

## 2. What do you consider your contribution to the field?

The first contribution – the less important but so far the more effective – is a philological-historical-associative one. Except for the studies of Nynfa Bosco and Rossella Fabbrichesi, the second part of Peirce's work, from phenomenological categories to cosmology and from Existential Graphs to metaphysics, was little known in Italy. The very late Peirce was completely unknown. Moreover, the chronological view of Peirce's studies that is so important in order to understand many Peircean topics, was not used at all in translations. So, I first translated some of Peirce's later manuscripts and then I composed a huge translation (750 pp.) that was meant to give an idea of the whole path of his thought, from "On a New List of categories" to "An Essay toward Improving Our Reasoning in Security and Uberty".

While studying and translating I found the great cooperation of Rosa Calcaterra, whose original reading of a kind of continuity among pragmatists, was an inspiring companionship. Both convinced of the importance of Peirce for the contemporary philosophical landscape, we started a series of meetings, conferences, and publications that culminated with the common direction of the series "Filosofia Americana" for the publisher Aragno, the enterprise of the *European Journal of Pragmatism and American Philosophy* (with Roberto Frega), and the formation of Associazione Pragma, a joint venture with the Centro Studi Peirce of Milan, led by Rossella Fabbrichesi. At this moment, Pragma is the real hub of studies on pragmatism in Italy.

The second contribution is a methodological reading of Peirce. I saw that Peirce's tools of inquiry led to the extreme borders of human knowledge. They enlarged the usual picture of reasoning, showing at the end several points in which reasoning needs an odd sort of metaphysical realism in order to be accomplished. This is my understanding of abduction as an aesthetical and ethical reading of signs that relies upon an order of reality, which will be proved only at the end of inquiry; the reading of the important and often neglected topic of assent as dynamic interpretant which works as an answer to the call of this evolving reality; the semiotic reading of the theory of reference in proper names and the proposal of nicknames as iconic proper names that tells the story of evolving reality and identity; and of course the reading of the independent discovery of Cantor's paradox as a proof *per absurdum* of a metaphysical "real continuity" and the clear hypotheses of a paradoxical foundationalism a posteriori.

In all these topics (collected in the book *Metafisica per assurdo*, 2009), Peirce found a new way to solve philosophical problems that he never completed but that is easily accomplished with Peirce's instruments. On the one hand, this shows the importance of using Peirce's philosophy to overtake some important topics of contemporary philosophy (reference theory, hypothetical reasoning, the role of normativity in science, the relationship between logic and metaphysics). On the other hand, this method of reading shows that Peirce did not accomplish his philosophy: at the borders of his epistemology he always found "vanishing points" that pointed out to this metaphysical real continuity, which cannot be an a priori foundation. He affirmed its reality but he could not finish his revolutionary project. However, these "vanishing points" also signaled a persistent failure, that one may also observe in other pragmatists. Notwithstanding their brilliant achievements, they could not figure out a satisfactory overall picture of reasoning in which all of their findings could fit. The inquiry about this failure brought me to the third part of what I see as my contribution.

The third contribution is an original theory that is based on Peirce's failures. At the end I realized that he could not build up a complete version of knowledge because he was still caught by the Kantian pattern, even though he progressively abandoned it over the years. In brief, Peirce was still thinking to provide an analysis of the synthesis that our reasoning operates without trying to revise the definition of analysis and synthesis according to the evolutionist metaphysical realism that he thought of.

Corroborated by the mathematical studies of Fernando Zalamea and following a semiotic reading of Existential Graphs, I proposed a different threefold view of reasoning where synthesis is understood as "recognizing identity through change", analysis as "loosing identity through change", and vague reasoning (to be added to Kant's scheme) as "being blind to identity through change" ("Peirce's incomplete synthetic turn", *The Review of Metaphysics, 2012*).

Synthesis in this different pattern needs a synthetic tool of inquiry, otherwise the analytic method would hinder the grasp of the synthetic pattern and its epistemological priority. Working on the pragmatic maxim and the acknowledged unity among practice and theory, I proposed the tool of "complete gesture" understood as "an action with a beginning and an end that carries on a meaning". A complete gesture is the synthetic tool with which we ordinarily synthesize not conceptual phenomena. It is a meaningful action which is composed by a dense blending of icons, indices, and symbols and, phenomenologically, by a dense blending of firstness, secondness and thirdness. Examples of complete gestures are public and private rites, scientific experiments, artistic performances. Those complete gestures account for creativity, full communication, functioning of memory according to a figural turn of narrative identity. As a matter of fact, our knowledge and memory are constituted by a continuity which is not simply homogenous, but it is a Peircean kind of continuity constituted by these dense meaningful moments.

I consider this new pattern and its proper tool a supplement to Peirce's view of reasoning that can dialogue with different disciplines as anthropology, psychology, pedagogy.

## 3. What is the proper role of Peirce's work in relation to philosophy and other academic disciplines?

As for philosophy, I really think that Peirce will be one of the most important authors to reference for XXI century.

I consider this epoch as the transition from the kingdom of analytic and continental philosophy to another, new conception of knowledge. Peirce can be one of the key authors of this important passage. I list with him several others who could work out not-rationalist way of thinking (Florensky, Barfield, the late Jung are those who immediately came up to my mind). As Rorty foresaw, the two leading philosophies of the past century came to a joint end. I think they both explored and exhausted their paradigms because it was the final stretch of the Kantian paradigm based on a static view of analysis as part-whole scheme. Something is necessary because it is necessarily part of a whole. With completely different intentions, Robert Hanna correctly explains that the scheme of necessity that presides over synthetic a-priori judgments is the same as the analytic ones. That is why Kant's or Husserl's (or Peirce's) attempts to account for synthesis were always finally caught up by the analytic drive. It is a defeating end above all for Peirce and pragmatists whose goal was to overtake all the dichotomies and all rationalisms.

Radical hermeneutics rejected the paradigm as such. However, in this way, they just accepted that reasoning coincides with that paradigm or you have to rely upon something else, which is not a structured reasoning anymore. Existence, emotion, taste, insights, events, are all very important findings but they do not reform or touch the Kantian canon of reasoning, which is still at the bottom of education and science in Western culture.

As I said above, pragmatists themselves could not reach a final reform of the canon. They stated to overcome all dichotomies but they still strived for a Kantian analysis of the synthesis that their tools of inquiry were proposing. But the tools, in particular Peirce's, were good and new. I think that time has come that these tools can open up new roads of inquiry: a different paradigm for reasoning and new tools that make use of Peircean semiotics, theory of reasoning, and metaphysics.

Besides to this general view, I would indicate two roles for Peirce's philosophy.

The first one is to explain the rational path at the extreme borders of rational field. This is the classic role of ordinary studies on Peirce.

One example is the rational path for creativity and hypothesis and the role of normative sciences. In 2008 I had the honor to participate in a Conference about Scientific Discovery in San Marino. So, with this opportunity, I had the chance to work for two days with C. Townes (Nobel prize, inventor of laser), J. Mather (Nobel Prize, discoverer of the deep background cosmic radiation), Y. Coppens (Collège de France, discoverer of the hominid Lucy). I was invited to explain abduction, and my particular reading of it as grounded in an aesthetical and ethical reading of signs. These precious, kind, and curious men confirmed Peirce's insights in many ways: discovery is not an extra-rational, pre-rational sort of inquiry. There is a rational path that goes from consequent to antecedent. And they also confirmed that the leading forces of the discovery are (in order!): 1) the sense of beauty; 2) dialogue; 3) technology. I think that all three have much to do with Peirce. Only in a pragmatist Peircean way you can consider all these items as part of the research without dividing up theory from practice, the normative from the descriptive, interpretation from precision of reference. What I understood on that occasion was that philosophers need scientists as much as the latter ones need the former. Often practitioners of science are not aware of what they are doing. Same discourse holds for artists and creativity, and so on. From this perspective, studies such as philosophy of science, of literature, of art, of communication, are all in need of Peircean contribution.

The second role is to be ascribed to a Peircean driven philosophies like the one I proposed.

As for my proposal, once one has discovered a new way to understand synthesis and a new tool like "complete gesture", one has also to understand the incompleteness of gestures, giving a comprehensive picture of knowledge. We may account for many different levels and nuances of phenomenological and semiotic structures of this new land. After the first perusal which will be published soon, the new soil seems to be more akin to the one in which our common sense moves than the complicated structures of the analytic pattern. We could say that the new completely synthetic pattern is the rational depth of the land of our common sense and common living. This is why the philosophy of complete gesture finds so many applications and, by nature of this embodied philosophy itself, any application illustrates the pattern and the tool better. Memory, personal identity, artistic creativity, morality, and education have been tackled already as examples of application because they seemed immediately relevant to understand the pattern better. But there are many other fields and topics that should be examined with the philosophy of gesture. Just to mention the former ones: philosophy of mathematics (of course, since the paradigm stems from there), sociology, psychology (is there a psycho-synthesis? I think so), law, anthropology, politics are the first ones that come to my mind. But many others can be thought of: an integrated vision of disciplines related to knowledge more than effective than interdisciplinary studies (which fail because you cannot unite what you consider to be divided at the beginning), a new account of the philosophy of language and the origins of language, a new theology. It is important to notice that in any field we have a tool to think comprehension as given or givable through action. Comprehension can really be conceived of as a non-intellectual affair as classic pragmatists dreamed.

**4. What do you consider the most important topics and/or contributions in the field of Peirce studies?**

There are two fundamental kinds of contributions. The first is the philological one. I do not think we will ever be grateful enough to the hard work of those who worked for the *Collected Papers* and for the *Writings of Charles S. Peirce*. In particular, I think that in this field we should give a homage to Max Fisch. I am sorry that I did not meet him. His published works are outstanding and insightful as his unpublished catalogue at the Peirce Edition Project and his living legacy in many scholars. De Tienne's care for philological precision and inspiring perspectives that has been so helpful to me is largely due to this legacy.

There are many scholars who gave wonderful contribution but here I will only state those who were immediately relevant to my work. I am much indebted to Hausman's conception of dynamical object and realism, to De Tienne's view of phaneroscopy and symbolic teleology, to Colapietro's account of the shift that Peirce took from Kant to Hegel, to Zalamea's view of continuity and to the position he ascribes to Peirce in the history of mathematics. Haack's studies on foundationalism and the continuous project of pragmatism advocated by Calcaterra had a significant role in clarifying the theoretical and historical background.

## 5. What are the most important open problems in this field and what are the prospects/avenues for progress?

I think that at this point we need perspectives and visions based on Peirce as much as we need that the work at the Peirce Project would be carried on and finished. Certainly, we need that philology completes its job. I think that modern tools allow for a cooperative action with the Peirce Project that would speed up the process.

However, above all we need courage! I am glad that William James curiously ascribed such a quality to the young Italian pragmatists he met in Rome in 1905: "They taught me courage".

There are many scholars who work on Peirce but few of them develop new patterns, new full interpretations or visions. We must avoid becoming a closed church and we have to launch Peirce's studies to the comparison with every field and philosophy.

I look with increasing interest to attempts which apply Peirce to different disciplines and fields where his philosophy can bring fresh air. Biosemiotics is obviously one of these fields, but I think that pedagogy, psychology, communication, heritage studies have much to learn from Peirce. The point is that the world of knowledge is changing according to a pragmatist turn, and of course I think that the synthetic drive of pragmatist and the philosophy of gesture will have a lot to say on this issue.

Let me take an example. Italy owns the majority of cultural artworks of the world. So far, there have been distinct disciplines for dealing with this immense legacy. Archivist activities and archeology had to discover and preserve, then museology thought to store and display, and communication had to think to make those goods as attractive and sellable as possible. However, things are changing and this ambit does not work in that way anymore. All practitioners understood there is a deep continuity among all those passages and disciplines. A Peircean view helps to understand that this happens because of the continuity of reality, it is rooted in the infinity of possibilities of the dynamic object and in the general understandings that logical interpretants can take. Understanding (including the physical or virtual discovering and storage) is part of the same process of representation in which we find the communicative drive of any object. Yes, the more we communicate the more we understand, and vice versa, if communication is rooted in a Peircean realism: it is the object itself that communicates some of its infinite possibilities through our interpretations. The rationalist separation among disciplines is fading away and the new conception of them needs Peirce's semiotic as common ground.

As for me, following the pattern I signaled on synthetic paradigm and complete gestures, I will concentrate my attention on vague reasoning. A threefold view of reasoning as the one I report here below needs a study of vagueness through vague tools (very different from the analytic study of it). So far I could not work on it, but I think that the constitution of vagueness and the ways of inquiring it are one of the top priorities of one who wants to understand reasoning.

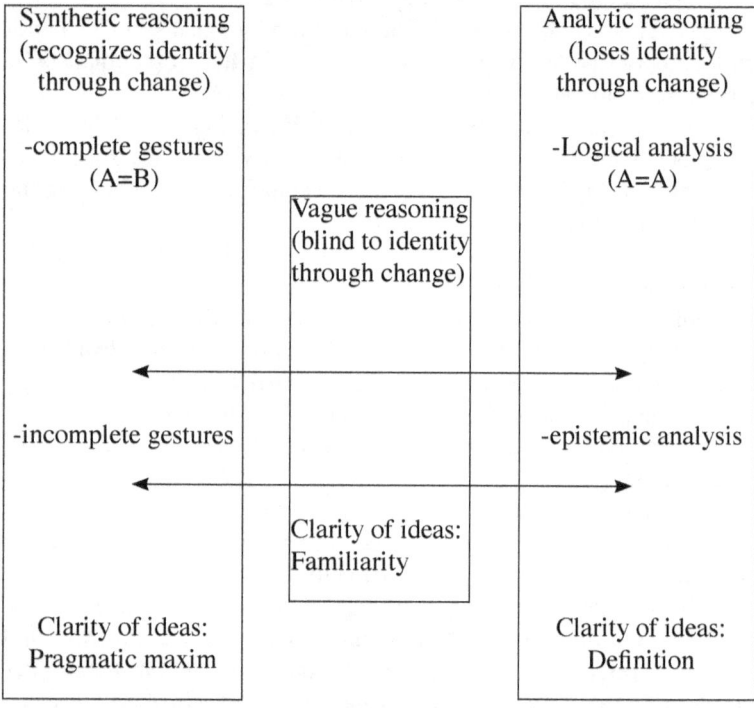

The last topic I want to mention is the study of metaphysics. Pragmatism can be compatible with some sort of metaphysics as held by some interesting scholars as Tiercelin and Zalamea. The direction that I see for these studies points toward an odd sort of a posteriori foundationalism, which should be justified both epistemologically and ontologically. It sounds like a paradox, but we must be courageous.

## References

Calcaterra R.M.

    2003    *Pragmatismo: I valori dell'esperienza. Letture di Peirce, James e Mead*. Roma: Carocci.

Colapietro V.

2004 "Portrait of an historicist: an alternative reading of Peircean Semiotic", *Semiotiche*, I/2004, 49-68.

De Tienne A.

2000 "Quand l'apparence (se) fait signe: la genèse de la représentation chez Peirce", *RS/SI* 20, pp. 95-144.

2004 "Is Phaneroscopy as a pre-semiotic science possible?", *Semiotiche* 2/2004, 15-30.

Fisch, M.H.

1986 *Peirce, Semeiotic and Pragmatism: Essays by Max H. Fisch*, ed. by K.Ketner and C.Kloesel, Bloomington: Indiana Univesity Press.

Haack S.

2009 *Evidence and inquiry*. Amherst (NY): Prometheus Books.

Hanna R.

2001 *Kant and the Foundations of Analytic Philosophy*, Oxford: Clarendon Press.

Hausman C.

*1993* *Charles S. Peirce's Evolutionary Philosophy*, Cambridge (Mass.): Cambridge University Press.

Maddalena G.

2000 *La lotta delle tradizioni, MacIntyre e la filosofia in America* ["The Struggle among Traditions: MacIntyre and Philosophy in America"], Cuneo: L'Arciere, 214 pp.

2003 *Istinto razionale. Studi sulla semiotica dell'ultimo Peirce (1908-1914)* ["Rational Instinct: Studies on Peirce's late semiotics (1908-1914)"], Turin: Trauben, 222 pp.

2005 "Abduction and Metaphysical Realism". *Semiotica* 153 1/4, 243–259.

2005 Editing, translation and introduction to the anthology, *C.S. Peirce, Scritti scelti* ["C.S. Peirce, Selected Writings"] Turin: UTET, 750 pp. Republished in 2009 in "I Meridiani", Mondadori, Milano.

2005 "The limits of experience: Dewey and Comtemporary American Philosophy", *Quaestio: annuario di storia della metafisica*, 4/2004, 387-406.

2006 Peirce, Proper Names and Nicknames". *Semiotics and Philosophy in Charles Sanders Peirce*. Ed. by R. Fabbrichesi and S. Marietti. Newcastle: Cambridge scholars Press, 22-35.

2008 "Un estremista dello scotismo: Charles S. Peirce" [A scotist of a somewhat extreme stripe: Charles S. Peirce], *Quaestio: annuario di storia della metafisica*, 8/2008, 569-584.

2009 *Metafisica per assurdo. Peirce e i problemi dell'epistemologia contemporanea* [Metaphysics per absurdum. Peirce and the problems of contemporary epistemology], Rubbettino, Soveria Mannelli, 247 pp. Preface by A. De Tienne, director of the Institute for American Thought.

2010 "Peirce's Theory of Assent" in *Ideas in Action* ed. by M. Bergman, A.V. Pietarinen, H. Rydenfelt, S. Paavola, Helsinki: Nordic Studies in Pragmatism, 211-223.

2010 "The belief story: Peirce's anti-Kantian open perspectives", *Cognitio* 2/11, 257-266.

2010 "La via pragmatista al senso comune" [The pragmatist way to Common Sense], *Paradigmi* XXVIII, 3/2010, 57-71.

2011 *Alle origini del pragmatismo. Corrispondenza tra Charles S. Peirce e William James* [At the origins of Pragmatism. Correspondence between Charles S. Peirce and William James] translated and edited by M. Annoni e G. Maddalena, Turin: Aragno.

2012 (with Fernando Zalamea) – "A New Analytic/Synthetic/ Horotic Paradigm. From Mathematical Gesture to Synthetic/Horotic Reasoning". *European Journal of Pragmatism and American Philosophy*, vol. VI, 208-224 .

2012 "Peirce's incomplete synthetic turn". *The Review of Metaphysics*, vol. LXV, 3, 613-640.

2013 "A Synthetic Pattern: Figural and Narrative Identity". *Contemporary Pragmatism* 10, 1, 145-165.

2013 "Creative gesture. A pragmatist view". *European Journal of Pragmatism and American Philosophy* V, 1/13, 65-76.

2014 "Gesto completo: uno strumento pragmatista per l'educazione" [Complete gesture: a pragmatist tool for education]. *SpazioFilosofico* 10, 31-41.

Zalamea F.

2008 *Filosofia sintetica de las matematicas contemporaneas.* Bogotà: Universidad Nacional de Colombia.

2010 *Los graficos existenciales peirceanos.* Bogotà: Universidad Nacional de Colombia.

2012 *Peirce's logic of continuity*, Chesnut Hill (MA): Docent Press.

2012 Seminario *Filosofía francesa de la matemática en el siglo XX*. Manuscripto.

# 20
# Rosa Mayorga

Miami Dade College

**1. Why were you initially drawn to Peirce?**

I was introduced to Charles Peirce in a Metaphysics class at the University of Miami in the fall of 1991 by a newly-arrived professor from the University of Warwick. The professor, who eventually became my dissertation director, was Susan Haack. The class covered Hume's impressions and ideas, Kant's analytic and synthetic judgments, the Vienna Circle's verification principle, and ended with Peirce's attempt at a "scientific metaphysics." I was already a fan of John Duns Scotus and his subtle metaphysical distinctions so I was intrigued (and a bit relieved!) to find a modern philosopher who shared my rather uncommon philosophical taste. The fact that Peirce's extreme scholastic realism was mostly ignored, if not misunderstood, by many, made it obvious what my calling would be.

**2. What do you consider your contribution to the field?**

I would like to think that I have contributed to a better understanding of the importance that realism had in Peirce's thought. That is one constant throughout his philosophy, on which he claims he "was never able to think differently,"[1] and it has been a constant in much of my work on Peirce. In my *From Realism to Realicism: On the Metaphysics of Charles Sanders Peirce*,[2] I trace the notion of universal realism beginning with Plato through Scotus' scholastic realism, and compare and contrast Peirce's "extreme" kind, which I dub his "realicism."[3] In my contribution to *The Normative Thought of Charles Peirce*,[4] I attempt to show how his views on realism and nominalism can explain his enig-

---

[1] CP 1.20

[2] Mayorga, Rosa. *From Realism to Realicism: The Metaphysics of Charles Sanders Peirce*. Lanham, MD: Rowman and Littlefield/Lexington Books, 2007. Second printing (paperback) November 2008.

[3] Ibid.

[4] Cornelis De Waal, Krzysztof Piotr Skowroñski, eds. "Peirce's Moral 'Realicism,'" *The Normative Thought of Charles Peirce*. New York: Fordham University Press, 2012

matic and seemingly-inconsistent claims about ethics. In "The Beauty of the Unbeautiful,"[5] I again use his anti-nominalism to clarify some of his most confusing pronouncements, and try to show that he began to lay the groundwork for an esthetic theory before his death. In "The Fairy and the Aleph: On Peirce's Esthetics,"[6] I explore further Peirce's notion of "concrete reasonableness" which he proposes as the highest ideal of esthetics, the first of his three normative sciences, followed by ethics and logic, according to his classification of the sciences.

### 3. What is the proper role of Peirce's work in relation to philosophy and other academic disciplines?

Peirce set out to create a new system to encompass all human knowledge, and in the process, distilled, filtered, re-combined, absorbed, and incorporated the thought of the greatest thinkers into his own original scheme. A true polymath, he wrote voluminously on an incredible array of topics, ranging from astronomy, spectroscopy, geodesy, physics, psychology, anthropology, history, to mathematics, logic, semiotics, metaphysics, all the while bringing a new perspective to old topics, and providing new solutions to old puzzles. I believe the proper role of his work in relation to all academic disciplines can be summarized, using his own terminology, as contributing to "concrete reasonableness," by making the world more reasonable through providing novel insights, making innovative connections, detecting new patterns, formulating new theories.

### 4. What do you consider the most important topics and/or contributions in the field of Peirce studies?

As Program Co-Chair of the 2014 Peirce Centennial Congress, I have seen first-hand the range of topics and contributions that Peirce's work has spawned, and it is truly astounding. In addition to the expected themes so dear to Peirce's heart, such as semiotics, logic, metaphysics, epistemology, and mathematics, the topics of economics, engineering, physics, systems analysis, education, Chinese medicine, medical imaging, psychoanalysis, anthropology, geology, biology, cosmology, theology, business, management, ethics, drawing, painting, photography, literature, poetry, music, dance, theatre, even sex, are also represented in the program. This is a clear indication that Peirce's work continues to grow in its influence across all fields of knowledge.

---

[5] "The Beauty of the Unbeautiful," *Cognitio*, v. 14, n. 1, p. 85-100, Jan./June 2013

[6] Presented at the Universidad Nacional de Colombia's International Colloquium on Peirce's Esthetics, August 2013

## 5. What are the most important open problems in this field and what are the prospects/avenues for progress?

For a Peircean, all problems, even those considered "settled," are open, in theory. This is, of course, Peirce's fallibilistic view, and his philosophy (including his especially fruitful semiotic theory and logic of relatives, categories, and cosmology) allows for continuous progress in the search for truth in all fields.

### Bibliography

Mayorga, Rosa. "Peirce's Normative Realism," *Acta Philosophica*. Rome: Fabrizio Serra Editore (forthcoming)

Mayorga, Rosa. Torkild Thellefsen, Bent Sorensen, eds. "Beauty and the Best," *The Peirce Quote Book*. Berlin: De Gruyter Mouton (forthcoming)

Mayorga, Rosa. "The Beauty of the Unbeautiful," *Cognitio*, v. 14, n. 1, p. 85-100, 2013

Mayorga, Rosa. Cornelis De Waal, Krzysztof Piotr Skowroñski, eds. "Peirce's Moral 'Realicism,'" *The Normative Thought of Charles Peirce*. New York: Fordham University Press, 2012

Mayorga, Rosa. Review of Mateusz Oleksy's *Charles S. Peirce and the Threat of Modern Nominalism* for *Transactions of the Charles S. Peirce Society* Vol. XLVIII, No. 3, 2012

Mayorga, Rosa. Review of Antonio Armas Vazquez' *El Pragmatismo En Cuba* for *Transactions of the Charles S. Peirce Society* Vol. XLVI, No.2, 2010: 327-336

Mayorga, Rosa. "On Talisse's' 'Peirceanist' Theory," *Transactions of the Charles S. Peirce Society* Vol. XLV, No.1, 2009: 65-70

Mayorga, Rosa. "Peirce y los ideales democraticos" *Revista Studium Filosofia y Teologia* Vol. 23, No.23, 2009

Mayorga, Rosa. Review of Lee Braver's *A Thing of This World: A History of Continental Anti-Realism* for *The Review of Metaphysics* Vol. LXII, No.4, 2009

Mayorga, Rosa. Review of Robert Talisse's *A Pragmatic Philosophy of Democracy* for *Social Theory and Practice*, Vol.35, No.1, 2009: 133-140.

Mayorga, Rosa. "Teaching Peirce to Undergraduates." *Transactions of the Charles S. Peirce Society*, Vol. XLIV, No.2, 2008: 189-235.

Mayorga, Rosa. "Rethinking Democratic Ideals in Light of Charles Peirce," *Contemporary Pragmatism* 5.2:1-10

Mayorga, Rosa. "Scholastic Realism" entry for *Routledge Encyclopedia of American Philosophy* (2008)

Mayorga, Rosa. "Review of Frances William Scott's C.S. Peirce's System of Science." *Transactions of the Charles S. Peirce Society*, Vol. XLIV, No.2, 2008: 181-87

Mayorga, Rosa. *From Realism to Realicism: The Metaphysics of Charles Sanders Peirce*. Lanham, MD: Rowman and Littlefield/ Lexington Books, 2007. Second printing (paperback) November 2008

Mayorga, Rosa. "¿El pragmatismo: un nombre antiguo para nuevas maneras de pensar?" *Anuario Filosofico*, Vol. XL/2, 2007: 301-318.

Mayorga, Rosa. "Peirce y la metafisica." *Anthropos*, Vol. 212, 2006: 121-132.

Mayorga, Rosa. "Diamonds are a Pragmaticist's Best Friend." *Transactions of the Charles S. Peirce Society*, Vol. XLI, No. 2, 2005: 255-271

Mayorga, Rosa. "Stimulating Student Discussion in an Online Course," *International Journal of Learning*, Vol.12, Issue 1, 2006: 206-219.

Mayorga, Rosa. "The Hair: On the Differences between Peirce's Nominalism and Realism." *Transactions of the Charles S. Peirce Society*, Vol. XL, No. 3, 2004: 433-457

# 21

# Cheryl Misak

Professor of Philosophy
University of Toronto

---

**1. Why were you initially drawn to Peirce?**

I was initially drawn to Peirce as an undergraduate. Working on a great philosopher who was underappreciated was exciting. I loved the detective work of trying to figure out, from original material, what he was trying to tell us.

**2. What do you consider your contribution to the field?**

I think that I have made some progress in both trying to make Peirce's view as compelling as it can be, while setting his views both in the context in which he worked and in a contemporary context.

**3. What is the proper role of Peirce's work in relation to philosophy and other academic disciplines?**

I think it's a bit of a shame that we tend to carve out academic disciplines so definitively. It's obvious that Peirce made significant advances in, for instance, logic, probability theory and statistical inference. But philosophers write about these topics, as well as those who are employed in other university departments. Peirce also made advances in thinking about signs. Again, philosophers think through these issues just as much as do those in semiotics programs.

**4. What do you consider the most important topics and/or contributions in the field of Peirce studies?**

I have focused mostly on Peirce's pragmatist account of inquiry, belief and truth. These topics certainly have been taken to be the major and new contribution that pragmatism has made to philosophical debate. They are what have shaped the view of pragmatism. I think that if you did a survey of philosophers, it is the pragmatist view of truth that would come up mostly frequently as being what marks pragmatism off from other traditions. That's not to say that it is the most important contribution made my Peirce. But it's one that can't be ignored.

## 5. What are the most important open problems in this field and what are the prospects/avenues for progress?

Right now I am looking at how Peirce's thoughts about the tie between belief, successful action and truth survived in the hands of Frank Ramsey. Peirce and James brought pragmatism into being in the 1870's in Cambridge Massachusetts. By the early 1900's, James' version of it had become much discussed on both sides of the Atlantic, with Russell and Moore in Cambridge England savaging James' view of truth. But in the early 1920's, the young and brilliant Frank Ramsey was taking a serious interest in Peirce's then-neglected work. Had Ramsey lived past the age of 26, pragmatism's fortunes would have been very different. For not only were Ramsey's important papers on truth and probability heavily and explicitly threaded with Peirce's thoughts about the relationship between belief and habits of action - at the time of his death in 1930, Ramsey was working on a book that would have delivered the best version of pragmatism. Ramsey is usually taken to be a straightforward redundancy theorist. But his view, contrary to that popular belief, is not that truth can be eliminated by asserting the sentences of which it is predicated. He takes his cue from Peirce and argues that all there is to the concept of truth is what we can get out of the practices of belief and assertion. And when we unpack the commitments we incur when we assert and believe, we find that our theory of truth must be substantive and normative.

## Bibliography

Misak, Cheryl

(1994) "Pragmatism and the Transcendental Turn in Truth and Ethics." *Transactions of the Charles S. Peirce Society*, 30/4: 739–75.

(2000) *Truth, Politics, Morality: Pragmatism and Deliberation.* London and New York: Routledge.

(2004) *Truth and the End of Inquiry: A Peircean Account of Truth.* 2nd ed. Oxford: Oxford University Press. [1991]

(2007) "Pragmatism and Deflationism." In Misak (ed.), *New Pragmatists.* Oxford: Oxford University Press. 68–90.

*The Origins of Cambridge Pragmatism: The Influence of Peirce and James on Ramsey and Wittgenstein*, Oxford University Press. (forthcoming)

# 22
# Ilkka Niiniluoto

Professor Emeritus
Department of Philosophy, History, Culture, and Art Studies
University of Helsinki

**1. Why were you initially drawn to Peirce?**
In 1964 I started my studies in mathematics at the University of Helsinki, but in the second year I was also attracted by theoretical philosophy as a minor subject. My favorite topic was probability theory, but the concept of probability was more interesting than the technical details of probability calculus. In 1967 I read about Charles S. Peirce's idea of induction as a self-corrective operation in Georg Henrik von Wright's book *The Logical Problem of Induction* (1957), but I had learned about Peirce's account of the scientific method already in 1965 by the lectures of Professor Oiva Ketonen. During his visit to Columbia University, New York, in 1949-50 Ketonen was impressed by John Dewey's naturalist pragmatism, and he chose as textbooks for his students works like J. H. Randall's and J. Buchler's *Philosophy: An Introduction* and Morris Cohen's and Ernest Nagel's *An Introduction to Logic and Scientific Method*.

In 1968 I wrote my Master thesis in mathematics to Professor Gustav Elfving. He was one of the first probability theorists and mathematical statisticians in Scandinavia who supported the Bayesian approach. The topic of my thesis was "On the Power of Bayes Tests". Later I have realized that this concept of power is a Peircean truth-frequency for rejecting a false null hypothesis. My interest in Bayesianism was also encouraged by Professor Jaakko Hintikka's lectures on subjective probability and semantic information. While I was critical of the frequency theories of probability, I was happy to learn later that Peirce had proposed the dispositional propensity interpretation of physical probability in 1910 (*CP* 2.664).

In my project for a doctoral dissertation, I applied Hintikka's inductive logic to study the role of theories and theoretical terms in scientific inference. For this purpose, all classics of probability and induction were mandatory reading. As Hintikka's inductive logic is an improvement of Rudolf Carnap's system, which is not able to handle inductive generalization and the probability of laws, the bitter controversy between Carnap and Karl Popper was also significant. Popper's criticism and rejection of induction was not convincing, but his attempt to combine scientific realism and fallibilism was important. However, I soon realized that Peirce had formulated his version of fallibilism in a richer and a more plausible way than Popper. I bought my first Peirce book, Justus Buchler's *Philosophical Writings of Peirce* (1955), when I was a visiting fellow of Stanford University as Hintikka's research assistant during the spring of 1972. I still remember the warm days which I spent in the parks of Palo Alto reading and underlining Peirce's texts in Buchler's book. After finishing my Ph.D. in 1973, I wrote my comparison of Peirce and Popper first in a Finnish paper on fallibilism in 1974, and then in the summer of 1975 in an essay "Notes on Popper as Follower of Whewell and Peirce", published in 1978. I have been an admirer of Peirce ever since.

## 2. What do you consider your contribution to the field?

I have applied many ideas from Peirce in my own work, among them probability as propensity, probabilistic and statistical explanation, distinction between weaker and stronger forms of fallibilism, evolution of knowledge, scientific progress as convergence to the truth, abductive reasoning, and semiotics as a theory of language – world relations. In my *Critical Scientific Realism* (1999), I treat Peirce as an important background figure of scientific realism (in spite of his objective idealism in metaphysics). My definition of the notion of verisimilitude in *Truthlikeness* (1987) explicates an idea which was significant both for Peirce and Popper. Some of my lectures and writings may have influenced younger scholars who have made Helsinki an important center of pragmatism and Peirce studies.

Perhaps my main contribution to Peirce scholarship is the suggestion, made originally in 1981, that on the basis of his 1867 and 1883 accounts of explanatory probable arguments "Peirce should be regarded as the true founder of the theory of inductive-probabilistic explanation". This is against Wesley Salmon's authoritative history which takes Carl G. Hempel's 1962 essay as giving birth to this idea. My systematic defense was given in a paper "Peirce's Theory of Statistical Explanation" in 1989 in the Harvard Sesquicentennial Congress, and later my point was accepted by Hempel himself who in a personal letter admitted that the orientation of the philosophers in the Berlin group and the Vienna Circle was "basically a-historical", so that Peirce's contributions were not acknowledged.

## 3. What is the proper role of Peirce's work in relation to philosophy and other academic disciplines?

Peirce made important contributions in mathematics, logic, probability theory, philosophy and history of science, semiotics and theory of communication. But his fragmentary writings contain also a philosophical system, ranging from the doctrine of categories to evolutionary metaphysics, ethics, and religion. In all of these fields Peirce is amazingly original and inspiring thinker.

## 4. What do you consider the most important topics and/or contributions in the field of Peirce studies?

As Peirce's manuscripts may still include surprising discoveries, it would be most important to continue the edition and publication of his writings. Peirce is more powerful and interesting philosopher than his pragmatist successors in America. Peirce's diagrammatic logic, as based on existential graphs, still inspires contemporary logicians working with game-theoretical ideas. Peirce's semiotics, based on a triadic notion of sign, is more advanced than the popular European trends and more promising in its potential applications in the theory communication and culture. Peirce's notion of abduction, as inverse reasoning from effects to causes or from surprising observations to explanatory theories, is a hot topic in philosophy of science and artificial intelligence.

## 5. What are the most important open problems in this field and what are the prospects/venues for progress?

I am currently writing a book on abduction and scientific realism. One of the tasks is to find new examples of abductive reasoning in different scientific disciplines. The role of abductive inferential steps in the logic of discovery, or heuristic truth-seeking, is still largely unexplored. As the best reasons for scientific theories appeal to their explanatory and predictive power, it is also important to study the function of abduction in the confirmation and acceptance of theories. Philosophers of science are currently debating on the no-miracle argument in defending scientific realism. This "ultimate" abductive argument concludes that the best explanation of the empirical success of scientific theories is their truth or truthlikeness. It is still an interesting open question how the pattern of abduction changes if its conclusion concerns the truthlikeness (rather than the truth) of a successful explanatory theory.

## Bibliography

"Notes on Popper as Follower of Whewell and Peirce", *Ajatus* 37 (1978), 272-327. Reprinted in *Is Science Progressive?*, D. Reidel,

Dordrecht, 1984, pp. 18-60.

"Probability, Possibility, and Plenitude", in James H. Fetzer (ed.), *Probability and Causality: Essays in Honor of Wesley C. Salmon*, D. Reidel, Dordrecht, 1988, pp. 91-108.

"Peirce's Theory of Statistical Explanation", in Edward C. Moore (ed.), *Charles S. Peirce and the Philosophy of Science: Papers from the Harvard Sesquicentennial Congress*, The University of Alabama Press, Tuscaloosa and London, 1993, pp. 186-207.

"Hempel's Theory of Statistical Explanation", in James H. Fetzer (ed.), *Science, Explanation, and Rationality: Aspects of the Philosophy of Carl G. Hempel*, Oxford University Press, 2000, pp. 138-163.

"Defending Abduction", *Philosophy of Science (Proceedings)* 66 (1999), S436-S451.

# 23

# Winfried Nöth

Professor of Cognitive Semiotics
Catholic University of São Paulo

---

**1. Why were you initially drawn to Peirce?**

Peirce is among the authors I quoted in my earliest book publications of 1972, 1975, and 1976. At the time, I was more deeply influenced by structuralist semiotics in the tradition of Ferdinand de Saussure and Louis Hjelmslev. Against this background, Peirce's icon-index-symbol trichotomy seemed to offer a promising semiotic tool in the attempt to extend the semiotic horizon and to overcome the limitations imposed by the Saussurean dogma of arbitrariness. Peirce's distinction between iconic, indexical, and symbolic signs became an indispensable tool in my studies in applied semiotics of these years. I applied it to the analysis of illustrated ads as well as to studies in the ontogenesis and phylogenesis of signs.

The next step was to make use of further Peircean tools of semiotic analysis and to apply all three trichotomies of Peirce's typology of signs. I did so in a series of studies on signs and semiotic reflections in Lewis Carroll's Alice books (1980, 1994). The privilege of focusing on the Peircean sign typology in studies of applied semiotics had an end when I saw myself confronted with the necessity of presenting a more complete panorama of Peirce's semiotics and phenomenology in the three versions of my *Handbook of Semiotics* (2000). Its chapter on Peirce's semiotics also became a part of my introductory *Panorama da semiótica de Platão a Peirce* of 1995 and appeared as well in a Russian translation in 2001 (Nöth 2001a).

Nevertheless, my research only took a decisively Peircean turn from the mid-1990s on, when I became a permanent visiting professor of semiotics in São Paulo and a member of the São Paulo Centro International Center of Peirce Studies directed by Lucia Santaella. The enthusiastic students and renowned scholars working there as well as the opportunity of meeting prominent Peirce scholars from all over the world at the occasion of the biannual "Advanced Seminars on Peirce's Philosophy and Semiotics" inspired me to intensify my research in Peirce.

## 2. What do you consider your contribution to the field?

My Peirce studies cover a broad range of subjects. Among the principal topic areas in my focus are Peircean Visual Semiotics, media semiotics, iconicity in language and Peircean linguistics in general, Peircean semiotics of maps, the semiotics of tools, instruments, and machines, ecosemiotics and the semiotics of nature, evolutionary semiotics, and the development of Peircean semiotics and his key concepts (such as representation, information, thirdness, symbol, habit, etc.; Nöth 2010a, 2012, 2014a). I need to restrict myself to three of these areas.

My writings with a focus on Peircean Visual Semiotics, besides the various chapters of my *Handbook* dealing with this topic, began with a paper written together with Lucia Santaella on the semiotics of images, paintings, and photography (Nöth and Santaella 2012), which also constitutes the centerpiece of a book on the semiotics of the image (Santaella and Nöth 2000). Fundamental positions of a Peircean Visual Semiotics are addressed in papers on the image in general (Nöth 2003), on abstract paintings in particular (2002b), and in a much-quoted paper on why pictures are signs (2005). The latter was written in reply to the anti-Peircean arguments of a group of German art historians and theoreticians who claim that works of the visual arts are usually not signs but "phenomena sui generis".

In 1990, I first wrote about iconicity in spoken and written language (Nöth 1990). In a series of ensuing studies, I extended the traditional view of iconicity as onomatopoeia to include Peirce's theory of the icon as image, diagram, and metaphor (Nöth 1990, 1999, 2001b, 2008b, 2014b). Further extensions of this topic area to a general Peircean linguistics resulted in papers on Peirce as a pioneer in linguistics (Nöth 2002a), on the Peircean foundations of linguistic pragmatics (Nöth 2011) and on the questions of meaning and vagueness (Nöth and Santaella 2011), among others.

My research in semiotic machines began with an invitation by Frieder Nake to contribute a paper to the 1996 Dagstuhl Colloquium on *Informatics and Semiotics* and his invitation to extend the study presented there to a lecture at the University of Bremen soon after. The paper on *Semiotic Machines* (Nöth 2002c), which I presented there has meanwhile been published six times in three languages. The most important sequels to this study are my papers on the instrumentality and semiotic agency of signs, tools, and intelligent machines (Nöth 2009). The question of semiotic agency and autonomy of signs is currently one of the hottest topic in philosophical and social studies, to which Peirce's semiotics can contribute important insights (Nöth 2010b).

## 3. What is the proper role of Peirce's work in relation to philosophy and other academic disciplines?

Peirce was a polymath, and it is well known that he contributed important insights to the most diverse academic disciplines, from cartography to photometric research and from mathematics to metaphysics (see especially Fisch 1986), but for Peirce, semiotics, the research field whose foundations he had laid, provided the missing link between all sciences, from the natural sciences to metaphysics. The relation of Peirce's work to philosophy and other academic disciplines can best be epitomized in the much-quoted words he addressed to Lady Victoria Welby in his letter of December 23, 1908: "It has never been in my power to study anything, – mathematics, ethics, metaphysics, gravitation, thermodynamics, optics, chemistry, comparative anatomy, astronomy, psychology, phonetics, economics, the history of science, whist, men and women, wine, metrology, except as a study of semiotic" (SS 1977, 85–6). However, despite this declaration on the ubiquity of sign, Peirce was not a pan-semiotician in the sense of an advocate of a hegemony of semiotics over other domains of research. He had a very clear vision of the place of semiotics within the concert of the sciences, as his ambitious outline of the classification of the sciences (CP 1.176-283) shows, in which semiotics is only one of the three normative sciences, after aesthetics and ethics, all of which are preceded by phenomenology and followed by metaphysics.

## 4. What do you consider the most important topics and/or contributions in the field of Peirce studies?

The ubiquity and general acknowledgement of Peircean ideas in the most diverse fields of study makes it impossible to determine any specific topic as most important among all others. It is impossible to say whether Peirce's theory of abductive reasoning is more important than his work on existential graphs, his classification of signs, his metaphysics, or his cosmology. Peirce was a thinker far ahead of his time. It took more than half a century until the great originality of his method of existential graphs became fully acknowledged. Peirce's general theory of signs took no less time to be understood. For decades, under the influence of behaviorism, his semiotic ideas were severely distorted, especially by Charles Morris's reinterpretation of Peircean key concepts. Although it is unfortunate that many of Peirce's ideas have only survived as fragments, even the challenge of reconstructing his ideas is awarding in itself.

One of Peirce's greatest general contributions to modernity consists in his achievement of overcoming dualisms of all kinds. From Peirce's doctrines of semiotic mediation, synechism, and fallibilism, we can learn that we cannot expect to find "ultimate truths" but only approximations to final interpretants.

## 5. What are the most important open problems in this field and what are the prospects/avenues for progress?

In the speculative sciences, as Peirce called them in a Scholastic fashion, it is always hard, if not impossible, to identify problems that are still unresolved. On the one hand, as Peirce's doctrine of synechism teaches, the identification of a problem is already the first step to its resolution. On the other, his doctrine of fallibilism teaches that final "resolutions" are never possible. However, there are insights from Peirce that are more and others that are less relevant to discussions of contemporary intellectual and cultural life. In an interview for the Tallinn cultural journal *Keel ja kirjandus*, Marek Tamm asked me about the greatest challenges to the humanities today. My answer was about the challenges to the humanist doctrine of the autonomous human mind in a posthuman world in which semiotic machines seem to be taking over (Nöth 2008a). From Peirce we can learn that semiotic machines will act no more and no less autonomously than human minds. In the long run, it is the agency of the sign that will prevail in the evolution of semiosis.

The most important open problem in the field of Peirce studies is certainly the slow progress in the edition project of Peirce's *Writings*. More than thirty years have passed since the first volume of was issued, but the number of volumes that have been published so far is still less than half of the number of volumes which deserve and need to be made available to scholars and students of philosophy, semiotics, and other sciences. The avenue for progress can only be the reconsideration of the research priorities in the country indebted to Peirce for the privilege of having one of the greatest philosophers of all times among its citizens.

## Bibliography

Fisch, Max H. 1986. *Peirce, Semeiotic, and Pragmatism*. Bloomington, IN: Indiana University Press.

Nöth, Winfried. 1972. *Strukturen des Happenings*. Hildesheim: Olms.

Nöth, Winfried. 1975. *Semiotik: Eine Einführung*. Tübingen: Niemeyer.

Nöth, Winfried. 1976. *Dynamik semiotischer Systeme*. Stuttgart: Metzler.

Nöth, Winfried. 1980. *Literatursemiotische Analysen zu Lewis Carrolls Alice-Büchern*. Tübingen: Narr.

Nöth, Winfried. 1990. The semiotic potential for iconicity in spoken and written language. *Kodikas/Code* 13.3/4: 191-209.

Nöth, Winfried. 1994. Alice's adventures in semiosis. In *Semiotics and Linguistics in Alice's Worlds*, R. Fordyce and C. Marello (eds.), 11-25. Berlin: de Gruyter.

Nöth, Winfried. 1995. *Panorama da semiótica de Platão a Peirce*. São Paulo: Annablume.

Nöth, Winfried. 1999. Peircean semiotics in the study of iconicity in language. *Transactions of the Charles S. Peirce Society* 35.3: 613-619.

Nöth, Winfried. 2000. *Handbuch der Semiotik*. Stuttgart: Metzler.

Nöth, Winfried. 2001a. Charles Sanders Peirce. *Kritika i semiotica* [Novosibirsk] 3/4: 6-32. Online: *http://www.nsu.ru/education/virtual/cs34content.htm*.

Nöth, Winfried. 2001b. Semiotic foundations of iconicity in language and literature. In *The Motivated Sign*, O. Fischer & M. Nänny (eds.), 17-28. Amsterdam: Benjamins.

Nöth, Winfried. 2002a. Charles Sanders Peirce, pathfinder in linguistics. *Interdisciplinary Journal for Germanic Linguistics and Semiotic Analysis* 7.1: 1-14.

Nöth, Winfried. 2002b. Semiotic form and the semantic paradox of the abstract sign. *Visio* 6.4: 153-163

Nöth, Winfried. 2002c. Semiotic machines. *Cybernetics & Human Knowing* 9.1: 5-22.

Nöth, Winfried. 2003. Semiotic foundations of the study of pictures. *Sign Systems Studies* 31.2: 377-392.

Nöth, Winfried. 2005. Warum Bilder Zeichen sind: Bild- und Zeichenwissenschaft. In *Bild-Zeichen: Perspektiven einer Wissenschaft vom Bild*, S. Majetschak (ed.), 49-61. München: Fink.

Nöth, Winfried. 2008a. Humanitaarteaduste olevik ja tulevik. *Keel ja Kirjandus* 51(8/9): 740–742. [Responses to two questions by Marek Tamm.] In English: W. Nöth, Eero Tarasti, and Marek Tamm. 2008. Humanities: State and prospects. *Sign Systems Studies* 36(2): 527-532.

Nöth, Winfried. 2008b. Semiotic foundations of natural linguistics and diagrammatic iconicity. In *Naturalness and Iconicity in Language*, K. Willems & L. De Cuypere (eds.), 73-100. Amsterdam: Benjamins.

Nöth, Winfried. 2009. On the instrumentality and semiotic agency of signs, tools, and intelligent machines. *Cybernetics & Human Knowing* 16.3-4: 11-36.

Nöth, Winfried. 2010a. The criterion of habit in Peirce's definitions of the symbol. *Transactions of the Charles S. Peirce Society* 46.1: 82-93.

Nöth, Winfried. 2010b. Instrumentalität, Autonomie und Selbstreferenzialität der Zeichen. *Kodikas /Code* 33.1-2: 139-148.

Nöth, Winfried. 2011. Semiotic foundations of pragmatics. In *Foundations of Pragmatics*, W. Bublitz & N. R. Norrick (eds.), 167-202. Berlin: de Gruyter Mouton.

Nöth, Winfried. 2012. Charles S. Peirce's theory of information: A theory of the growth of symbols and of knowledge. *Cybernetics & Human Knowing* 19.1-2: 99-123.

Nöth, Winfried. 2014a. The life of symbols and other legisigns: More than a mere metaphor? In *Peirce and Biosemiotics: A Guess at the Riddle of Life*, V. Romanini & F. Eliseo (eds.), 171-182. Heidelberg: Springer.

Nöth, Winfried. 2014b. Three paradigms of iconicity research in language and literature. In *East Meets West: Iconicity in Language and Literature*, K: Shinohara, K. Akita & M. Hiraga (eds.). Amsterdam: Benjamins.

Nöth, Winfried and Lucia Santaella. 2000. Bild, Malerei und Photographie aus der Sicht der peirceschen Semiotik. In *Die Welt als Zeichen und Hypothese*, U. Wirth (ed.), 354-374. Frankfurt: Suhrkamp.

Nöth, Winfried and Lucia Santaella. 2011. Meanings and the vagueness of their embodiments. In *From First to Third via Cybersemiotics – A Festschrift Honoring Professor Søren Brier on the Occasion of his 60th Birthday*, T. Thellefsen, B. Sørensen, and P. Cobley (eds.), 247-282. Copenhagen: SL forlagene.

Peirce, Charles S. 1931-58. *Collected Papers*, vols. 1-6, ed. Hartshorne, C. and P. Weiss; vols. 7-8, ed. A. W. Burks. Cambridge, MA: Harvard Univ. Press (quoted as CP).

Peirce, Charles S. 1977. *Semiotics and Significs*, ed. Charles Hardwick. Bloomington IN: Indiana University Press (quoted as SS).

Santaella, Lucia and Winfried Nöth. 2012. *Imagem: Cognição, semiótica, mídia*, 6th ed. São Paulo: Iluminuras.

# 24

# Jaime Nubiola

Professor of Philosophy
University of Navarra, Spain

---

CHARLES S. PEIRCE: A PHILOSOPHER FOR THE 21ST CENTURY

### 1. Why were you initially drawn to Peirce?

After my graduation in 1975 from the University of Valencia in Spain, I worked in the broad field of analytical philosophy. I wrote my master's thesis on John L. Austin's theory of truth (1977) and my doctoral dissertation at the University of Navarra (1982) on the essentialist commitment of modal logic, focusing on the debate between W. V. O. Quine and S. Kripke. My attention in those years was concentrated on philosophical issues related to language, following mainly the insights and the style of Ludwig Wittgenstein, Hilary Putnam and other analytic philosophers of a pragmatist stripe. In 1991 my mentor Alejandro Llano suggested to me that it was the right time to look for a single author to devote my study to in order to compensate for the piecemeal character of my analytic training. I talked with several colleagues to find out who the philosopher was who *deserved* my attention. Leonardo Polo, an old colleague from Navarra, suggested that since I was a pragmatic person and I was interested in Communication Theory perhaps Charles S. Peirce was the right choice.

In the summer of 1992 I found myself as a Visiting Scholar at Harvard University trying to write an introduction to contemporary philosophy of language, looking to show how a historical understanding of analytic philosophy enabled one to predict that this philosophical tradition would undergo a renovation of a markedly pragmatic nature. At the same time, given that I found myself in the homeland of Charles S. Peirce, I was hoping to familiarize myself with his thought, his writings and with the scholarship that had recently sprung up around him. One day a lawyer friend of mine suggested that I read the American novelist Walker Percy's (1916-90) Jefferson Lecture "The Fateful Rift: The San Andreas Fault in the Modern Mind," which appears in the posthumous volume of his essays published in 1991 under the general title *Signposts in a Strange Land*.[1] That reading of his wonderful lecture had an effect on me very similar to Helen Keller's remarkable experience with the water from the fountain, referred to so many times by Percy.[2]

In the reading of that text—which can be considered the intellectual testament of Percy, at that time already very ill—I discovered the unification of my diverse intellectual interests that had long been pursued separately. For some time I had been interested in seemingly disparate segments of our culture, such as the philosophy of language, semiotics and the theory of communication, the argument concerning the limits of artificial intelligence, the possibility and limitations of mechanically processing human language, the attempts to teach language to primates, feral children and their linguistic capacities, the language of the deaf-mute, the creativity of language and even the revolution in linguistics provoked by Chomsky's generative grammar. My reading of that text by Walker Percy, physician and humanist, astonished me, because it revealed as clear as day both the diagnosis of the most serious disease afflicting our present-day culture, and its cure.

Percy was suggesting that the unifying element in all those topics that had attracted me so much was to be found in the insufficiency of the scientistic narrative that, permeated with a simplified Darwinism, had dominated the Anglo-American academic scene during the second half of the past century, with the aim of explaining the most characteristic behaviors of human beings such as language and communication. The cure—in Percy's judgment—ought to be looked for in Charles Peirce and his discovery of the irreducibly triadic nature characteristic of all linguistic behavior. Indeed, the remedy for overcoming the gap that divides our culture between the natural sciences and the humanities, and which made an integrated understanding of human beings and their activity impossible, was to be found in "the work of a human scientist who, I believe," Percy concluded, "laid the groundwork for a coherent science of man, and did so a hundred years ago".

Scientism, promoted by the Vienna Circle and its positivist heirs, became the dominant philosophical culture from the 1950s onwards, converting itself into that dominant mainstream naturalism which trusts in the progress of human reason and its ability to explain all problems definitively in the immediate future. As a reaction to this scientistic op-

---

[1] This lecture was given by Percy on the 3rd of May, 1989 as the *18th Jefferson Lecture* at the *National Endowment for the Humanities* (Washington D.C.). It was published with the title "The Divided Creature" in *The Wilson Quarterly* 13 (1989), pp. 77-87, and was included by Patrick Samway in the posthumous book *Signposts in a Strange Land* (Farrar, Straus and Giroux, New York), 1991, pp. 271-291.

[2] W. Percy, *The Message in the Bottle*, Farrar, Straus and Giroux, New York, 1976, pp. 34-36 and in many other places.

timism, post-modern thought, widespread in the last three decades, has oscillated between the presentation of science as a mere power structure or as just another form of literature.

Following Hilary Putnam, it is my conviction that Peirce's thought may help us not only to reassume our philosophical responsibility—which has been largely abdicated by much of 20th century philosophy—but also to tackle some of our most stubborn contemporary problems. More specifically, the founder of pragmatism not only identified most of these problems one century ago, but he also mapped out some paths that we could follow to overcome the poverty of contemporary scientistic reductionism.

## 2. What do you consider your contribution to the field?

My contribution to Peirce scholarship is mainly in three areas: 1) the launching in 1994 in Navarra of a Grupo de Estudios Peirceanos [http://www.unav.es/gep/] in order to promote the study of the work of Charles S. Peirce (1839-1914), especially in Spain and in the Spanish speaking countries, in the belief that his thought may offer some key insights into problems related to the culture, science and philosophy of the 21st century; 2) the detailed study of Peirce's "cosmopolitan period", to use Max Fisch's expression (1870-1883), in particular through his correspondence; and 3) some specific studies of the connections between C. S. Peirce and other authors like John H. Newman, Richard Rorty, George Searle, Alfred N. Whitehead and Ludwig Wittgenstein.

In connection with the first area, I want to say that I have been extremely fortunate in having outstanding doctoral students during the last twenty years. I've learned together with them all that I know about Peirce and pragmatism. In particular, I am extremely grateful to Dr. Sara Barrena, who has been the main translator of Peirce into Spanish [http://www.unav.es/gep/Peirce-esp.html] and to Dr. Izaskun Martínez who has worked as the webmaster of the Group for years. Together with Fernando Zalamea we have edited the volume *Peirce y el mundo hispánico* (2006), which includes an exhaustive and commented catalogue of all that has been written in Spanish about Peirce from 1883 until the year 2000. For twenty years we have been hosting monthly seminars with scholars from all around the world, particularly from the Spanish-speaking countries. In this sense, I also like to recall the great number of courses that I have given throughout the Spanish-speaking America in order to spread the word about Peirce and pragmatism: Bahía Blanca, Buenos Aires, Santa Fe and Tucumán (Argentina), Bogotá (Colombia), Santiago (Chile), Chihuahua, Ciudad Juárez, México D. F., and Monterrey (México). I was always impressed by the great attraction that Peirce exerted in all these places. The motto of our Group is that quotation from Peirce that reflects well the spirit of agapastic collaboration: "I do not call the solitary studies of a single man a science. It is only when a group of men, more or less in intercommunication, are aiding and stimulating one another by their understanding of a particular group of studies as outsiders cannot understand them, that I call their life a science." (*MS* 1334, Adirondack Summer School Lectures, 1905).

Regarding the study of Peirce's "cosmopolitan period", we have transcribed, translated into Spanish and published on the web, in heavily annotated form and with links and illustrations, all the letters by Peirce or to Peirce related to his first and second European trips (7/18/1870 — 3/7/1871 and 4/2/1875 — 8/26/1876). Scarce attention has been paid until now to Peirce's correspondence and we think that it is of great importance for understanding the real Peirce. In the course of our research, we have discovered some documents completely unknown until now, for instance, his signature in the book of visitors of the Alhambra and in the registration book of the British Library Reading Room, the galleys of "Fixation of Belief" with handwritten corrections sent by Peirce to W. K. Clifford; however, it seems to me that our main contribution is just the publication with open access of thousands of images of Peirce's pages, illustrated and annotated.

Although Peirce was a philosopher and a logician, he was first and foremost a real practitioner of science. Peirce insisted that the popular image of science as something finished and complete is totally opposed to what science really is. Science is for Peirce "a living historic entity" (*CP* 1.44, c.1896), "a living and growing body of truth" (*CP* 6.428, 1893), and above all a communicative mode of life. For this reason I have been always interested in the connections between Peirce and other authors. In my studies on Peirce's relations with J. H. Newman, R. Rorty, G. Searle, A. N. Whitehead and L. Wittgenstein I have tried to combine careful and thorough evidence-based scholarship with intellectual relevance.

### 3. What is the proper role of Peirce's work in relation to philosophy and other academic disciplines?

Peirce has been gaining an ever-increasing relevance in very different areas of knowledge: in astronomy, metrology, geodesy, mathematics, logic, philosophy, theory and history of science, semiotics, linguistics, econometrics, and psychology.[3] In all these fields Peirce has been considered a pioneer, a forerunner or even a "father" or "founder" (in the cases of semiotics and pragmatism). Bertrand Russell's comment

---

[3] M. Fisch, "The Range of Peirce's Relevance", *The Monist* 63, (1980), pp. 269-276; 64, pp. 123-141.

is representative: "beyond doubt ... he was one of the most original minds of the later nineteenth century, and certainly the greatest American thinker ever".[4] Even among academic philosophers it has become a commonplace to say that Peirce is the most original philosophical mind that the United States has yet produced[5] and his seminal role in a wide range of philosophical problems has been alluded to by many philosophers: Popper described Peirce as "one of the greatest philosophers of all times"[6] and Putnam called him "a towering giant among American philosophers".[7]

Peirce is usually identified as a *philosophers' philosopher* since he always gives food for thought. My colleague Sara Barrena and I have published a co-authored book on the occasion of the centennial of Peirce's death with the title *Charles S. Peirce (1839-1914): A Thinker for the 21st Century*.[8] In our book we have collected most of the papers jointly prepared along twenty years. Much of the work we have gathered there reflects those central aspects of his thought—abduction, creativity, pursuit of truth, reasonableness, God—that have attracted our attention over the years, and the volume as a whole provides a fairly accurate view of the nature and scope of the work of Peirce. We wanted to provide easy and direct access to the richness and depth of this scientist, logician and philosopher, who is so relevant and still so little known in the Spanish-speaking world. We are persuaded that Charles S. Peirce is not a nineteenth-century author who can be relegated to oblivion, but, on the basis of our knowledge of him, we claim is really a thinker for the twenty-first century. Peirce invites the reader to always to go deeper, to think more. This is for me his greatest legacy.

## 4. What do you consider the most important topics and/or contributions in the field of Peirce studies?

It is not easy and perhaps not fair to answer this question simply by highlighting some names of persons and their contributions. On the door of my office I have a sign with Peirce's expression: "The life of science is in the desire to learn" (CP 1.235, c.1902). In this sense, I would like to say that the most important contribution is each time that

---

[4] B. Russell, *Wisdom of the West*. Garden City, NY: Doubleday, 1959, p. 276.

[5] E. Nagel, "Peirce's Place in Philosophy", *Historia Mathematica* 9, (1982), p. 303.

[6] K. R. Popper, *Objective Knowledge: An Evolutionary Approach*, Oxford: Clarendon Press. 1972, p. 212.

[7] H. Putnam, *Realism with a Human Face*. Cambridge, MA: Harvard University Press, 1990, p. 252.

[8] S. Barrena & J. Nubiola, *Charles S. Peirce (1839-1914): Un pensador para el siglo XXI*, Eunsa, Pamplona, 2013.

a new graduate student finishes his or her doctoral dissertation on some aspect of Peirce's thought. In that situation this new scholar is opening the door of Peirce scholarship to new promising developments. Along this line, I want to mention, for example, Santiago Pons' recent dissertation on the laws of nature according to Peirce, Hedy Boero's thorough dissertation on Peirce's ethics (which was awarded the Extraordinary Prize of my university), and Ignacio Redondo's superb work on Peirce's communication theory.

From a general perspective, the most relevant contribution is without any doubt the *Chronological Edition* of Peirce's writings developed by the Peirce Edition Project in Indianapolis during decades. It is a pity that the pace of publication of the volumes is slow, due mainly to limitations of funding.

## 5. What are the most important open problems in this field and what are the prospects/avenues for progress?

When I entered the field of Peirce scholarship something that surprised me was the relatively scant attention paid throughout the years to the religious dimensions of Peirce's thought. Since my first readings of Peirce twenty years ago I had been deeply struck by this neglect, which contrasted so much with the ubiquity of religious references in his writings, especially in his mature years. In my meetings with well-known Peirce scholars I used to ask them about God and religion in Peirce, and mostly the answer that I received was that there was plainly a lot of religious stuff in Peirce, but that they were not interested in it. On the other hand, I was pleasantly surprised by Walker Percy when in his correspondence with Kenneth Ketner he called himself "a thief of Peirce", intending "to use CSP as one of the pillars of a Christian apologetic".[9] It seemed to me that Percy was in some sense nearer to the real Peirce than those scholars whom I had asked about God and religion in Peirce.

My reaction to these conflicting approaches was to decide that the whole matter deserved careful attention and I suggested this area of research to three of my graduate students. The first of them, Sara Barrena, did the first translation of "A Neglected Argument for the Reality of God" into Spanish and published it in 1996 with a long introduction dealing in detail with the subject (she later wrote a doctoral dissertation on creativity and reasonableness in Peirce); the second, Gonzalo Génova, wrote his dissertation on abduction and Peirce's logic of discovery, published in Spanish in 1997 and available on the web [http://www.unav.es/gep/Genova/Genova.pdf]. Since Peirce's Argument was

---

[9] P. H. Samway (ed.), *A Thief of Peirce. The Letters of Kenneth Laine Ketner and Walker Percy*, University Press of Mississippi: Jackson, MI, 1995, p. 130.

a particular form of abduction, going deep into this type of inference would support the study of Peirce's thought about God; the third, Rolando Panesa wrote a doctoral dissertation on science and religion in Peirce (1996), which is available on our website [http://www.unav.es/gep/TesisDoctorales/TesisRPanesa.pdf].

During these years we have studied and translated into Spanish a good amount of Peirce's religious texts, but the world is still eagerly awaiting the book that Douglas Anderson and David O'Hara are preparing of *Peirce's Religious Writings*. This is for me the most urgent need in Peircean scholarship.

**Bibliography**

Barrena, S. (2007), *La razón creativa. Crecimiento y finalidad del ser humano según C. S. Peirce*, Rialp, Madrid.

Barrena, S. y Nubiola, J. (2013), *Charles S. Peirce (1839-1914): Un pensador para el siglo XXI*, Eunsa, Pamplona.

Nubiola, J. y Zalamea, F., (2006), *Peirce y el mundo hispánico. Lo que C. S. Peirce dijo sobre España y lo que el mundo hispánico ha dicho sobre Peirce*, Eunsa, Pamplona.

Nubiola, J. y Zalamea, F. (eds.), (2006), *Charles Sanders Peirce. Razón e invención del pensamiento pragmatista*, monographic issue, *Anthropos*, 212, 3-206.

Peirce, C. S. (2010), *El amor evolutivo y otros ensayos sobre ciencia y religión*. Edition and translation by S. Barrena, Marbot, Barcelona.

# 25

# Sami Paavola

University Lecturer
Institute of Behavioural Sciences, University of Helsinki

---

**1. Why were you initially drawn to Peirce?**
I do not remember exactly but central influences were Ilkka Niiniluoto's courses on philosophy of science at the late 1980s. I must have read on Peirce already before but these courses sparked more detailed interest to Peirce's work. Important themes on those courses were the growth of knowledge and different views on conceptual change. Popper, Kuhn, Laudan, Lakatos and others were then prominent figures. Early on I got interested in N. R. Hanson's ideas on patterns of discovery where abduction has a crucial role. For me it seemed that abduction was a very promising way of characterizing issues concerning discovery. At that time abduction was often criticized especially as a logic of discovery, and I started to wonder why.

I also got interested in methodological issues more generally. I had started my university studies in sociology but was drawn towards philosophy more and more. Abduction seemed as a way of looking for an alternative position in relation to central dichotomies prevalent in methodological literature. I think that my basic philosophical temperament has always been to look for mediating positions instead of strict dichotomies. I think that those corners of research where things seem to be clashing against each other are the ones where new mediating processes are lurking. The quarrel between inductivism and the hypothetico-deductive model was a good example of this. Abduction seemed to have elements from both of these approaches but something new besides.

There were heated debates between analytically oriented philosophy and "continental philosophy" (or more generally philosophy emphasizing the role of "human sciences") at that time. There were, however, some philosophers who explicitly aimed at overcoming such dichotomies. I think that Peirce provided an interesting option because Peirce's philosophy seemed to have elements from both of these parties, and gave a promise of conceptual tools for developing a versatile outlook on various philosophical issues (on logic, phenomenology, signs, practices, realism, idealism, etc.). I still think that the situation is the same: Peirce's philosophy is not automatically giving means for avoiding polarities but it includes a promise, with its broad arsenal of conceptual tools, of a very wide-ranging and versatile perspective on philosophical issues and phenomena.

Very important was also that I found people in Helsinki who were interested in Peirce's philosophy. At late 1990s we established our own "Metaphysical Club" to the University of Helsinki (with Mirja Kela, Kimmo Pentikäinen, Erkki Kilpinen, Mats Bergman, and others) dedicated especially to Peirce's philosophy. With Mats Bergman we constructed 'Commens', a web-site dedicated to Peirce, with a dictionary on Peirce's terminology. I also found out that there was a learning model called progressive inquiry model (founded by Kai Hakkarainen and his colleagues) where abductive search for explanatory hypotheses was emphasized. I think that we felt that our Peirce endeavours were treated somewhat marginal in relation to mainstream philosophical approaches but this kind of a social network of students and researchers gave confidence on the importance of Peirce.

## 2. What do you consider your contribution to the field?

My focus has definitely been on abduction. It might seem like a narrow approach but I think that abduction can function as a central key to many fundamental philosophical questions. I have tried to argue that abduction (with various forms) gives a way of conceptually analyze the area of discovery. Abduction has been – and I think in many ways still is – a neglected topic in the philosophy of science and methodology. I hope that I have been involved in bringing some fresh ideas and perspectives on abduction.

I have tried to argue that there are various phenomena related to abduction, and by opening up these different forms of abduction new avenues for understanding processes of discovery opens up. I have tried to maintain that the discussion on abduction has been concentrated on questions of justification and validity. They are important perspectives as such but those discussions should be complemented with analyses on uses of abductive inference in dynamic processes of inquiry. This highlights *strategic* outlook on abductive reasoning. Hintikka has emphasized the meaning of strategies in inquiry processes in general, and I think that this should be developed further especially when it comes to abduction. This gives also means for understanding better the nature of abductive guessing instinct (which Peirce in his later writings emphasized) besides abductive inference. Abduction has important visual and iconic characteristics. Besides these, I think that human cognition more generally should be seen through lenses of distributed cognition.

Human beings are using culturally, socially, materially, and temporally distributed processes in their thought and activities. I have tried to develop further also those kinds of approaches to abduction. Traditional philosophical approaches (also on Peirce's philosophy) have not taken these kinds of phenomena much into account.

### 3. What is the proper role of Peirce's work in relation to philosophy and other academic disciplines?

I think that the main strength of Peirce's work comes from its broad and systematic concepts. At the same time this provides a challenge for Peirce studies, especially for students on Peirce. It takes time to get to know Peirce's conceptual apparatus, and when that is done, there is a risk of getting "trapped" to Peirce's work. I think that Peircean approach to research and philosophy should mean that one aims at developing novel and better explanations and approaches also on those issues that Peirce was developing; so not to be content (necessarily) with Peirce's own formulations. This was also one key message on N. R. Hanson's outlook on research and why he empahsized abduction: researchers have always "pressed on" for new explanations and interpretations on the basis of previous ones, and in relation to new observations. This is not easy with Peirce whose works are dispersed in many writings with a large amount of ideas and perspectives. Actually it might be a bit easier in relation to abduction which has nowadays many roots, not all tightly related to Peirce (like the inference-to-the-best explanation model started by G. Harman).

For me Peirce's one strength is then to give potential means to transcend many dichotomies in philosophy, and find fertile research areas on the basis of this. Of course, it is not self-evident if this is a good goal in itself but I think that Peirce's work provides interesting means for fresh outlooks. These dichotomies include, for example, logic vs. human experience, justification vs. discovery, theories vs. practices, natural sciences vs. hermeneutics, or science vs. art.

### 4. What do you consider the most important topics and/or contributions in the field of Peirce studies?

This is a difficult question to answer when nowadays Peirce's works are used and developed in many areas of research. This is then my own very personal perspective. As I argued above my own interest is especially on that kind of research which is not just Peirce research but aims at using Peirce's concepts and approaches clearly in relation to other approaches. For me, a good example of this kind of an use of Peirce has been Peter Skagestad's discussion on "augmentationism". Skagestad has compared Peirce's semiotics to Douglas C. Engelbart's ideas of augmentationism (what is the role of computers, artifacts and tools in human mind), and to Donald Campbell's and Karl Popper's evolutionary epistemology. This is not just about Peirce studies but more on using Peirce's conceptions also for phenomena which existed in a very crude form when Peirce wrote his own texts.

For me the most important aspects of Peirce studies have been understanding of dynamic processes where different kinds of signs are involved. This means sign theoretical studies but in a sense which does not stay only within signs. Peirce's philosophy emphasizes those issues which are central for understanding modern epistemology, that is, fundamentally social character of human knowledge, indexicality, the role of objects, or visual and emotional characteristics of human knowledge, fundamental fallibilism with practical and theoretical orientation, and constant search for novelties; among others.

## 5. What are the most important open problems in this field and what are the prospects/avenues for progress?

This is also a difficult question to answer except in relation to my own research interests and hunches in this field. On abduction I would say that we probably still have quite poor understanding on what it is and what it might be, and also on how different forms of abduction are used. As far as I see it, new formulations of abduction are still to be developed, as well as more specific understanding on sign processes and activities involved. There are many special areas where abduction is developed further like practical syllogism, or the use of visual thinking and iconicity in the hypothesis generation.

Abduction could be seen more from the *methodological* point of view, that is, how hypotheses are constructed and modified bit by bit in the course of research processes. There is a growing literature on abduction from a methodological perspective in various empirical fields and within different methodological approaches (like grounded theory, case studies, or ethnography). There could be more interaction between methodological literature and philosophy of science.

My own interest is also to interpret sign processes and abduction more in relation to those things emphasized in distributed cognition (or what Lorenzo Magnani has called manipulative abduction). How to understand abductive processes of search which take into account the fundamental role of social interaction and the use of materials from the environment in the human inquiry. In summary, abduction is then a bunch of interesting ideas and formulations to be developed further!

## Bibliography

Paavola, S. (2004). Abduction as a logic and methodology of discovery: The importance of strategies. *Foundations of Science* 9 (3), 267-283.

Paavola, S. (2004) Abduction through Grammar, Critic and Methodeutic. *Transactions of the Charles S. Peirce Society* 40 (2), 245-270.

Paavola, S. (2005) Peircean abduction: instinct or inference? *Semiotica* 153-1/4, 131-154.

Paavola, S. (2006) Hansonian and Harmanian Abduction as Models of Discovery. *International Studies in the Philosophy of Science* 20(1), 93-108.

Paavola, S. (2007) Abductive Logic of Discovery with Distributed Means. In Olga Pombo & Alexander Gerner (eds.) *Abduction and the Process of Scientific Discovery* (pp. 47-62). Colecção Documenta, Centro de Filosofia das Ciências da Universidade de Lisboa.

Paavola, S. (2011) Diagrams, Iconicity, and Abductive Discovery. *Semiotica* 186-1/4, 297–314.

Paavola, S. (2012). *On the Origin of Ideas. An Abductivist Approach to Discovery*. Revised and enlarged edition. Saarbrücken: Lap Lambert Academic Publishing.

Paavola, S. (2014) From steps and phases to dynamically evolving abduction. A paper at the Charles S. Peirce International Centennial Congress 2014. *Invigorating Philosophy for the 21st Century*. Lowell, USA, 16-19 July.

Paavola, S. & Hakkarainen, K. (2005). Three abductive solutions to the Meno paradox – with instinct, inference, and distributed cognition. *Studies in Philosophy and Education* 24(3-4), 235-253.

Paavola, S., Hakkarainen, K., & Sintonen, M. (2006) Abduction with Dialogical and Trialogical Means. *Logic Journal of the IGPL* 14(2), 137-150.

Paavola, S. & Järvilehto, L. (2011). Action Man or Dreamy Detective. In Josef Steiff (Ed.) *Sherlock Holmes and Philosophy. The Footprints of a Gigantic Mind* (pp. 45-54). Popular Culture and Philosophy series, vol 61. Chicago and La Salle, Illinois: Open Court.

# 26
# Helmut Pape

Professor of Philosophy
Universität Bamberg

---

**1. Why were you initially drawn to Peirce?**
When I started studying philosophy in the winter term of 1971/72 at the University of Hamburg I enrolled for almost all the courses - seminars and lectures - offered in philosophy. There were, as far as I can remember, a total of sixteen courses on offer, ranging from dialogues of Plato and Kant's *Kritik der Reinen Vernunft* to Popper's *Logic of Scientific Discovery* and a lecture course by Gotthard Günter on non-Aristotelian, three-valued logic. Among the sixteen was a lecture course by Klaus Oehler on Peirce. Oehler presented Peirce as a philosopher who was able to combine the ontological and transcendental aspirations of the German idealist tradition with the focus on logic and scientific method of analytic philosophy and modern philosophy of science - and in doing so providing a better, comprehensive alternative to both. My interest quickly turned into fascination as, in the course of my first term, I began exploring Hartshorne's and Weiss's edition of Peirce's *Collected Papers* (CP). I read around somewhat wildly, and as I did so my attention was caught in particular by Peirce's strong claims about ethics and science. What does it mean that there are "ultimate goods", even a *summum bonum*? How come that a community of investigators has to share truth as a common purpose in order to produce theories that are empirically meaningful? The first paper I ever wrote in philosophy addressed these issues. I somehow managed to apply Peirce's ethics to the findings of the Club of Rome in their first report "The Limits of Growth". I argued that mankind needs a way of arriving at a *summum bonum* if we are to prevent the depletion of natural resources and the collapse of the environment. To this paper I appended a translation into German of the "Ultimate Goods" chapter in CP 1. Although Klaus Oehler liked my translation, he did not like the thesis I had argued for. My interpretation of Peirce's ethics in connection with this ethical account of sustainability was too "leftist" for his taste. Nevertheless, he offered me a job as a student assistant, which I became eligible for two terms later. During

this period my initial impressions of Peirce's work developed and stabilized: I was struck and impressed by Peirce's way of bringing together a fascinatingly broad range of systematic questions, challenging ideas, a broad historical outlook and detailed, systematic arguments. I read Peirce as a contemporary thinker addressing philosophical problems we still face today. One of my early efforts was a paper on fallibilism and logic in which I compared Peirce and Popper. Of course, it took me some time and effort before I could make explicit what my impression of superficiality in Popper's account of science and logic consisted in. But the result was a better appreciation of Peirce's philosophical power. Whereas Popper's somewhat limited conception of deductive logic and fallibilism struck me as one-sided and dangerously narrow-minded, Peirce's ideas about logic, science and fallibilism made it possible to situate knowledge within a practical context which also took account of its social conditions, providing a realistic and philosophically salient account of empirical meaning. So from the very beginning I saw Peirce as a contemporary and original partner in a dialogue that made ample use of logical and mathematical concepts and the methods I saw at work in his semiotics and pragmatism. I still think that my early rather harsh judgment is correct: that not Popper but Peirce presents the best way to pursue the project of philosophy, providing us with a comprehensive account of the logical and conceptual structures by virtue of which human beings are able to find their place in the overall scheme of reality. My fascination with the immense breath of Peirce's thought has stayed with me, though - under the influence of analytic philosophy of language – my focus has been primarily on the theory of knowledge, semiotics and logic, and the ontology of visual properties.

## 2. What do you consider your contribution to the field?

It is difficult to estimate the importance of one's own contribution to a field such as Peirce studies. What is the criterion of a good or lasting contribution? My own judgment on this question is bound to be partial. One measure is the range and breadth of this contribution. I have published some six volumes to date which include translations of Peirce's unpublished manuscripts into German together with philosophical introductions (also in German). The first of these volumes contains the group of manuscripts constituting the syllabus on logic written for the 1903 Lowell-Lectures. It was published in 1981 under the title *Charles Peirce. Phänomen und Logik der Zeichen*. This first volume has sold almost 8,000 copies and continues to sell well. This, if not my best, is certainly one of my longest-selling contribution to Peirce studies in Germany!

There are of course a number of topics, claims and theses that I have repeatedly presented and discussed over the last 30 years in some 150 papers and 3 monographs about Peirce, and which I consider to be important contributions to Peirce scholarship - even if other philosophers and Peirce scholars may disagree. From the very beginning I have represented Peirce as a systematic philosopher and not just as the grandfather of semiotics or the progenitor of pragmatism. Peirce developed a rich, systematically interrelated network of theories on a wide range of topics, using all sorts of conceptual and, in particular, mathematical concepts and tools. I have argued that the systematic philosophy that Peirce developed in this way is in fact a specific variety of objective idealism. Admittedly, after working at this task for more than thirty years, I find that many of my German (as well as Austrian and Swiss) contemporaries remain unconvinced. However, there are also exceptions, including Jürgen Habermas who has consistently supported my work over the past decades.

But I want to mention some of my more specific contributions to Peirce studies. Starting in the early eighties, I drew attention to the importance of the concept of an object in Peirce's semiotics, logic and methodeutic. My claim (*contra* D. Greenlee, for example, in his *Peirce's Concept of a Sign*) was that the semiotic concept of an object is part and parcel of Peirce's relational, process account of semiosis. This claim I developed in my first book on Peirce: *Erfahrung und Wirklichkeit als Zeichenprozess. C. S. Peirce' Entwurf einer spekulativen Grammatik des Seins* ("Experience and Reality as Semiosis. C. S. Peirce's Concept of a Speculative Grammar of Being"), Suhrkamp, Frankfurt 1989. In the second part of the book I argued that the semiotic concept of an object is crucial to a phenomenological account of communication and interpersonal experience. Indeed, Peirce makes use of a sophisticated normative notion of an object. He thereby develops an implicit theory of desire and normativity, something which many Peirce interpreters and other philosophers, e.g. Robert Brandom in his criticism of classical pragmatism, completely overlook. In sum, Peirce's semiotic account of an object is part of a phenomenology of intersubjective common sense experience that serves as a backdrop for his formal account of sign-processes. This insight – which may be both my most important and most overlooked contribution to Peirce-scholarship! – was the starting point for a series of papers in which I argued that Peirce's semiotics uses the properties of ordered relations (e.g. transitivity) to explain how we are able to keep track of identical objects in sequences of radically different, even contradictory interpretations. For me, Peirce's theory of the semiotic object paves the way for a philosophical understanding of the success conditions of communication, in general, and a philosophical theory of translation in particular. This thesis I developed in detail in the 2002 paper "Wovon war eigentlich die Rede? Missverstehen als Scheitern von Identitätsunterstellungen", (What were you actually talking about? Misunderstanding as a Case of False Identity Assumptions). If the relational properties of sign-sequences allow us to grasp the identity relations implicit in the use of signs by different people at different times, then the properties of semiotic processes provide the basis for an ontological and dialogical account of how we are able to think and communicate successfully about identity. There emerges along these lines a more comprehensive understanding of Peirce's semiotics, logic and philosophy within the scope of a theory of mind and semiotic normativity. For this approach helps us to understand the performative role of events of sign-use, and the way in which they carry forward their "identity-load" within the flow of experienced signs. Another consequence is that the distributed events of visual experience may be used as a common, interpersonally perceptible basis for dialogical processes to which people are obliged to refer back. This insight, which is at work in the background in Peirce's observations about "quasi-mind" and "commens", provides the philosophical, ontological and semantic foundation of Peirce's understanding of signs in general and his graphical logic – and the Existential Graphs in particular.

I developed a somewhat more general version of this argument for an ontology of visual properties in the book *Die Unsichtbarkeit der Welt. Eine visuelle Kritik neuzeitlicher Ontologie* (The Invisibility of the World. A Visual Critique of Contemporary Ontology), Frankfurt 1997. This book argues (alongside a number of other claims about visual properties) that Peirce's work contains fragments of a phenomenology of the relational structure of the dialogical, interpersonal nature of visual experience. And it is this visually based phenomenology that allows Peirce to break away from a Cartesian subjective account of mind and visual experience and to discover the semantical and logical force of visual structures in his Existential Graphs. In a later paper, titled "Was ist Peirce' bildnerisches Denken?" ("What is Peirce's Pictorial Thought?"), Berlin 2010, I interpreted the semiotical, logical and ontological role of visual experience in Peirce's philosophy as a sort of constructive, formative principle in the development of his philosophy and his thought in other disciplines.

Another way to appreciate the importance Peirce's semiotic theory of objects arises from a generalized interpretation of his conception of indexical signs. In several papers about indexical signs, some of them in English, I argued that this kind of sign provides us with an implicit account of the dynamics and success conditions of sign-use in general. Peirce's account of indexical signs has crucial implications for rhetoric, epistemology and ontology as well as for the methodology of the humanities. This is the point of a paper published 2008 in the *Transactions of the C. S. Peirce Society*, "Searching For Traces. Towards a Peircean Account of an Indexical Methodology for the Humanities". Implicit in Peirce's notion of an index is an important general thesis: that the use of signs of all kinds has an implicitly indexical aspect. If indices are formulated explicitly some of the facts about the situation within which they are used are captured by the indexical sign: they are correlated performatively with the present experience, that is, with the perceptual attention of speaker and interpreter. The force of the semiotic event of the use of an index token is grasped by both parties in a given dialogical exchange only if the index is understood correctly. For what the index does is to allow the interpreter to share the compulsion, forces and other existential relations the utterer of the index is subject to. That is to say, indices are our only semiotic option to combine communication with a participation of human existence in biographical space and time.

The editorial work for which I am perhaps best known in Germany is an edition of a group of published and unpublished manuscripts dealing with Peirce's philosophy of nature, his evolutionary cosmology and his semiotics and philosophy of science. For this book *Charles S. Peirce. Naturordnung und Zeichenprozess: Schriften über Semiotik und Naturphilosophie*, ("The Order of Nature and Semiosis: Writing on Semiotics and the Philosophy of Nature"), Aachen 1988, I persuaded Ilya Prigogine to write a preface. I had sent Prigogine some of Peirce's manuscripts on chance and dissipation. When I visited him at the Université Libre in Bruxelles, I convinced Prigogine that Peirce's writings anticipated conceptual elements of Prigogine's non-equilibrium thermodynamics. Prigogine had developed this theory against the background of his work on chemical clocks. In my introduction to the volume – which includes among other things 32 of Peirce's entries on topics like "chance", "probability", "time" etc. in the *Century Dictionary* – I discussed the relation of Peirce's approach to modern physics: The relation of his work to probabilistic approaches to microphysical events in quantum physics, for example, and to the role of the anthropic principle in cosmology. I also showed that Peirce's philosophy of nature and cosmology is internally related to and can even be described using the same concepts he employs in his account of mind and signs. Prigogine's work is foreshadowed, I suggested, in Peirce's hopes for a non-Newtonian physics that would accommodate the chance events occurring far from the thermodynamic equilibrium. Peirce had been looking for "real" laws of nature that would allow for irreversible growth of regularities. Human habits provided him with a model because they are regularities of action with a time-structure and invariant order that may change irreversibly. In a number of papers, especially in "Chance, Time and Methodology in Peirce's Philosophy of Nature", in: *Philosophy and the Many Faces of Science,* London/Landham 1999, and in "The Emergence of Time and Singularity in Peirce's Philosophy of Nature", in: *Philosophia Naturalis*, 2/2001, I argued that Peirce's philosophy of nature was consistent both with his pragmatic methodology and with his version of objective idealism. For this reason, in my introduction to "*C. S. Peirce: The Order of Nature and Semiosis*", I suggested it might be appropriate to characterize Peirce's philosophy as a form of "logical idealism". Another reason for favoring the term "logical idealism" was my discovery that Peirce posited a sort of fuzzy, partial identity between physical and mental processes, physical qualities and mental qualia. I argued for this in two papers, the first of which is "The Logical Structure of Idealism. C. S. Peirce and the Search for a Logic of Mental Processes", in: *The Rule of Reason: The Philosophy of C. S. Peirce*, Toronto 1997. A more detailed argument is developed in my later study "What Thought is For. The Problematic Identity of Mental Processes with Chance Events in Peirce's Idealistic Metaphysics", published in the Transactions of the C. S. Peirce Society, 2002. In these papers I also presented some arguments for my view that the theory of mind associated with Peirce's logical idealism and the evolutionary ontology/cosmology are entirely compatible with his semiotics and logic.

## 3. What is the proper role of Peirce's work in relation to philosophy and other disciplines?

Any body of thought that deserves to be called a "philosophy" consists in a unique configuration of conceptual and methodological tools that provides a distinctive approach to the overall structure, features and practical character of human reality. Peirce's work satisfies this criterion: his emphasis on an open, fallibilistic conception of scientific method and scientific knowledge, his phenomenological claim that all experience has a universal categorical qualitative structure which everybody has at his or her disposal, even though this structure is largely implicit, and his thesis that there is a developmental and evolutionary process structure, embodied in habits, that connects all sorts of natural, cultural and moral phenomena form the quasi-systematic core that is characteristic for his philosophy. This philosophical character will surely continue to influence the development of other philosophical and scientific approaches. One role of Peirce's work, for quite a considerable time to come, will therefore be to act both as a source of inspiration, irritation and new approaches to philosophy and perhaps also to some of the twenty-four disciplines to which he made various contributions. Given the scope and richness (and in some cases not fully developed) state of much of his work, I expect that there are still surprises in store for philosophers and scientists in a variety of fields. Although his semiotics, philosophy of science and pragmatism define the main scope of his philosophical influence, I expect that this picture will if anything tend to broaden and become more highly differentiated in the course of time. To give just one example from philosophy of science: I once spent some time thinking about the theory of scientific measurement, and in particular the question of how the elementary unit of a system of measurement should be established. On checking into Peirce's writings on this issue I found a passage where he suggested that a good strategy would be to determine the value of a number of unit-elements and to calculate a mean value. As far as I know, nobody in philosophy of science has written anything on this issue taking Peirce's proposal into account.

## 4. The most important topics or contributions to Peirce studies

When I started studying Peirce in the 1970s, M. G. Murphy's *The Development of Peirce's Philosophy* was *the* book about Peirce. But in the meantime the situation has changed completely; many good books and articles have by now been devoted to the study of Peirce's work, addressing a wide range of topics, and sometimes stemming from disciplines outside philosophy. A growing number of editions of Peirce's manuscripts and in particular the critical edition of the *Writings* have provided one of the most important impulses for a new generation of contributions to Peirce study. By now there a number of excellent collections of essays, some more general in character (e.g. *The Cambridge Companion to Peirce*, ed. By C. Misak) and others addressing a special topic (e.g. *The Normative Thought of C. S. Peirce*, ed. by C. de Waal & K. P. Skowronki). For those interested in Peirce's semiotics the most important and influential study is surely T. L. Short's *Peirce's Theory of Signs*. This book combines detailed discussions of various concepts, approaches and projects pursued by Peirce, and situates his ideas on semiotics in the wider philosophical context of contemporary discussions in philosophy. The chapters on final causality, in particular, are unsurpassed. Short concentrates for the most part on semiotics in a narrow sense, on speculative grammar. For this reason, J. J. Liszka's *A General Introduction to the Semiotic of Charles Sanders Peirce*, which discusses the status and claims of Speculative Rhetoric (or Methodeutic) — the third branch of semiotics — is an important addition to Short's book and can be usefully combined with M. Bergman's *Peirce's Philosophy of Communication* which addresses the bearings of Peircean semiotics and rhetoric on human interaction. One important and extremely helpful book - especially if it is read in connection with A. Pietarinen's *Signs of Logic* - is the comprehensive volume of *Studies in the Logic of C. S. Peirce*, edited by N. Houser, D. D. Roberts and J. V. Evra, in which a large number of contributors discuss Peirce's formal logic from a variety of perspectives. Also of particular importance are studies that develop and test the systematic potential of Peirce's numerous conceptual innovations. Peirce studies derive much benefit from works such as Frederik Stjernfelt's impressive *Diagrammatology. An Investigation on the Borderlines of Phenomenology, Ontology, and Semiotics*, that develops and applies one of Peirce's systematic conceptual tools—the idea that the iconic or diagrammatic form is the most basic one for all sorts of reasoning and theoretical thought.

## 5. What are the most important open problems in this field and what are the prospects/avenues for progress?

Open problems and the progress of Peirce studies will no doubt continue to be closely connected. But exactly how and to what degree is hard to tell. Of the five questions this is the one most likely to stimulate wild speculation. Peirce studies undoubtedly suffer from blind spots of succumbing to which every Peirce scholar, myself included, will be found guilty by future researchers. In making prognoses one is bound to be guided by what one believes or implicitly takes for granted. If what I have described so far (especially in answering question 3) is to some degree correct, then progress in the use, interpretation and influence of Peirce's work is to be expected in a wide range of fields and scientific disciplines, indeed throughout human culture. But exactly what course such developments – in the social sciences, in the theory of culture, in literature and linguistics – may take it is hard to be specific about. This guess is based in part on the reception of my own work, which provides evidence of the way in which theoretical concepts developed in the study of Peirce's semiotics can be taken up by scholars writing about topics such as the meaning and semiotic structure of paintings, or the status of obviously false self-descriptions. However, it is obvious that neither I nor anybody else will be able to foresee all or even the most important avenues of progress. Whether and in what way any of Peirce's thoughts – whether about economics, the history of science, the role of mathematics in philosophy or his idea of a unique *summum bonum* that culminates in the proposal that the growth of concrete reasonableness is an ultimate good – will turn out to be fruitful to the further progress of philosophy and other disciplines is an open question. At a methodological level, however, one prediction does seem safe: that a widening interest in Peirce's work and the problems and questions it raises in a variety of fields, will stimulate Peirce scholars to develop the conceptual potential implicit in his rich and diverse thought with greater care and ever more scrupulous attention to detail.

On the basis of my own experience in the field I would welcome both more general and more specific studies. Peirce says somewhere that there are two errors in philosophy: to generalize too much and to generalize not enough. It seems to me that in some areas of Peirce studies, the lack of generalization is a serious problem. One area of generalization that might prove fruitful concerns the ontology implicit in Peirce's work. It seems that a process ontology is assumed or implicit, not only in his evolutionary cosmology but also in his epistemology, pragmatism, logic and semiotics. Peirce never made this ontology explicit and one or more careful studies of this archeological-ontological layer of his thought would surely prove a worthwhile undertaking.

On the other hand, the third part of semiotics, the speculative rhetoric, cries out for attention and will surely be studied and better understood in the near future. Such research should take place on a number of different levels in order both to make Peirce's thoughts and assumptions more explicit and to give them a more definite and systematic theoretical shape. A number of complementary research programs along these lines would be feasible. A rhetorical study of the style and language of Peirce's manuscripts and letters might be of value. And we also need careful and detailed studies of how Peirce uses rhetorical properties in his semiotic writings to describe signs, sign processes and discursive and interactional settings that take as their point of departure and even integrate the different developmental stages, layers and issues of his semiotics.

To make progress along all these lines may call for a new methodological approach, a new rhetorical interpretation of Peirce's "experimental" method of writing. The style of Peirce's writing in many of the unpublished manuscripts has a quality which at first impresses the reader with a labyrinthine, confused and obscure quality that is sometimes attributed to a defect of the author's philosophical thought. But this impression is to some extent mistaken. In many cases Peirce's manuscripts are the archeological remains, the traces of his method and rhetoric. Peirce often develops several possible lines of thought more or less simultaneously. The alternative versions branch off at a certain point critical for the issue at hand. Like most other Peirce scholars, I have tended to select just one of the possible lines of arguments that seemed to me to be the most promising. However, in studying the *logica utens* of his work, it may be more fruitful, especially with the richest and most extensive manuscripts, to pursue and interpret a number of possible lines of argument and the way they relate to each other simultaneously.

Let me conclude with some remarks concerning some more concrete avenues of progress. As I suggested above, in the theory of communication, in linguistics, in the theory of translation, in pragmatics, and in many other areas of the humanities, the theory of art and culture, Peirce's semiotics could help to broaden the range and scope of questions to which theory seeks to provide an answer. Over the last four or five years a number of scholars, M. Bergman, V. Colapietro and J. Liszka in particular, have emphasized the role of Peirce's speculative rhetoric or methodeutic. At present, philosophical interest in rhetoric is rapidly growing. A kind of rhetorical turn may be about to take place in the near future. Any research that tends to highlight the rhetorical components in Peirce's thought will undoubtedly place his work at the center of contemporary discussions in the philosophy of language.

A similar process involving Peirce's role in contemporary philosophy of mind may also be underway. Recent "enactivist" approaches to mind and consciousness elaborated in the work of Alva Noë (*Action in Perception*), S. Gallagher, D. Hutto and others interpret cognitive processes and capabilities in terms of the interactions of humans with each other and with their environment. This approach might be seen as building on Peirce's early claim that inner events stand in need of outer facts, applying the pragmatic dictum that the meaning of theoretical thought is clarified only in terms of its practical consequences. The environmental relation embraces for Peirce as for Hutto and others the relationship between beliefs, intentions and the social group to which the knowing and believing subject belongs. Indeed, the rhetorical theory implicit in Peirce's semiotic writings can also be interpreted as a way of spelling out the enactive meaning of signs in terms of their interactional function: they embody the relational properties that hold in every kind of situation or environments in which the various specific types of sign function successfully.

**Bibliography**

**Books:**

*Charles Peirce. Phänomen und Logik der Zeichen*, (Syllabus to the 1903 Lowell Lectures) edition, introduction & translation into German, Frankfurt 1982

*Erfahrung und Wirklichkeit als Zeichenprozess. C. S. Peirce' Entwurf einer spekulativen Grammatik des Seins* ("Experience and Reality as Semiosis. C. S. Peirce's Concept of a Speculative Grammar of Being"), Suhrkamp, Frankfurt 1989

*Die Unsichtbarkeit der Welt. Eine visuelle Kritik neuzeitlicher Ontologie* (The Invisibility of the World. A Visual Critique of Contemporary Ontology), Frankfurt 1997

*Charles S. Peirce zur Einführung* (Introducing C. S. Peirce), Hamburg 2004

**Papers:**

"The Logical Structure of Idealism. C. S. Peirce and the Search for a Logic of Mental Processes", in: *The Rule of Reason: The Philosophy of C. S. Peirce*, ed. by J. Brunning & P. Forster, Toronto U.P., 1997, 153 - 184

"Chance, Time and Methodology in Peirce's Philosophy of Nature", in: *Philosophy and the Many Faces of Science*, hrsg. von D. Anapolitanos, A. Baltas, S. Tsinorema, Landham/London, 93-116, 1999

"Wovon war eigentlich die Rede? Missverstehen als Scheitern von Identitätsunterstellungen" (What were you actually talking about? Misunderstanding as a Case of False Identity Assumptions), in: *Übersetzung als Medium der Integration und des Kulturverstehens*, ed. J. Renn, J. Straub, S. Shimada, Campus Verlag Frankfurt, 2002, 62 - 92

"What Thought is For. The Problematic Identity of Mental Processes with Chance Events in Peirce's Idealistic Metaphysics", *Transactions of the C. S. Peirce Society*, Vol. XXXVIII, 2002: No. 1/2, S. 215-251

Was ist Peirce' bildnerisches Denken?" ("What is Peirce's Pictorial Thought?"), in: *Charles S. Peirce: Das bildnerische Denken*, hrsg. von F. Engel, M. Queisner und T. Viola, Berlin 2012, 65 - 94.

# 27
# Ahti-Veikko Pietarinen

University of Helsinki & Tallinn University of Technology

---

**1. Why were you initially drawn to Peirce?**

I graduated from the universities of Turku and Helsinki, Finland, the land strangely contracted by a Peirce-virus early on and where nearly all philosophy professors became prominent Peirce scholars. The first to introduce me to Peirce was Risto Hilpinen, who in the early 1990s commuted between Turku and Miami and whose philosophy of science class I sat and enjoyed. I had studied computer science and mathematics, and Hilpinen correctly emphasized the probabilistic nature of all sciences and explained in his lectures Peirce's theory of probabilities, why the semantics of questions is important in understanding the nature of scientific discovery, and how logic – in the wider sense than what they teach you in your commonplace mathematics and CS departments – becomes the method for discovery. Hilpinen was the student of the mighty Hintikka who had inspected the *Collected Papers* in the early 1960s although he published on Peirce only much later. Hintikka's philosophy is in fact so intensely in consort with Peirce's thought as almost to make one believe in reincarnation.[1]

Hintikka was the student of Georg Henrik von Wright, who referred to Peirce very positively in his works since the early 1940s. And von Wright's teacher, in turn, was Eino Kaila, a legendary educator in the Finnish history of philosophy. Kaila took part in the Vienna Circle meetings and wrote on pragmatism as early as in 1912. Hintikka taught and influenced a legion of philosophers, including also Leila Haaparanta, Simo Knuuttila, Ilkka Niiniluoto, Juhani Pietarinen, Veikko Rantala, Gabriel Sandu, Matti Sintonen and Raimo Tuomela. The third, even the fourth, generation of Hintikka's students is already active in the Peirce scene and beyond. As can also be observed from such lineages

---

[1] To this remark Jaakko replied that "Ok but who reincarnated whom?" In his biography on his second wife (*She Chose to Be Called Merrill Hintikka*, in Finnish, WSOY 2014), Jaakko tells the tale of how their mutual life got started after having met during the Eastern APA in a Manhattan hotel in Christmas 1975. Peirce met Juliette in the Brevoort House, a few blocks away, during the Christmas ball in 1875. On the outlines of the common traits in the philosophies of Hintikka and Peirce see Pietarinen (2007).

the so-called analytic philosophy has always thrived in the wider context of the sciences, pragmatism, humanism, and even phenomenology, in these freezing corners of the continent.

My thesis work was on independence-friendly logic and game-theoretic semantics, with Hintikka as the opponent. (Jaakko is also a *Doktorvater* of my father, Juhani.) Although Peirce was not the showpiece of my dissertation, understanding his logic and philosophy would soon gain prominence. Hilpinen had already shown in the 1980s that Peirce had what effectively is the game-theoretic interpretation of quantifiers, a finding which I documented in detail and extended in Pietarinen (2003, 2006, 2013c). Recently, it turned out that Peirce, in investigating certain peculiar issues his graphical logic in relation to the meaning of complex natural-language sentences and Weierstrassian mathematical conceptions, had put forth considerations that at once lead one to the graphical counterpart of independence-friendly logic (Pietarinen 2004a, 2014b).

**What do you consider your contribution to the field?**

I have been working on issues to do with the philosophy of Peirce's algebraic, quantificational and graphical logics, his semantic and pragmatic theories for logic, and the development and relation of these theories to contemporary notions in theories of logic, among others. In more than one occasion, it has struck me that Peirce understood the nature of problems better than his successors, no matter how famous the latter may have become in the cabinets of contemporary philosophy of language and mathematics. He developed a theory of quantification with the game or action-theoretic semantics which at the same time models mathematicians' spontaneous conceptual thinking superiorly to the logic that we have been exposed to for too long. He set out to find out, in a painstaking fashion, what our expressions mean – and whatever the medium in which expressions are presented may be – and so had to undertake the colossal task of logically analysing, both in terms of his general algebraic logic and ultimately by means of his method of existential graphs, what amounts possibly to thousands of very complex natural-language assertions, rife with donkey-type anaphora; distributive, cumulative, collective, branching and generalized quantifiers; modalities of different kinds; knowledge statements; modalities interspersed with quantification; and so on.

Peirce's research directions took a near century to be re-established and reinvented in any half-adequate manner, and often in considerably different, historically isolated or otherwise inferior forms. Such developments typically paid little or no attention to what Peirce or his tradition had attempted to accomplish. As a result, we have witnessed inflexible theories of quantification, tendencies to over-formalize, and separation of semantic and pragmatic sign-object and sign-interpretant relationships, the latter of which were erroneously thought to correspond to Peirce's critic and speculative rhetoric, respectively. The modern trend further overlooked the notational and philosophical aspects of one's key symbols, terms and concepts, and what their signification and use in the context of logical theories is intended to be.

These are just a small set of examples of what I have attempted to address in my research on Peirce's logic and philosophy – his writings are an inexhaustible well of ideas that put into sober perspective what has been achieved in the areas of philosophical logic, formal semantics and pragmatics, in cognitive sciences, in philosophy of science, and elsewhere, a century later. Even if we might well want to resist becoming full-blown Peirce scholars in the scholastic senses of the term, it is apparent that, as a seasoned scientist and polymath he had deep insights into the nature of a host of timeless problems, the solving and the development of which he largely had to leave for the future to carry out.

Together with Francesco Bellucci, we have been investigating the analytic virtues of existential graphs. In Peirce's algebraic and graphical logics the relation of illation is the primitive one, which becomes a fundamental motive in his philosophy of notation (Bellucci & Pietarinen 2014a). Peirce's aim, in algebra and in graphs, was to represent both the notion of scope and the truth function with same logical constants. Our analysis of the analyticity of Peirce's logic shows, among others, that Sun-Joo Shin's (2002) argument for multiple readings of existential graphs is circular.

Why has philosophical logic these days become quite un-philosophical? Why has philosophy of logic lost its prominence? While interest in logic has persevered in departments outside philosophy, the relevance of logic to philosophy has faded. Maybe existential graphs can re-instate the lost status of philosophical logic by analysing and generalising such notions as scope, identification, modality, abstraction etc. under the unifying efficacy of diagrammatic languages – languages that we cannot speak but which can preserve the structures between meaning and cognition better than the symbolic and conventional expressions do.

The pride and joy of philosophical logic, quantified modal logic, was developed by Peirce in 1906 and he used it to address questions of identity and identification, what quantifying into the scope of modalities means, and what the nature of real possibilities is (a kind of Scotistic realist possible-worlds semantics), quite ahead of others in more than one sense of 'ahead'. A lesson may be that philosophically informed logical investigation is not an exercise in different kinds of formalised languages with unanalysed semantic components, and not an expedient tool for distinguishing correct forms of human reasoning from incorrect ones, but that business devoted to the search for the principles on which the most general forms of timeless thought depend. Among others, I have attempted to discern what the full value of diagrammatic logics is in fulfilling the criteria for logical analysis and analyticity.

The 1903 gamma theory of existential graphs was Peirce's boutique of modal (including propositional, multi-modal and quantified) and higher-order logics. There was the open question of a regular definition of classes of transformation rules for the broken-cut gamma that correspond to a number of systems of modal logic. It turned out that Peirce's preferred modal system was the deontic one. Far from being surprising the result agrees well with his statement that logic, including thus modal logic, is a normative science.

What follows from the diagrammatic version of quantification in which the extremities of lines of identity range over individuals is equally interesting, as it tells us that the elements that are being quantified are those that are in principle identifiable. In addition to quantification, the lines serve as such identifying devices. Qualities in the phaneron are not occurrences and have no manifest duration. They give rise to assertions with non-propositional content. Thus with gamma Peirce is quantifying over *might-be*s and thus modal logics need to take such possible objects as constitutive of their real domains. This comes close to the modern, model-theoretic idea of the semantics of quantified modal logics. And here one more function emerges from the diagrammatic representation of the line of identity in the language of graphs: besides quantification, existence/possibilia, predication and class-inclusion, the lines serve as denotations of the modes of identification.

Peirce was interested in logic as a theory of normative, conventional, habitual and strategic action. This has some wider implications, not least since later Grice came to erect his theory of the logic of conversation on the Peircean background. But cooperation is a property of model-building games and an integral part of Peirce's method. Cooperative model-building resorts to the same theoretical construct as the strictly competitive semantic games do. It can be shown that the two kinds of games, the semantic and the model-construction games, are in this sense two sides of the same conceptual coin (Pietarinen 2013c). What is more, general principles governing mathematical practices are related to model-building activities. In Pietarinen (2012a) I argued that normative assertions not grounded in rules governing meaning-constitutive practices lead to inconsistency. This argument is really the same as what lies at the heart of Peirce's 'proof' of pragmaticism; a proof which he did not spell out in so many words but which can nevertheless be reconstructed in the light of modern logic and semantics in terms of quantified modal logics ('the possible is what *can become actual*') and the semantics that relates *habits* to general *strategies of action* (Pietarinen 2008b, 2011a; Pietarinen & Snellman 2006).

Having mentioned Grice, it turned out that he studied and meditated on Peirce's semeiotic writings while he was elaborating his own ideas on non-natural meaning, and that his account of meaning developed, at least in part, from his reaction to Peirce. This story is not known and thus worth a brief recount. Two aspects of the influence that Peirce's semeiotic ideas exercised upon Grice's thought are particularly pertinent: the distinction between natural and non-natural meaning, and the distinction between "what a sentence means" and "what the speaker means by using a sentence". As to the first, he attempts to re-state Peirce's claims about "signs" in terms of "meaning". As is well-known, Grice presents the definition of the conditions of non-natural meaning as an improved formulation of the traditional distinction between natural and conventional signs. He addresses this point in connection with Peirce's division of signs into icons, indexes and symbols. According to Grice, indices approximate natural meaning while symbols approximate non-natural meaning. Icons do not correspond to either type, but Grice's conclusion is that icons do not mean naturally but may be *used* to mean non-naturally. Second, Grice takes Peirce's type-token dichotomy as the starting point of his own account of the distinction between "what a sentence means" and "what the speaker means by using a sentence": the former corresponds, in Peirce's terms, to the meaning of a type-sentence (timeless meaning) the latter to the meaning of a token-sentence (speaker's meaning). Grice takes the same account to be found in Peirce's theory of signs. Grice's theory of the speaker's meaning was, in his own words, merely a "rhapsody on a theme by Peirce".

In Pietarinen (2004b) I had investigated several commonalities between Grice's and Peirce's pragmatic theories of meaning. I hypothesized that Grice most likely had to know something about Peirce's original work, so near are his normative accounts of speaker's meaning, conversational implicatures, cooperative principle, and several other central concepts of his theory to Peirce's semeiotic ones. But he never referred to Peirce in his published papers. For a while it seemed as if that the puzzle could not be solved unless asked from Grice himself. A few years later, this is what effectively happened: Grice's archives turned up striking material that testified that not only did he know about Peirce but also that by mid-1950 he had written a full set of lecture notes entitled "Peirce's Theory of Signs", which predate any of his publications. Those lecture notes, a living testimony of the depth of Grice's studies on Peirce that far exceed any other attempt at Peirce's theory of meaning until then, are now being published (Pietarinen & Bellucci

2014b). it has only gradually began to dawn to the philosophers of language and cognitive sciences that the usual order of explanation (from syntax to semantics, semantics to pragmatics) may need to be reversed.

## 3. What is the proper role of Peirce's work in relation to philosophy and other academic disciplines?

Peirce is a very technical philosopher. His ideas cannot be understood without understanding the highly technical apparatus that they involve. And that apparatus, its notation and vocabulary are largely of his invention. At his time, there was no set method available. Logic was to become the method of discovering the methods. And that logic had to be created first. To come clear at the meaning of anything in Peirce's philosophy is an application of the methods of logical analysis (or, if you want, pragmaticism). To come to possess the right methods is then to attune, in minute details, to the theoretical, philosophical, conceptual and notational aspects of logic. All signs and rules of logic need to be assigned their proper and justified significations. Sometimes we can understand him better in terms of what we now know about logic, about model theory, about the semantics and pragmatics of natural language, about epigenetics, and so on, but using our vantage point of knowledge can also be deceptive. In some respects, Peirce managed to do better than his successors. He was not conditioned on certain restrictive ideas of what logic is, such as being a formal theory of inferences or logical truths, or the home for all mathematical propositions, or a theory of mental models, or talking about one structure or logical universe or logical thought. For him, logic is the living connection between reasoning, imaginative action and habits that govern intellectual pursuits. Perhaps also importantly, he was free from burdensome academic professionalism. He lived during the times when overspecialization, disciplinary entrenchment, physics-envy or the two-cultures thinking had not yet disfigured the occupation. Maybe we can consider him lucky after all. We need to carry and improve on what he set out to do, while exercising critical common sense in those endeavours. Here the work to be done is virtually endless.

Teaching Peirce to students in the arts and general humanities not well versed in scientific methodology and precise meanings may be frustrating; all you get to do is to present the sign triad (not as a triangle, though!) with its main sub-trichotomies, from which endless classifications may then be derived. This never reaches the bottom of the well, however: the logical analysis of one's basic concepts and meanings, or the kinds of specific notations that are needed to become clear of those meanings, have routinely to be let pass. Great harm was done by Charles Morris's degenerate triads and his erroneous description of

Peirce's speculative grammar-critic-methodutic trichotomy – and Carnap's appropriation of it – as entire generations of linguistic theorizing were misplaced due to this compartmentalization of linguistic sciences. Peirce's theory is not prone to simplifications. Formalistic studies flourished in the masquerade of semiotics. *The Collected Papers* was the target of constant ridicule by people like Russell, Quine and Schiller. Very few took the effort to really venture into his logical forest. Perhaps Roman Jakobson salvaged what could have been salvaged, but he was not a logician and the damage was already done and Peirce had already gotten into the wrong crowd. As a consequence, those who could have had potential to understand Peirce thought it wiser to stay away from those crowds.

In contrast, Morris Cohen's 1923 *Chance, Love and Logic* was instrumental during those decisive years, as indeed was Ogden & Richard's *Meaning of Meaning*, although the latter was over ten years overdue and ill-conceived in its composition when finally published. And it was not only the former that Ramsey and Wittgenstein had an eye on – Ramsey even studied the 1906 *Prolegomena* which Ogden had transcribed from Welby's copy of the *Monist*, the journal which was not available in Cambridge during the years when Wittgenstein first arrived there.

These events, which may at first sight seem like minor-looking incidents, nevertheless changed the course of the history of logic. Russell was reportedly furious when he found out that Peirce had publicly dismissed his *Principles of Mathematics* (Pietarinen 2009). He would seek for other allies as far-off from the algebraic school as possible.

Beyond philosophy, I cannot help feeling that some of the most refreshing work on Peirce and some vindication of his visions is being accomplished by scientists and professionals outside philosophy, in fields such as geology and earth sciences, mathematics, physics, biology, economics, archaeology, anthropology, even medical practice – in a word, in fields of real discovery. But this is only how it should naturally be: Peirce's stages of reasoning are, after all, an attempt to articulate what is going on in the sciences and in the actual practices of the scientists. Again, it took something like a century before the practice-based philosophy of science was allowed to emerge, although I fear that today that approach is more like yet another interest-group or a professional society with its secluded agendas that have emerged from distressed reactions to the dead ends of the epistemologically overloaded philosophy of science on the one hand, and to the constructionist fancies on the other, rather than offering a genuinely pragmatistic analysis of what is going on in the scientific practices and imaginative discovery.

## 4. What do you consider the most important topics and/or contributions in the field of Peirce studies?

Passing judgment on the importance of scientific contributions is the task for distant posterity. Generally speaking, anything that makes Peirce's unpublished writings available to the world is bound to be an important contribution, as the case of Cohen's early volume testifies. The critical chronological edition will not reach Peirce's most productive years or the massive correspondence in a lifetime, which is very unfortunate. The most valuable asset for now is the *microfilm edition of manuscripts*, available in PDF, and the *Robin-Kloesel Catalogue* prepared for it. But the microfilm omitted nearly half of the correspondence material and not everything is stored in the Houghton Library's secretive vaults. Luckily the *Peirce Edition Project* has accumulated a fantastically rich archive which, clearly, would make that project the most important posthumous contribution to Peirce studies to date, if only the rate of churning the volumes out would be better.

But when it comes to the published works, the list of really important contributions grows thin. *Studies in the Philosophy of Charles Sanders Peirce* (Moore & Robin 1964) is a finely crafted volume from the era when books were still prepared with care and attention. *Studies in the Logic of Charles Sanders Peirce* (Houser et al., 1997) testifies the breadth of Peirce's logical thought. Of monographs, I can only enlist Don Robert's *The Existential Graphs of Charles S. Peirce* (1973); still to date the only reliable book-length source on Peirce's *chef d'œuvre* and with enough coverage and historical and logical accuracy to be of use for the wider and future community. But that volume gives only a glimpse of the vast territories of his method of existential graphs. I am about to publish an edition of about 900 pages consisting of his mostly unpublished writings devoted to the theory, method and applications of existential graphs (Pietarinen 2014e).

Contributions to Peirce studies took place during Peirce's lifetime, too. The earliest achievement was his 1883 edition *Studies in Logic by Members of the Johns Hopkins University* in which some of Peirce's first-year graduate students published their doctorate works. All of the topics addressed were related to the ongoing research to develop new logics, to address open problems in the past, present and future of reasoning, and to spell out the logic of science and the nature of probabilities. Many of his students and colleagues continued the research that dates from the Hopkins era, and came to shape the course of the future research in their respective fields, often elsewhere than strictly in logic or philosophy. This, I think, is a living testimony to how the method of logic traverses. Therefore, *Studies in Logic* must be nominated as the most important contribution to Peirce studies to date.

## 5. What are the most important open problems in this field and what are the prospects/avenues for progress?

Peirce's thought overall is an open problem, and not meant to be closed and completed. What are the logical structures of thought and action? How to find the best method to analyse mathematical reasoning? Did he have a solution to the quest for the method of inventing methods? Are diagrams that? But what are they? Is there a general diagram concept? Is this a non-empirical question? What else can such a diagram be but what the theory of logical diagrams can provide? What is an icon? Can we communicate, beyond self-communion, with icons? Are existential graphs the true logic of our cognitive processes? (Pietarinen 2011c.) If their primitive notations (spots, interpreted as images) correspond to the indecomposable elements of thought and to the interpretation of non-logical constants of the logical alphabet in symbolic terms, is our qualitative imagery bounded by what can be expressed by these primitive notations of the system of graphs? According to the logic of graphs, inferentialism fails but would the theory of diagrammatic logic answer what the meaning of logical constants is? Would it answer to what the meaning of metaphors is beyond the mere conceptual level? Exactly how do diagrammatic transformations facilitate deductive reasoning? (The answer cannot only be that they may be visual.)

Does Peirce's pragmatic theory of proper names provide a genuine alternative to the descriptive and the causal theories, without becoming a dull hybrid of these? (Pietarinen 2010c.) Is natural language non-compositional, as the full account of existential graphs seems to suggest? (Pietairnen 2005c.) What is this different, endoporeutic and diagrammatic account of 'compositionality'? What is the 'language' of graphs, after all, for in order for its assertions to be expressed we might need to scribe them in the space of three (or possibly four) dimensions? Is it really so that every assertion can be expressed and the logical structure analysed in such a space or a projection of the space? Does the most expressive language of graphs amount to the system of logical diagrams that corresponds to a higher-order logic (Peirce's logic of potentials)? Are the expressions of that logic any more of the nature of a language? Would such expressions then reduce to 'mathematics in a diagram's clothing'? What will happen to diagrammatic pragmaticism seen as a philosophy of mathematics? (Pietarinen 2010a,d.) Would it become one of the main currents in the philosophy of mathematics if only more attention would be paid to his ideas? What precisely speaking is Peirce's doctrine of substantive possibility and its relation to such graphs of potentials? ('No entity without substantive possibility'.) How does higher-order quantification come to be about such qualitative and substantive possibilities? What are the criteria of identity that go into the notation of identity lines which quantify these possibilities? Might Peirce have invented the full IF (independence-friendly) logic, had the Carnegie grant been given to him to complete the Minute Logic project? Would the subsequent history of logic become different? Would our theories of logic and mathematics be different, had he been granted that modest support he applied for with his massively persuasive application? Would the subsequent history of semiotics be different, had he managed to complete and publish the paper solicited for the Welby volume on significs, or the dozens or hundreds of other drafts for books and journals that were lying around in his attic in his later years?

Moreover, what did he intend to be included in his preferred systems of modal logics in the gamma part of his theory of graphs? Did he want to develop epistemic logic, as it seems? What sorts of things are supposed to be there in the universes of discourse of Peirce's gamma modal logics? Do they exist? What might the diagrammatic logic of various kinds of non-declarative assertions look like? (Pietarinen 2008c.) Can we complete the work he began on the diagrammatic logic of collections? What was to become of his theory of collections, contrasted with set theory? Precisely what were the steps and lines of thought that lead him from his universal algebra of logic into the method of existential graphs, and to lay claim to the latter as the most analytic method that has yet been invented? What would the non-visual logical diagrams, such as auditory or tactile diagrams, sound and feel like? (Pietarinen 2010b.)

How compelling are his arguments that there are precisely three types (or stages, kinds, or orders) of reasoning? How to explain his view that retroductive reasoning draws its validity from deductive reasoning? Is all reasoning deductive at bottom? How does logical analysis, recommended by Peirce to be carried out in existential graphs, relate to the diagrammatic in the first, retroductive, stage of inquiry? What are the rules of retroduction? What could they be in the system of existential graphs? Do they explain all mathematical inferences? Would that be the ultimate logic of discovery? Can only a living intelligence perform it? If we were to teach these graphical systems of reasoning to children, and, as Peirce suggested "before they learn grammar", what would the impact be?

I have some preliminary thoughts and approximate ideas about how to approach, investigate and maybe in the future to find some workable arguments to settle some of these question in one way or another, but I would like to see a lot more research being done alone these lines. Peirce's logic and philosophy of logic harbour countless fascinating and well-formed research questions. Although one might feel that

I have here highlighted merely some technical or specifically logical problems, these problems do illustrate not only the wider relevance of logical issues to philosophical concerns in general but the fundamentally logical nature of all thought. The implications of what follows from the complex network of possible answers to the aforementioned puzzles are too many to be even attempted here, but they would have repercussions to how the other parts of Peirce's architectonics are conceived. But without logical analysis nothing can be done and complex meanings would remain hidden. Without the method of analysis, investigation either would not even get started or would not deliver the kind of assurance, security or uberty that the stages of reasoning can provide.

A good deal, if not nearly everything, in Peirce's thought and in his writings is strongly interconnected, continuous, and overlapping. This presents also a formidable challenge. He wanted to erect a theory of signs, or semeiotic, but also a general theory of meaning and action, pragmaticism, and the general theory of the logic of science, the three-pronged theory of reasoning, and so on. All of these interlock. A specialist in the philosophy of mathematics may be able to evaluate some claims about mathematics, another specialist may be able to do the same for logic, and yet another one for geology, and another one for theory of action, and so on. But how about mastering all his areas in a sufficient depth? Will the one, unifying thought 'to rule them all' ever be possible or even conceivable?

I do not know, but here is an encouraging thought: It may not matter so much whether we want to phrase the underlying issues in terms of his semiotic, or in terms of pragmaticism, and so on, as long as we know what we are talking about. Abduction is a case in point: the kind of reasoning, or a phase or a stage of reasoning, which is able to germinate a new idea. But how do the new ideas emerge? Where do they come from? If you ask some good, right sorts of questions, then new answers may be possible, or there may be some unforeseen implications or helpful unintended consequences or even something that is in fact necessitated by the earlier questions and answers. Hence the nature and meaning of questions is so important. And abduction is the process of creation amidst these question-answer cycles. And the questions here should not be taken to be entirely linguistic ones but those schemata and representations that take place in cognition. Cognition seems to work well with icons and especially with diagrammatic representations as its signifying material, for example, as numerous scientists have testified over the years.

While I was working out Peirce's so-called 'proofs' of pragmaticism it occurred to me that a couple of steps in that argument are about procedures that concern questioning and answering. Thus they are about abductive reasoning. And thus abductive reasoning becomes, in late Peirce, part of what pragmaticism is. In his 1903 Harvard lectures he even had attempted the 'proof' by effectively assimilating abduction and pragmatism. But his semeiotic attempt from 1907 is more successful and admits of a somewhat more precise reconstruction, as I have attempted to present in some works of mine. But it is not quite right to state that abduction is the basic method, as there are three types of methods of reasoning, which also form a complex and partially interlocking system, the nature of which has dawned to me only recently in collaboration with others. For example, the validity or justification of abduction for Peirce draws from deductive reasoning and in certain senses the deductive form of reasoning is the more basic one over the others. But at the same time, there are further justifications, including some abductive and inductive ones (the latter drawing from the history of science). And deduction itself is not free from its abductive moments, and has to involve non-trivial and creative aspects, including theorematic types of reasoning, as well as abstraction. The true nature of abduction, or even that of deduction, is not yet clear from mist.

The interconnections between logic, semeiotic and pragmaticism are thus intimate and uberous. In a way Peirce wanted pragmaticism to be a theory of meaning, and so it is located within his attempts to develop the methodeutic or speculative rhetoric part of his semiotic theory. It is here that we find some further explanations on what his ideas may have been concerning the nature of meanings, concerning habits of acting in certain ways in certain kinds of circumstances. But that development was by no means finalized and pragmaticism may indeed be conceived in wider senses of amounting to a theory of intellectual action, behavior, and conduct, including collective and social intentional action. I think the latter could become a novel direction to revitalize the research taking place on collective intentionality and team reasoning, for instance. The quips such as "a person is not absolutely an individual" suggest that the stark contrast between the intrapersonal, multiple-minds perspective on conversational dialogues and the evolution of thought, on the one hand, and the interpersonal, social communication, on the other hand, assumes much less importance than is typically thought of in research on action and reasoning in the social sciences (Pietarinen 2013b).

In the light of the acuity of these questions it is also clear that no loose talk about Peirce, various and potentially endless classifications of signs, or what meaning or pragmatism in the broad sense may amount to, or what the categories are or how they apply, suffices to address the fundamentally philosophical issues. Conceptualizations that neatly slot object representations into icons, indices and symbols may provide fine aide to logical investigations, but they can only cater the prelude to the actual work, or an elucidation. This is clear in Peirce's writings as soon as you investigate the entire sequences of manuscripts and not the collected snippets.

Equally misleading would be to take Peirce's explicitly logical investigations to be more difficult than his semeiotic or pragmati(ci)sm: for Peirce, logic is (formal) semeiotic. Logic and semeiotic are inseparable. This is just how it always was in the past, too. Aristotle and the Stoics in the Greece, Leibniz, Locke, and so many others in the great chain of ideas, set out to construe systems of signs for the betterment of human reason. Peirce investigates this entire history and its heritage until his own days and gives full yet never uncritical credit to the great contributions of the past. He states that nothing as such of what he has to say about the topic in general is entirely new. He would investigate and analyse the tradition in depth and then produce his own articulation of what he took to be the outcome those painstaking investigations. What I feel really difficult is to decide how pragmatism could apply to ethical or religious or political or managerial questions and so on. I do not see how one could even begin to address such questions before pragmatism (in Peirce's sense) is laboured into some other, relevant and probably richer and more detailed theories than what it was in the classical pragmatists' works. And I do not think that anyone has done the job yet. To excitedly apply pragmatism or to think that the 'pure' and 'applied' come with some different characteristics of reasoning is to be monochromatic about the key terms in one's possession. Peirce's methodology, in contrast, is a pluralist one and admits of recurring reinterpretations (Pietarinen 2008a). It is scholastic realism and methodological pluralism that go hand in hand. Likewise, it is the pragmatism of Peirce's contemporaries that resembles what may be termed a *one-world philosophy* – not unlike a revisionist metaphysician's image of the world that must satisfy some predetermined criterion. Yet there is nothing that ultimately guarantees such a vision or makes it compelling, and so universalism and conceptual relativism follow. The alternative is the Peirce-type *many-worlds philosophy*, which permits indefinite variability of meaning and hypotheses.

For example, the Peirce–Schiller correspondence reveals that Peirce and Schiller, interestingly enough, shared a common enemy in the emerging 'Russellisation' of logic that is hyper-formal, in which the totality of language is uninterpreted, and which leaves no room for anthromorphism. Accepting such totalities would only amount to endorsing one more dogma of empiricism: a compartmentalisation of things into logical and extra-logical (Pietarinen 2011b). At the end, however, the true differences are revealed as Schiller is an actualist pluralist while Peirce a many-world philosopher about the reality of modalities and a pluralist about methodology. Peirce had pressed Schiller to define the notions that he used in vague senses such as 'reality'. In his review of Vol. III of the *Collected Papers* Schiller thinks it might be a good time to pay back: what he does is to complain that Peirce never defined 'exact logic'! Schiller is oblivious of actually making advances towards his alleged enemy Russell here: ignorant of the theories of logic, Schiller believed that the exact and the formal coincide and that once something is made exact, its interpretation does not change, thus can no longer be 'applied' or 'useful' and thus is of no interest.

Another set of problems concerns the methods of Peirce research. How are we to understand a thinker who did not – or so it is believed – weave together the endless pieces and threads of his writings, however continuous his corpus or the underlying thought may eventually turn out to be? We do not need Peirce industry. We do not need enthusiasts. Look what happened to Wittgenstein: broken down to schools of thought with no communication between, the least with Wittgenstein himself. Letting community to bog down into exegetic discourses about what others may have said about others works, ad nauseam, may be a creeping problem and may have paralyzed segments of analytic philosophy. Losing touch with the living sciences is another: for the Johns Hopkins community, which managed to make marvellous progress in research during those formative years when Peirce lectured there on the topics of logic, the method of sciences and the nature of probabilities, it would have been inconceivable not to connect philosophy to other fields of inquiry (Pietarinen 2014c). Dewey was inspired by E.M. Hartwell's experiments presented in the Metaphysical Club concerning his research on purposeful action of brainless frogs. No euphemisms or managerial whip to fund aimless interdisciplinary projects were needed to make progress. Today we need to strike a balance between overspecialization and shallow generality, and to exploit our ignorance well in both regards.

**References**

Pietarinen, Ahti-Veikko

> (2003). "Peirce's Game-theoretic Ideas in Logic", *Semiotica* 144, 33-47.

> (2004a). "Peirce's Diagrammatic Logic in IF Perspective", in A. Blackwell, K. Marriott and A. Shimojima (eds), *Diagrammatic Representation and Inference, Lecture Notes in Artificial Intelligence* 2980, Berlin: Springer, 97-111.

(2004b). "Grice in the Wake of Peirce", *Pragmatics & Cognition* 12, 295-315.

(2005a). "Cultivating Habits of Reason: Peirce and the *Logica Utens* versus *Logica Docens* Distinction", *History of Philosophy Quarterly* 22, 357-372.

(2005b). "The Composition of Concepts and Peirce's Pragmatic Logic", in E. Machery, M. Werning and G. Schurtz (eds), *The Compositionality of Concepts and Meanings: Foundational Issues*, Ontos-Verlag, 247-270.

(2005c). "Compositionality, Relevance and Peirce's Logic of Existential Graphs", *Axiomathes* 15, 513-540.

(2006). *Signs of Logic: Peircean Themes on the Philosophy of Language, Games, and Communication*, (Synthese Library 329), Dordrecht: Springer.

(2007). "To Peirce Hintikka's Thoughts". *The Epistemology and Methodology of Jaakko Hintikka*, Carlsberg Academy, Copenhagen, November 2007.

(2008a). "The Place of Logic in Pragmatism", *Cognitio* 9(1), 247-260.

(2008b). "The Proof of Pragmatism: Comments on Christopher Hookway", *Cognitio* 9(1), 85-92.

(2008c). "Diagrammatic Logic of Existential Graphs: A Case Study of Commands", in G. Stapleton, J. Howse, and J. Lee (eds.), *Diagrammatic Representation and Inference*, Lecture Notes in Computer Science 5223, Heidelberg: Springer, 404-407.

(2009). "Significs and the Origins of Analytic Philosophy", *Journal of the History of Ideas* 70(3), 467-490.

(2010a). "Pragmaticism as an Antifoundationalist Philosophy of Mathematics", in B. Van Kerkhove, R. Desmet and J. P. Van Bendegem (eds.), *Philosophical Perspectives on Mathematical Practice*, London: College Publications, 305-333.

(2010b). "Is Non-visual Diagrammatic Logic Possible?" In A. Gerner (ed.), *Diagrammatology and Diagram Praxis*, London: College Publications.

(2010c). "Peirce›s Pragmatic Theory of Proper Names", *Transactions of the Charles S. Peirce Society* 46, 341-363.

(2010d). "Which Philosophy of Mathematics is Pragmaticism?", in M. Moore (ed.), *New Essays on Peirce's Mathematical Philosophy*, Chicago: Open Court, 59-80.

(2011a). "Moving Pictures of Thought II: Graphs, Games, and Pragmaticism›s Proof", *Semiotica* 186, 315-331.

(2011b). "Remarks on the Peirce-Schiller Correspondence", in E.H. Oleksy & W. Oleksy (eds.), *Transatlantic Encounters: Philosophy, Media, Politics*, Frankfurt am Main: Peter Lang, 61-70.

(2011c). "Existential Graphs: What the Diagrammatic Logic of Cognition Might Look Like", *History and Philosophy of Logic* 32(3), 265-281.

(2012a). "Why Is the Normativity of Logic Based on Rules?", in C. De Waal & K.P. Skowronski (eds.), *The Normative Thought of Charles S. Peirce*, Fordham: Fordham University Press, 172-184.

(2012b). "Peirce and Deacon on the Meaning and Evolution of Language", in F. Stjernfelt & T. Schilhab (eds), *New Perspectives on the Symbolic Species*, Dordrecht: Springer, 65-80.

(2013a). "Christine Ladd-Franklin's and Victoria Welby's Correspondence with Charles Peirce" (Special Issue on Significs and Victoria Welby), *Semiotica* 196, 139-161.

(2013b). "Pragmaticism Revisited: Co-Evolution and the Methodology of Social Sciences", *Cognitio* 14(1), 123-136.

(2013c). "Logical and Linguistic Games from Peirce to Grice to Hintikka", *Teorema* 33(2), in press.

(2014a). "A Scholastic-Realist Modal-Structuralism", *Philosophia Scientiae*, in press.

(2014b). "Exploring the Beta Quadrant", Special Issue on Peirce's Philosophy of Logic and Language, Pietarinen, A.-V. (ed.), *Synthese*, to appear.

(2014c). "The Second Metaphysical Club and Its Significance in the Development of the Sciences in the US", to appear.

(2014d). "Iconic Logic of Metaphors", *Journal of Cognitive Science*, in press.

(2014e). "Is There a General Diagram Concept?", in Sybille

Krämer & Christina Ljundberg (eds.), *Thinking with Diagrams*, Amsterdam and Philadelphia: John Benjamins, in press.

(ed.) (2014e). *Logic of the Future: Charles S. Peirce's Writings on Existential Graphs*, to appear.

(with F. Bellucci) (2014a). "Existential Graphs as an Instrument for Logical Analysis. Part 1: Alpha", to appear.

(with F. Bellucci) (2014b). "'A Rhapsody on a Theme by Peirce': Grice's Lecture on Peirce's Theory of Signs", to appear in *International Review of Pragmatics*.

(with L. Snellman) (2006). "On Peirce's Late Proof of Pragmaticism", in T. Aho and A.-V. Pietarinen (eds), *Truth and Games*, Helsinki: *Acta Philosophica Fennica* 78, 275-288.

**Five most valuable contributions to Peirce studies**

Peirce, Charles S. (1883, ed.), *Studies in Logic by Members of the Johns Hopkins University*, Little, Brown, and Company, Boston, MA, 1883. (Reprinted in *Foundations of Semiotics*, Vol. 1, A. Eschbach (ed.), Max H. Fisch (intro.), Johns Benjamins, Amsterdam, 1983.)

The Houghton Library Microfilm Edition & The Robin-Kloesel Catalogue.

THE PEIRCE EDITION PROJECT

Moore, Edward C. & Robin, Richard S. (eds.) (1964). *Studies in the Philosophy of Charles Sanders Peirce*, Amherst: University of Massachusetts Press.

Houser, Nathan, Roberts, Don D. & Van Evra, James (eds.) (1997). *Studies in the Logic of Charles Sanders Peirce*, Bloomington & Indianapolis: Indiana University Press.

# 28

# Nicholas Rescher

Distinguished University Professor of Philosophy
University of Pittsburgh

---

**1. Why were you initially drawn to Peirce?**

I never studied Peirce in college or in graduate school. At the time (the late 1940s) he did not figure much on the agenda of academic philosophy. My involvement with him emerged much later, in the 1970s, when my own work in epistemology evolved a decidedly pragmatic direction and I increasingly embarked on lines of thought where I found that Peirce had already been on the ground many years before. In particular, my thinking about the methodology of science and the conduct of rational inquiry in general unfolded along the lines pioneered in Peirce's project of an economy of research. It was thus the systematic rather than the historical side of my thought and work that initially motivated my closer encounters with Peirce.

**2. What do you consider your contribution to the field?**

For me, personally, Peirce has been a guide and role model, albeit subordinate to—but only to!—Leibniz and Kant. And as I see it, my prime contributions to Peirce studies has been to extend and project lines of thought that have opened up in new and hopefully promising directions.

The first step was the development of the sort of pragmatic epistemology that I myself thought to be mandated by the problem of knowledge extension and validation. This came to expression principally in two books: *The Primacy of Practice* (1973) and *Methodological Pragmatism* (1977).

Next came two books focusing on issues in inductive reasoning in which Peirce himself figured frontally, namely *Peirce's Philosophy of Science* (1978) and *Induction* (1980). I see these books as contributions not just to philosophical pragmatism but to Peircean studies as such.

Closely associated with these studies were two investigations in the spirit and direction of Peirce's project of an economy of research. These were *Scientific Progress* (1978) and *Cognitive Economy* (1989). My ongoing interest in this area was also resumed in a much later publication, *Epistemetrics* (2006).

Peirce's preoccupation with issues of evolutionary development also figured in this theory of science, a connection was mirrored my *A Useful Inheritance* (1990).

At this stage I brought together the various strands of my pragmatic thinking in a trilogy entitled *A System of Pragmatic Idealism*. It comprised three volumes: *Human Knowledge in Idealistic Perspective* (1992), *The Validity of Values* (1993). And *Metaphilosophical Inquiries* (1994). These books were the ultimate result of an endeavor to formulate, synthesize, and defend a pragmatism which, like that of Peirce himself, was formed under the stronger influence of Kant and post-Kantian German idealism. It sought to project Peircean inspirations into the changed conditions and circumstances of the late 20$^{th}$ century philosophizing.

With the basic structure of my pragmatic system well in place by the mid 1990s I now proceeded to carry out a series of investigations in pragmatic metaphysics and epistemology that over the next twenty years yielded some half-dozen books devoted to the consolidation of a concrete and instructive pragmatic synthesis. The resultant set of publications included: *Communicative Pragmatism* (1998), *Realistic Pragmatism* (1999), *Cognitive Pragmatism* (2001), *Rationality in Pragmatic Perspective* (2003), *Epistemic Pragmatism* (2008), *The Pragmatic Vision* (2014). The project at issue here has as an ongoing theme the restoration of Peirce's own realistic vision of the prospective program. For as I saw it, the latter-day self-styled "pragmatists" of the post WWII era succumbed to the siren call of William James psychologistic pragmatism to which Peirce himself has already strongly objected. (He even proposed to change the designation of his own position to "pragmaticism" to achieve what he deemed to be an essential contrast.) Countering this wishy-washy, psychologistic pragmatism of William James and the returning this approach to its original realistic Peircean roots has been the definitive Leitmotiv that ran throughout all my own efforts in this field.

## 3. What is the proper role of Peirce's work in relation to philosophy and other academic disciplines?

As I see it, Peirce's philosophy stands at a crossroad in that it marks the end of one era and the beginning of another. In relating to the past, Peirce, along with A. N. Whitehead, marked the end of the period of the large-scale, many-sided, heavily science-influenced systems of thought that had typified systematic philosophy in the era of Kant, Hegel, and Lotze. On the other side, Peirce's work represented a new turning in that sought to restore the Leibnizian strategy for using *praxis* to illustrate *theoria*, looking to successful practice in inquiry and speculation not only as a guide to theorizing but as an arbiter of its adequacy. The leading idea here is to bring the practice of the laboratory, the work-bench, and the public forum as an indispensable guide for the deliberations of the study and the library. Thus as I see it the paramount importance of Peirce's work lay in its emphasis on seeing practice not as a replacement for theory (as per experiment sceptics since classical antiquity) but rather as an assessment standard and arbiter for adequate theorizing. Ironically, it has been Peirce, the most impractical of men, who reoriented theoretical philosophy in a practicalistic direction.

Among the leading ideas of Peirce's philosophical perspective is that of an evolutionary conformation of the human mind with the nature of the environing world within which it has come to be developed. This puts Peirce squarely into alignment with the ancient idea of a conformity of mind and nature. But it also effectively invests the stance of the Platonic tradition. For now the idea is no longer that mind shapes nature but rather that nature shapes mind. But despite this difference the fundamental stance remains the same, viz. that we live in a world that is user-friendly for intelligence (albeit now for evolutionary rather than theological reasons). This aspect of Peirce's thought seems has been rather underappreciated and is decidedly deserving of further inquiry and exposition.

**4. What do you consider the most important topics and/or contributions in the field of Peirce studies?**

Two highly important recent contributions to Peirce studies are (1) the magisterial edition of his *opera omnia* now well underway at the University of Indiana Press, and (2) Joseph Brent's excellent Peirce biography. I see these publications as indispensable tools for getting a firm grip on Peirce as a person and a thinker.

The presently most important topics in Peirce studies seem to me to be his theory of scientific method, economy of research, and scientific progress. His ideas on the evolutionary metaphysics of "love" are intensively interesting, but his science-related ideas of are greater present-day interest and relevance.

**5. What are the most important open problems in this field and what are the prospects/avenues for progress?**

A leading idea of Peirce's philosophical program is that there is an evolutionary conformation of the human mind with the nature of the environing world within which it has come to be developed. This puts Peirce squarely into alignment with the ancient idea of a conformation of mind and nature. But it effectively inverts the stance of the Platonic tradition. For now the idea is no longer that mind shapes nature but rather that nature shapes mind. And yet despite this difference the fundamental stance remains the same, viz., that we live in a world that is user friendly for intelligence (albeit now for evolutionary rather than theoretical reasons). Accordingly, Peirce operates an intelligent design theory of an interesting and idiosyncratic sort. This aspect of Peirce's thought seems to be somewhat underappreciated and well deserving of further inquiry and exposition.

Moreover, it would be nice to get a fuller, more detailed picture of Peirce's relating to his sources of inspiration and provocation. This would include such matters as what he thought of the work of the leading figures of the preceding generation in Germany (Lotze), Britain (Mill and Whewell) and France (Renouvier). I don't think that any of this will dramatically *change* our picture of Peirce and his contributions, but it offers good promise of *deepening* this understanding.

**Bibliography**

*Peirce's Philosophy of Science* (Notre Dame: University of Notre Dame Press, 1978).

*Methodological Pragmatism* (Oxford: Basil Blackwell, 1977. Co-published in the USA by the New York University Press).

*Realistic Pragmatism: An Introduction to Pragmatic Philosophy* (Albany: State University of New York Press, 1999).

*Cognitive Pragmatism* (Pittsburgh: University of Pittsburgh Press, 2001).

*Pragmatism* (New Brunswick: Transaction Books, 2012).

# 29

# Lucia Santaella

Prof. of Semiotics and Communication Studies
Catholic University of São Paulo

---

SOME DECADES OF PEIRCE STUDIES

**1. Why were you initially drawn to Peirce?**

In the 1970s, I was a student of the Brazilian concrete poets, Decio Pignatari and Haroldo de Campos, both responsible for the introduction of Peirce semiotic studies in Brazil. Besides being poets, Pignatari and Campos were important theorists and critics of literature, arts and culture. Pignatari also had great familiarity with the field of mass communication, especially advertising, film and television. For some years, he kept a column in one of the most renowned newspapers in Brazil as a TV critic. It is worth reminding that both, Pignatari and Campos, held the position of Vice-Presidents of the International Association for Semiotic Studies, during the first, second, and third periods of the board of this Association. I was elected and re-elected for the same position in the fourth and fifth periods, from 1989-1999.

Both Campos and Pignatari approached the work of Peirce, in particular semiotics, due to their contacts with Max Bense, on the one hand, and Roman Jakobson, on the other. Bense visited Brazil in the first half of the 1960s, and Jakobson, in the second half. Both reported the work of Peirce in their lectures and left behind the great interest that semiotics awoke in the mind of the concrete poets who, in the early 1970s, became professors and researchers of the graduate program in Literary Theory at the Catholic University of São Paulo. This interest spread to most students of the program in which I was at that time writing my PhD. Already in 1972, seminars on the work of Peirce were developed and his theory of signs was being applied to the arts, music, architecture, literature, and also to mass communication phenomena. That same year, Cultrix, an important publishing house in São Paulo, brought to light the first collection of translations of some of Peirce's texts, edited by two Brazilian logicians, Octanny Silveira da Mota and Leonidas Hegenberg. The enthusiasm of the students on Peirce's semiotics seethed.

At that time, I was immersed in the structuralist and post-structuralist texts. From my earliest contacts, phenomenology and especially the theory of the iconic sign led me to territories of thought and sensitivity of which I had dreamed without finding answers in the structuralist context. It was very difficult to import books in Brazil at that time. They had the same high tax rate of products as whiskey etc. But Pignatari already possessed the Collected Papers and lent me the volumes so that I could take xerox copies of some of the writings concerning phenomenology and the theory of signs. I spent six months deciphering these texts for hours every night. My PhD thesis, defended in 1973, already contained a whole chapter extensively dealing with this subject.

In 1976, I became a professor at the same program in which I had concluded my PhD studies and started then to transmit to my students the same enthusiasm concerning Peirce that had been transmitted to me years before. But Peirce's horizon only ushered in a broader and indelible way when I had the great opportunity to be a student of Joseph Ransdell, in 1983, during the famous summer courses organized by Thomas Sebeok at the Research Center for Language and Semiotic Studies. With unparalleled generosity, Ransdell gave to the students copies of all his published articles on Peirce and also the work in progress of a book on Peirce's Semiotics, a work which, to the misfortune of Peirce scholarship, never came to be published. I spent the entire month in Blomington devouring Ransdell's writings deep into the nights. This month was undoubtedly the most blissful period of my intellectual life. It was also during this period that I met Dines Johansen, who had spent many months in the Peirce Project at Indianapolis, studying Peirce's manuscripts. Also in a gesture of admirable generosity, Johansen gave me copies of the hundreds of pages of his manuscript notes. Returning to Brazil, I read those pages again and again, and I keep them until today. In my suitcases I also brought several texts of Max Fisch, Potter's precious book on Charles S. Peirce on norms and ideals (1967 [1997]). Thereafter, for decades until now, my interest in the work of Peirce has never faded, in his own writings and in the publications of his many excellent commentators. I returned several more times to Bloomington (to Sebeok's joy, I used to say that the campus was my Omphalus) and paid many visits to the Peirce Project collecting hundreds of pages of the manuscripts. Many of my books on Peirce were written thanks to those pages. In some of the periods in Bloomington I had the opportunity of following courses given by Christian Kloesel and by Nathan Houser.

## 2. What do you consider your contribution to the field?

Since 1976, I give courses on Peirce's philosophical semiotics once a semester every year at the graduate program in Communication and Semiotics/Catholic University of São Paulo. Counting 20 students per semester in the last 38 years, 760 master and doctoral students have passed through my classes. Not all of them have continued studies in Peirce's semiotics, finding their way into other authors and theories. But since 1978, 220 students received their master and PhD titles under my supervision. Among these students, at least half of them somehow made use of Peirce's concepts. Some of them went quite far in their study. These MAs and PhDs are now professors at various universities throughout Brazil and some continue disseminating Peirce's texts and concepts. It is my impression that there is no researcher in the field of the arts and communications in Brazil that has no knowledge, even precarious, of Peirce's semiotics.

In 1980, I published my first book, *Production of language and ideology*, a collection of chapters devoted to semiotic themes, all based in Peirce's semiotics. In 1983, I published a a less comprehensive book about Peirce, in a very popular collection whose name is First Steps. Under the title What is semiotics, the book is entirely devoted to Peirce, from a brief biography to phenomenology and some elements of his theory of signs. This book is now in its 25th. edition, having sold over 140,000 copies. At present, there are at least 10 websites that pirate the book under my full consent. As I already published in a long essay (Santaella, 1990), "Brazil is a culture in tune with semiotics", given the great attraction that semiotics provokes on young students. It is true that Greimasian semiotics has enough repercussion in the country, but no more than Peirce's semiotics.

From 1992 onwards, I have published several books on Peirce's work, each of them dealing with a different aspect of his thought. In 1992, I published *The signature of things*, a presentation of Peirce's philosophical edifice in the context of his classification of the sciences. For this, the book by Beverly Kent (1987) was of great value to me. In 1993, I published a small book on Peirce's theory of perception, a publication that was expanded in 2012. In 1994, my interest fell on the normative sciences, with emphasis on Peirce's aesthetics. In 1995, the publication was turned to a thorough discussion of the doctrine and classification of signs. Most of these books were written during research grants in Bloomington, with visits to the Peirce Edition Project.

In 2001, I published an extensive book on *Matrices of language and thought. Sound, Vision, Verb*, entirely based on Peirce's classification of signs. With this book, I received an important literary prize in Brazil. In 2004, the publication was about the anti-Cartesian method of C. S. Peirce. In this book, the three types of reasoning were explored in detail, abduction, induction and deduction, with close attention to Peirce's manuscripts on Methodeutics. In 2007, I published *Applied Semiotics*, a book that seeks to translate the complex Peircean concepts for an audience who wants to apply them to processes of cultural, literary and communicative signs. These are the books that deal exclusively with Peirce's thought. But there are others were the presence of semiotics if not so exclusive is still relevant, such as *Image* (1998), *Communication and semiotics* (2004b), *Semiotic strategies in advertising* (2010), these three are co-authored with Winfried Nöth, and *Metascience*, co-authored with Jorge A. Vieira (2008).

Since 2003, I have published extensively on digital culture. Apparently, Peirce is not present in these books. In one of them, however, I studied the profiles of immersive readers of hypermedia webs, in the light of Peirce's three kinds of reasoning (Santaella 2004b). Although not explicitly, all the other books have their foundations in the cognitive map that the theory of signs and pragmaticism provide. I published abroad several articles on Peirce, especially in *Semiotica*, Sebeok's legacy which is edited today in Canada, by Marcelo Danesi. The articles that I find most relevant appear in the bibliographical list at the end of this article. Following Hoffmeyer's path (1996, 2008), I am currently involved in research on a broad concept of Semiosphere under a Peircean point of view.

In 1996, I founded the Center for Peirce Studies at the Catholic University of São Paulo. Since then, every year, we hold a Colloquium with the participation of researchers, students and former students. Every two years, the Colloquium is accompanied by the Advanced Seminar on Peirce's Philosophy and Semiotics. These seminars have relied on the participation of international experts in Peirce, among which Vincent Colapietro and Fernando Andacht have repeatedly been present. Deliberately these events have been small, because every second year a theme is chosen to be studied in depth. These seminars have a publication that is delivered to the participants before the beginning of the seminar so that they can have time to read and study the subject in order to allow a richer discussion.

## 3. What is the proper role of Peirce's work in relation to philosophy and other academic disciplines?

First of all, although Peirce's phenomenology is not as influential as that of Husserl, it has the merit of getting rid of any transcendental residue. Moreover, from his phenomenology a new ontology can be derived which is much more universal than Heidegger's. Peirce's normative sciences, "the very most purely theoretical of purely theoretical sciences" (CP 1.282), present an extraordinary originality, especially due to the inseparable character of the three sciences and to the notion of the aesthetic *summum bonum* which lies in the growth of concrete reasonableness. From the indissoluble links of the three sciences his pragmaticism is extracted, which cannot be understood without recourse to the phenomenological categories (CP 8.255-56). In fact, the normative sciences get us "upon the trail of the secret of pragmatism" (CP 5.129). His theory of abduction is a gemstone for the study of the logic of discovery. Last but not least, his metaphysics, which flows directly from the normative sciences and is based on the concepts of synechism and tychism, builds an evolutionary theory of natural law, in which the human mind is presented as the most plastic reality of the whole universe, thanks to the potential of the human mind at changing habits.

I am convinced that Peirce accomplished his *desideratum* "to outline a theory so comprehensive that, for a long time to come, the entire work of human reason, in philosophy of every school and kind, in mathematics, in psychology, in physical science, in history, in sociology, and in whatever other department there may be, shall appear as the filling up of its details. The first step toward this is to find simple concepts applicable to every subject" (CP 1.1). In fact, his phenomenology and especially his classification of signs act as general concepts which can be applied to any phenomena and to any theories. I fully agree with M. Nadin (1983: 162) when he says that "the typology of the sign classes (the ten, the 28, the 66), as confirmed by the mathematical theory of categories (...) should be understood as a network of fundamental reference points in the generalized semiotics field. Whenever this typology is transformed into an end in itself it leads only to formalistic semiotics. To give a name to a sign (to identify it) does not solve the problem of the way it functions in the semiotic field. The sign can be conceived and interpreted only within the framework of the logic of vagueness and with the participation of the doctrine of the *continuum*".

In 1983, I published an article under the title of "C. S. Peirce, a philosopher for the XXI century". The intuition of some decades ago seems truer at present. The development of the sciences from the twentieth century on is bringing challenges that Peirce's philosophy helps to face, not only in the field of hard sciences such as chaos theory, dissipative structures (see about that, for example, Prigogine's reference to Peirce in his book *Order out of chaos* (1984: 302-303) and also in the humanities, in the contemporary non-human philosophical movement that Peirce anticipated in his essentially anti-anthropocentric philosophy. The semiosis of the non-human, of the biological, of vegetables, and even of the physical and astrological realms found in Peirce's semiotic guides us to an understanding whose coherence is subject to very little controversy. After all, we are in a moment of human thought that urges the exploration of the semiosis of the environment and geology, a time when books such as *How forests think* (Kohn 2013) are coming out and claiming for a powerful non-anthropological theory of semiosis.

This does not mean that Peirce's philosophy has relegated the anthropological question to shadows. Rather, Peirce introduced a new conception of human beings, of subjectivity and human action, as has been extensively explored in the writings of Vincent Colapietro, since the publication of his seminal book on *Peirce's approach to the self. A semiotic perspective on human subjectivity* (1989).

Peirce's semiotics is mainly a modern theory of representation and mediation. In cultural studies the concepts of representation and mediation are widely used, but never precisely defined, resulting in a wide spread conceptual confusion. Unfortunately, the complex and multifaceted Peirce's theory of representation is not usually remembered in that context. It is a theory that has variants such as presentation, quasi-representation to the limit of presentification. Semiotics also includes the distinction between representation and reference, and between representation and interpretation (Santaella 2003). Despite its complexity, representation is just one facet of a more general concept of mediation. The key to the comprehension of all these notions is in Peirce's definitions and classifications of signs, provided they are not taken in a narrow sense, but as it was reminded by Buczynska-Garewicz (1983: 27) they should be taken as "a pattern for comprehensive sign analysis rather than a classification *sensu stricto*. This pattern includes all epistemological and ontological aspects of the sign universe, the problem of reference, of reality and fiction, the question of objectivity, the logical analysis of meaning, and the problem of truth".

Mediation is defined as any process in which two elements are placed in articulation by or through the intervention of a third element. The role played by the third element is therefore to allow the passage of some property of an element to another element. Therefore, Peirce held that the notion of communication is an essential trait of all semiosis, since in any communication process there must be a mediation that allows the passage, communication, cognition of one element to the other. This mediation is exercised by the sign. So much so that, in his later writings, the mediating function of signs led Peirce to postulate that the sign mediates between two ideas or between an object and an idea, or rather between an object and an interpretant idea that the sign produces or modifies. It is by the mediation of the sign that something of the object can reach or influence an interpreting mind (MS 634: 24).

Mediation is inalienable because there can be no immediate connection between mind and mind, between an object and a mind. In this sense, mediation cannot be confused with what, from the first decades of the 20th century on, came to be called media. These actually refer to the mass media: newspaper, radio, cinema, television, and recently digital media. In their roles of vehicles of communication, they do not meet mediating functions. These functions are performed by the flows of signs circulating within them.

However, we cannot ignore that in order to fulfill the mediating function the sign must be embodied in a vehicle of communication that is, the media. Indeed, Peirce has always stressed the need to study the expressive forms or external representations instead of trying to examine thought itself through some form of unmediated introspection (CP 1.551).

Besides these more conceptual aspects if we come to the field of application of Peircean semiotics, the explosion of digital networks and hypermedia languages require a theory of signs that goes beyond a vision still attached to linguistic signs that, for Peirce, are but one of the possible types of symbols. Although the graded network of signs, the 10 classes of signs and ten trichotomies that give rise to 66 classes of signs, seem overly detailed, they can actually do justice to the intricate mesh of differentiated signs spouting by digital networks.

## 4. What do you consider the most important topics and/or contributions in the field of Peirce studies?

In the last four decades Peirce scholarship has continually grown in quality. There are now a large number of publications that deal with each of the multiple facets of his work which begins in mathematics, in logic and its system of existential graphs, passes through all the disciplines of Peirce's philosophical edifice, phenomenology and the normative sciences, the three branches of semiotics, to end in metaphysics.

There are also publications that deal with topical issues such as pragmatism, realism, Peirce's theories of truth, his theory of continuity, his cosmology, his theory of evolution, his conception of science, his classification of the sciences, his conception of method, his theory of vagueness, his fallibilism, his conception of diagrammatic thought, his theory of perception etc. There are publications that explore the various aspects of his theory of signs, especially the relationships that it establishes with information theory, with cybernetics, and with communication theories.

Furthermore since there are publications which establish the relationship of semiotics to biology, a field that is constituted today in a truly international school of biosemiotics, also the relationship of semiotics with cognitive sciences, with literature and the arts, with media and issues of everyday life.

Some time ago, it was believed that Peirce's work was merely a disconnected patchwork. Peirce himself seemed to be against this idea when euphorically he declared that his harvest time had finally arrived (CP 1.12). His euphoria came from the vision of the coherent integration between the parts of his work. Fortunately, the current state of the art of Peirce scholarship is revealing that consistency, presenting to the readers a set of *magna* works able to design a synthesis which is loyal to the originality and complexity of Peirce's thought.

That is the reason why I cannot indicate one or another aspect of Peirce studies which I think to be the most important. All of them are important in order to obtain a more holistic configuration of Peirce's thought. This indicates that what I think to be the most fundamental question concerning Peirce studies is to make the effort to avoid bias and sectarianism. Peirce's work is sufficiently broad and multifaceted to provide space for the most distinct choices. More than that, it is a work that requires the exploitation of its multiple facets.

## 5. What are the most important open problems in this field and what are the prospects/avenues for progress?

What I find as the most fundamental problem in Peirce scholarship here for the future lies in the discussion of the relevance of his thought for the scientific and cultural issues that are emerging nowadays. Peirce's work is inherently dialogical and anticipatory of the crucial issues that are emerging in the sciences, philosophy and the arts. It seems urgent that at least a volume on the relevance of C. S. Peirce for contemporary thinking is organized and turned public.

### References

Buczynska-Garewicz, H., Sign and Dialogue. *American Journal of Semiotics*, volume 2, number 1-2, 27-43, 1983.

Colapietro, V., *Peirce's approach to the self. A semiotic perspective on human subjectivity*. Albany: State of New York University Press, 1989.

Nadin, M. The logic of vagueness and the Category of Synechism. In *The Relevance of Charles Peirce,* Eugene Freeman (ed.). La Salle, Illinois: The Monist Library of Philosophy, 1983, 154-166.

Hoffmeyer, J., *Signs of meaning in the universe*, translated by Barbara J. Haveland, Bloomington and Indiana: Indiana University Press, 1996.

Hoffmeyer, J., *Biosemiotics. An examination into the signs of life and the life of signs*, translated by J. Hoffmeyer and Donald Favareau. Scranton and London: University of Scranton Press, 2008.

Kohn, Eduardo. *How forests think. Toward and anthropology beyond the human*. Berkeley: University of California Press, 2013.

Peirce, C. S., (1931-58). *Collected Papers*, vols. 1-6, ed. C. Hartshorne & P. Weiss, vols. 7-8, ed. A. W. Burks. Cambridge, MA: Harvard Univ. Press (quoted as CP). MS refers to the unpublished manuscript as paginated by the Institute for Pragmaticism. Lubbock, Texas.

Peirce, C. S., *Semiótica e filosofia*, Octanny Silveira da Mota and Leonidas Hegenberg (orgs and translators), São Paulo: Cultrix, 1972.

Potter, Vincent G. *Charles S. Peirce: On norms and ideals*. New York: Fordham University, [1967] 1997.

Prigogine, Ilya and Stengers, Isabelle. *Order out of chaos. Man's new dialogue with nature*. London: Flamingo, 1984.

Ransdell, Joseph. *Peircean semiotics*. Copy of a Work in progress, 1983.

Santaella, Lucia.
*Produção de linguagem e ideologia*. São Paulo: Cortez, 1980.

*O que é semiótica*. São Paulo: Brasiliense, 1983.

Brazil: A culture in tune with semiotics. In *The Semiotic Web*, 1989. Thomas Sebeok and Jean Umiker-Sebeok (orgs.). Berlin: Mouton de Gruyter, 1990.

*A assinatura das coisas*. Rio de Janeiro: Imago, 1992.

*Percepção. Uma teoria semiótica*. São Paulo: Experimento, 1993.

*Estética. De Platão a Peirce*. São Paulo: Experimento, 1994.

*Teoria geral do signos*. São Paulo: Ática, 1995.

Methodeutics, the liveliest branch of semiotics. *Semiotica* 124, 3-4, 1999a, 377-395.

A new causality for the understanding of the living. *Semiotica* 127, 1-4. Special issue, Biosemiotica, T. Sebeok, J. Hoffmeyer, C. Emmeche (eds). 1999b, 497-520.

*Matrizes da linguagem e pensamento. Sonora, visual e verbal*. São Paulo: Fapesp/Iluminuras, 2001a.

Esthetics, the supreme ideal of human life. *Semiotica* 135, 1-4, 2001b, 175-189.

Why there is no crisis of representation according to Peirce. *Semiotica*, 143, -14, 2003, 45-52.

*O método anti-cartesiano de C. S. Peirce*. São Paulo: Unesp, 2004a.

*Navegar no ciberespaço. O perfil cognitivo do leitor imersivo*. São Paulo: Paulus, 2004b.

*Semiótica aplicada*. São Paulo: Cengage Learning, 2007.

Santaella, Lucia and Nöth, Winfried. *Imagem. Cognição, semiótica, mídia*. São Paulo: Iluminuras, 1998.

### 29. Lucia Santaella

*Comunicação e semiótica*. São Paulo: Hacker, 2004.

*Estratégias semióticas da publicidade*. São Paulo: Cengage Learning, 2010.

Santaella, Lucia and Vieira, Jorge A. *Metaciência. Por uma semiótica sistêmica*. São Paulo: Mérito, 2010.

# 30

# Demetra Sfendoni-Mentzou

Professor of Philosophy of Science
Aristotle University of Thessaloniki

---

**1. Why were you initially drawn to Peirce?**
My first acquaintance with Charles S. Peirce started in the seventies, when I was trying to find a topic for my doctoral thesis in the field of Philosophy of Science. At that time the development of Quantum Mechanics and the impact of Werner Heisenberg's indeterminacy principle had already opened a serious discussion not only among scientists, but also among philosophers, as to the consequences of this principle. All this was bringing to the forefront the concept of indeterminacy and the claim that the scientific world-picture, based on a deterministic scheme of Newtonian Mechanics, could no longer be maintained. I found this idea, which at that time was not embraced by the majority of scientists and philosophers, fascinating and I started studying the development of those theories in Quantum Mechanics that had serious implications for the interpretation of causality, probability and determinism. It was then that the Oxford Philosopher Jonathan Cohen gave me a hint that a not very well known American Philosopher of the end of the nineteenth and early twentieth century, Charles S. Peirce, had put forward a theory of probability and chance. At that time C. S. Peirce was almost completely unknown in Greece and there was no piece of his work in our libraries. So, right away I ordered the eight volumes of the *Collected Papers* and started reading his scattered writings on Tychism, which I found extremely interesting and ahead of Peirce's time. My two years at Oxford University as a Recognized Student, gave me the opportunity to broaden my horizon in Philosophy of Science, so as to be able to appreciate Peirce's contribution in this field. I must say that it was my supervisor Rom Harré, who encouraged me for my decision to conduct research on the idea of indeterminacy and chance both in Peirce and Quantum Mechanics, as well as not to be afraid to stress the importance of the Aristotelian idea of potentiality—an idea that would not be easily accepted by many at those days—as an essential element for a construction of a dynamic model of physical reality.

## 2. What do you consider your contribution to the field?

As an introductory remark let me say, that my general approach is that there is an essential unity in Peirce's thought, although what he himself left to us is only scattered writings on an extremely large number of topics. So, right from the beginning, I set myself the task to explore the inner structure of Peirce's philosophical edifice in an effort to discover the fundamental ideas that can serve as an explanatory basis for a unified account of his philosophy, filling in between gaps. This, I believe— if we take for granted Peirce's confession—is the only way that could allow us to arrive at a coherent overall picture of his thought. What I have in mind is a letter to William James of December 1, 1902, where Peirce remarks: "Were all the parts of my system separately published, the mathematician would approve of the mathematical part, the physicist of the physical part, the ethicist would admit the ethical part to be a contribution of some weight, and so on; but the principal thing would remain unpublished; which is not the most obvious of things, and would then wholly escape notice" (MS 599, 1902). I must also add here, that in my overall work on Peirce, one can trace my particular interest in Peirce's relation to Aristotle and my preference for the Aristotelian idea of potentiality. This is not only, because I believe that it plays a central role in Peirce's thought, but also because I am convinced for the necessity of its involvement in any attempt for a realist account of reality. Let me, now, explain how all this works in the way I have thus far tried to understand Peirce's views on some fundamental issues, all of which have as a common element Peirce's realism.

### C. S. Peirce's realism

Peirce's model of reality, as I understand it, is grounded on his ontological categories of *Firstness, Secondness, Thirdness*. These are the pillars of his version of realism at least in those aspects of philosophy that I have been dealing with, i.e. Tychism, Synechism, laws of nature, truth and fallibilism. The interesting thing about Peirce's realism is this: It combines, in a most fruitful way, Aristotelian -Scholastic realism with the most significant scientific discoveries of his time. In this respect, my first aim has been to show, how *Thirdness*, or, the triadic relation of reality-generality-law, functions through the key-concept of "potentiality," a concept in many respects analogous to the Aristotelian "*potentia*" or "*dynamis*". Subsequently, I have tried to combine all this with some basic ideas of scientific realism, as we understand it today.

Let me, now, start with placing Peirce's ideas in the playground of philosophy of science of his day. It is important to note that Peirce developed a defense of scientific realism in an age when the dominant trend was that of positivism. He was critically opposed (a) to the ideas of A. Comte, E. Mach, H. Poincaré, K. Pearson and other significant philosophers and scientists of his time, all of which were stamped by Peirce as nominalists, and (b) to the Newtonian mechanistic determinism and atomism. His work, therefore, on those issues was developed within the context of the classical opposition between *realism*, on the one hand, and *nominalism/empiricism/ positivism/ atomism,* on the other.

It is also worth noticing, that the basic questions that have given rise to this kind of opposition, remain essentially the same: (i) what is the character of our knowledge and theories? (ii) what is the nature of reality as the object of our knowledge? In my opinion, the second question is at the heart of Peirce's thought. In particular, he was eager to provide an answer to the following question: Is the real represented by the singular, individual, actual things and events, i.e. by what the scholastics called *haecceitas*, or shall we say that there is something more—beyond experience—that is real?

Peirce's answer, as opposed to the *positivists/empiricists/nominalists* is this: Description of experienced phenomena is not all scientists are looking for; what they are mainly interested in, is to discover the permanent and real ties between phenomena, so as to provide explanations of a deeper level of reality not open to observation. This is what the scholastics called *fundamentum universalitatis*, or *quidditas*. It is located in things (*in rebus*) as the common element (*natura communis*) shared by all members of the same *kind* or *species*. This is exactly, in my opinion, the essence of Peirce's realism, which is initially based on scholastic realism, and particularly on that of Scotus (see e.g. 6.605,1893; cf.5.77n.1, 5.423. 5.503, 6.361). This finally culminates in the *Monist* period, 1890-1914 (see e.g. 6.605, 1893) in a whole-hearted commitment to Aristotelian-Scholastic realism.

I must say here that, although Peirce's commitment to scholastic realism is an idea shared by the majority of his commentators, what I have tried to establish is the close connection of Peirce's realism to the Aristotelian ontological scheme. Peirce himself expressed his admiration for Aristotle by characterizing him as "the greatest intellect that human history has to show" (6.96), or as the "prince of philosophers" (6.36; cf. 5.611, 5.423, 6.361). And, in his "Guesses at the Riddle", Peirce explained that his aim was, "...to make philosophy like that of Aristotle, that is to say to outline a theory so comprehensive that, for a long time to come, the entire work of human reason shall appear as filling up of its details. The first step towards this is to find simple concepts applicable to every subject" (1.1).

## Ontological categories

Let us now see, how the whole edifice of Peirce's scholastic realism is built on the ontological categories of *Firstness, Secondness,* and *Thirdness,* which express the structure of reality consisting in *potentiality* (or ontological possibility), *actuality* and *law* (see 6.32). Hence, the categories represent the three *"modes of being"* (6.342), or, we should rather say, the three *"modes of becoming."* The sum total of reality, even laws of nature, is in a continuous process of growth and development which should be thought to be analogous, in many respects, to that of Aristotle, as a transition from potential to actual being is taking place.

*Firstness* is described by Peirce as "mere possibility", an "atmospheric" possibility, or a possibility "floating in vacuo". It thus has a feature of "may-be" which belongs to the simple idea that has not been actualized yet. *Secondness,* represents the world of dyadic relation, of action and reaction, of struggle of thisness, *haecceitas*. It is that part of reality which belongs to the positivist world of actual existence, of what could be called in one word *observable* as opposed to the *unobservable* of *Thirdness*. The latter is the category, which represents the most essential part of reality and offers the grounds for the mediation between *Firstness* and *Secondness* (see 5.121). This mediation is accomplished through "generality".

## Generality-Continuity

Peirce adopts the scholastic definition of generality: *"Generale est quod natum aptum est dici de multis"* (5.102) and emphasizes that the word *multis* refers to an infinite number of differentiations, "which no multitude of existent things could exhaust" (5.103). Thus, *infinity* is intimately related with *generality* and *continuity:* "A true continuum is something whose possibilities of determination no multitude of individuals can exhaust" (6.170) and "the form under which alone anything can be understood is the form of generality which is the same thing as continuity" (6.173).

"Continuity", claims Peirce, " is an indispensable element of reality"; it is "the leading conception of science" and the most essential concept, which "enters into every fundamental law of physics"; Synechism, therefore, or the doctrine of continuity, is "the master key which adepts tell us unlocks the arcana of philosophy."

## Laws of Nature

All the above characteristics of *generality–continuity* stand as the corner stone of Peirce's conception of (a) laws of nature and (b) time. The definition of law given by Peirce in the "Logic of Mathematics" (c.

1896) is analogous to that of continuity and generality: "No collection of facts can constitute a law; for the law goes beyond any accomplished facts and determines how facts that may-be, but all of which never can have happened, shall be characterized" (1.420, c. 1866).

This is an explicit claim against the nominalism or positivism of Peirce's time. Laws of nature do not confine themselves to any actual number of individual facts. They go beyond the level of observable experience (see, MS 320, c.1907, p. 21). Moreover, laws of nature for Peirce are "formulations of relations"; for this reason, they should be expressed in "conditional proposition[s] whose antecedent and consequent express experiences *in a future tense*" (8.192, 1904), which future tense is connected with the idea of an *endless future*. This is why law can never be considered as completely actualized.

It is exactly this idea that constitutes, according to Peirce, the difference between a positivist and a realist attitude towards *unobservable entities, generals, laws* of nature and *time*. In the "Logic of Mathematics", c. 1896, he had already claimed that "the nominalist does object to the word 'law' and prefers 'uniformity' to express his conviction that so far as the law expresses what only might happen, but does not, it is nugatory" (1.422). Peirce repeatedly emphasizes the essential difference between *physical law*, as he understands it, and *uniformity* used by philosophers as Hume or Mill: "while uniformity is a character which might be realized in all its fullness, in a short series of past events, law, on the other hand, is essentially a character of an indefinite future" (8.192; see also *Minute Logic* 1902, 2.148).

## Time

All the above characteristics of *generality* and *continuity* applied to laws of nature are also applied by Peirce to the idea of time. It is interesting to see how Peirce's theory of time brings to light the traditional antithesis between the static a-temporal Parmenidean universe, and the dynamic model of becoming. Peirce emphasizes the idea of the *flux of time*, as he connects it with the becoming of nature. What makes his theory extremely interesting is the fact that it bears a kinship to contemporary theories of the *arrow of time,* such as that of Ilya Prigogine, and at the same time has striking similarities with Aristotle.

What both thinkers share in common is their deep concerns to give to *change-motion-becoming* its proper place in nature. They are, therefore, both opposed to the static model of reality, each of his own time: Aristotle to the Eleatic school and the atomists, whereas Peirce to Newtonian mechanics and atomism. To provide an answer to those theories, respectively, they both saw that it was necessary to defend continuity, as "an indispensable element of reality" (5.436). Thus, Peirce, exactly as

Aristotle had makes an appeal to time as a "continuum *par excellence*, through the spectacles of which we envisage every other continuum" (6.86, 1898). This is expressed by the idea, that time is not a collection of discrete instants; "[t] heir being is welded together" (MA 137, pp. 4-5, 1904), so that they loose their identity. Hence, instants of time as points on a line, become a *collection of possible points*, a collection of *possibilia* which, as *possibilia*, lack distinct individuality but are nontheless real.

This view is essentially interwoven with the idea of the *potential infinite*. The *actual* infinite (in the Zenonean-atomists' sense) is that whose infinitude exists, or is given all at the same time. The *potential* infinite is that whose infinitude is given over time and is never present as a whole. This is exactly what endows it with the character of a constant state of becoming, which never passes to actually in its entirety. Peirce seems to have been perfectly aware of the Aristotelian view that, "Time and movement are indeed unlimited, but only as processes..." (*Physics* 208a 20-23). In this dynamic-realist conception of reality, of laws of nature and of time, the triadic relation of *continuity-infinity-generality* appears in all its fullness. And, certainly, we must not forget that they are all essential features of *Thirdness*.

**Scientific theories**

My claim, therefore, is that, if the central role of *Thirdness* be accepted in Peirce's conception of reality, of laws of nature and of time, then we could be led to a deeper understanding of Peirce's attitude towards the whole body of scientific theories. It is essential to see here how Peirce defines the goal of scientific inquiry in his "Review" of Pearson's *Grammar of Science*, 1901:

As he [the man of Science] gradually becomes better and better acquainted with the character of cosmical truth... he conceives a passion for its fuller revelation... The very being of law, generality, truth, reason consists in its expressing itself in a cosmos and in intellects which reflect it, and in doing this progressively. (8.136)

Of particular interest here is the fact that Peirce, not only interrelates, but also identifies law—which is another expression for generality— with general truth. What then is truth for Peirce?

**Truth**

We must keep in mind that Peirce develops his theory of Truth in two levels: (a) The *epistemic* and (b) the *ontological* one. He is dealing not only with the problem of our knowledge of the world, but also with the problem of the nature of the world as the object of our knowledge. The main lines of Peirce's theory of Truth, as I understand it, are the following: Truth is the final opinion that would be reached by the unlimited community of inquirers, if their pursuit of Truth—through various paths—were to continue into an indefinitely prolonged future. The object represented in this opinion would be reality —covering both actuality and potentiality—considered as an open possibility, indefinitely projected into the future. Truth, therefore, is the result of the "ongoing community of investigators" which will (is destined to) arrive at the final opinion. Agreement with final opinion may be postponed "indefinitely", says Peirce. Its distinctive characteristic is that it has an *esse in futuro*, i.e. it remains an open possibility that would be reached "in the long run".

At this point, there has been a long discussion as regards a tension that appears to exist between Peirce's Fallibilism and his theory of Truth. A question has also been raised as to how much dogmatism/optimism, on the one hand, and/or skepticism/pessimism, on the other, is to be found in Peirce's doctrine of Truth. The prevailing view has been that Peirce's theory of Truth is a third solution in between rationalism and empiricism, as it expresses less pessimism than Descartes' skepticism and less optimism than Descartes' dogmatism. I certainly share the view that Peirce offers a third solution. However, I believe that we should not measure this difference with quantitative criteria. The important thing is that Peirce offers a qualitatively third solution. To establish my thesis I have tried to shed light on the intimate connection between Fallibilism and Peirce's Tychism.

In an extremely enlightening manuscript of 1897 Peirce poses the question: "what is the significance of Fallibilism?" (1.152). He then goes on to analyze "the three basic notions of science": *potentiality, continuity, evolution* (1.154). In this context, he examines the ideas of *statistical regularity, chance, spontaneity, novelty* and *differentiation*, all of which are the constitutive elements of his Tychism. The conclusion he arrives at is his doctrine of *probability, indeterminacy* and *chance* (see, 1.162). Therefore, in order to make clear how Peirce tries to connect Fallibilism with *indeterminism*, I think it is necessary to say a few words about his theory of chance.

## Tychism

"The hypothesis of chance-spontaneity," Charles S. Peirce claims in 1892, "is one whose inevitable consequences are capable of being traced out with mathematical precision into considerable detail." And he continues: "I mention it to indicate to future mathematical speculators a veritable gold mine, should time and circumstances and the abridger of all joys, prevent my opening it to the world" (CP 6.62). In fact, the gold mine was opened almost half a century later. The dramatic development of Quantum Mechanics brought in a spectacular way into the scene the idea of indeterminacy, which offered the ground for the claim that the scientific world-picture, based on Newton's deterministic model, could no longer be maintained. This is exactly what Peirce claims.

At the center of Peirce's theory of chance is his conception of that kind of law, which belongs, as we have seen, in the category of Thirdness. This is the "law of habit", which is the expression of a "generalizing tendency" and is intimately connected with Peirce's notions of probability, "would-be" and chance. What is also essential to note here, is that the law of habit is the opposite of the blind law of mechanics. It is endowed with a plasticity (6.86; cf. 6.261) and can only function through chance (6.63). This is how Peirce believes that *growth, evolution, variety and diversification* in nature can be explained (see, 6.613).

In fact, in Peirce's world-picture, there is a continuous evolution along the lines of the three modes of becoming (see 6.32; see also, CP 6.191). The process of diversification, Peirce claims, began in "the utter vagueness of completely undetermined and dimensionless potentiality" (6.193). This has a marked similarity to the Aristotelian definition of matter, which is also identical with the indeterminateness of freedom and potentiality. "By matter I mean that which in itself is neither a particular thing nor a quantity nor designated by any of the categories which define Being" (Metaphysics, 1029a 20-22). "The embryonic being, for Aristotle," remarks Peirce, "was the being he called matter" (1.22). And on another occasion, he remarks: "The original potentiality is the Aristotelian matter or indeterminacy from which the Universe is formed" (6.206).

All the above, I believe, can serve as the necessary material for the connection of *Falllibilism* with *Tychism*, by using an extremely interesting analogy between *Fallibilism* and *indeterminism*, that Peirce, himself, makes. In this context he uses the term *fallibilism* in the place of *indeterminism* and the term *infallibilism* in the place of *determinism*, and remarks: "the multitudinous facts of all experience" cannot be explicated by infallibilism, "but that which has opened our eyes to these facts is the principle of fallibilism" (1.162). And he continues: in order to appreciate fallibilism, we must take into consideration two basic ideas: evolution and continuity (see, 1.173). "Evolution means nothing but *growth* in its widest sense of that word...And what is growth?". His answer is of crucial importance: "Not mere increase", but "diversification" (1.174). "And yet mechanical law, which the scientific infallibilit tells us is the only agency of nature, mechanical law can never produce diversification...And anybody can see ... that mechanical law out of like antecedents can only produce like consequences...So, if observed facts point to real growth, they point to another agency, to spontaneity for which infallibilism provides no pigeon-hole" (1.174). But the infallibilist "makes the laws of nature absolutely blind and inexplicable"... This is something that blocks the road of Inquiry (1.175). By contrast, the fallibilist "will not do this" (1. 175). On the basis of this view Peirce proceeds to the following remark: there is "a natural affinity" of the principle of continuity with the theory of fallibilism... "The principal of continuity is the idea of fallibilism objectified. For Fallibilism is the doctrine that our knowledge is never absolute but always swims, as it were, in a continuum of uncertainty and of indeterminacy. Now the doctrine of continuity is that *all things* so swim in continua" (1.171). We can thus claim that, fallibilism is a theory which has both an *epistemic* and an *ontological* aspect, as it refers both to our knowledge (uncertainty) and to the world (indeterminacy).

All this, as I have argued, can also be applied to Peirce's theory of truth. Truth, on the one hand, cannot be the outcome of the effort of a finite number of investigators. This is why an uncertainty in the process of inquiry always remains; on the other hand, the totality of physical reality—natural laws included—has a character of *indeterminacy*. This *indeterminacy* is interrelated with the idea of *infinite possibility*, which remains open in the future, in such a way that the possibility/probability for the discovery of new aspects and levels of reality is never exhausted. As a result, the continuous process towards truth brings us all the time closer to our goal, final opinion, which is indefinitely prolonged into the future.

## 3. What is the proper role of Peirce's work in relation to philosophy and other academic disciplines?

Peirce has produced an extremely significant work to nearly every basic field of philosophy, such as Logic, Symbolic Logic, Mathematical Logic, Ontology, Metaphysics, Epistemology, Theory of Meaning, Ethics, Religion, Aesthetics, Semeiotics (he himself invented the term and the science of the meaning of signs), as well as in History and Philosophy of Science, in Mathematics, in Psychology (he carried out, together with Joseph Jastrow, Johns Hopkins University, some significant experiments in psychology), etc. it is important to note, that all the work Peirce produced was built on a firm knowledge of the classical philosophical tradition, as well as of various scientific theories. To be more specific, Peirce studied thoroughly the work of great classical European philosophers, such as Descartes, Kant and Hegel; he also studied Duns Scotus, as well as Aristotle in the original. On the other hand, we must not forget that Peirce himself was a scientist. He received a bachelor of science in chemistry in 1863 and he worked as an assistant at the Harvard Astronomical Observatory (1869-1872), where he made a series of astronomical observations (1872-1875). He was also employed for more than thirty years by the United States Coast and Geodetic Survey as a physicist and "made many important scientific and technical contributions". As a result, he took profit of his knowledge in all those areas, so as to produce an extremely significant work. In some cases he created new fields, as for example his *semeiotic* or theory of signs, and in some other cases he put forward some pioneering ideas, as is the case with his *Tychism*.

**4. What do you consider the most important topics and/or contributions in the field of Peirce studies?**

I am inclined to say, that all the topics in Peirce's studies are equally important and that there have been excellent studies on almost all areas of Charles S. Peirce's Philosophy. What one would choose would mostly be a matter of one's special interests.

**5. What are the most important open problems in this field and what are the prospects/avenues for progress?**

If I want to follow Peirce, I should say that all problems are open and no problem could be considered as already solved; this would "block the road of inquiry". If, however, I should give my opinion as to what field of Peirce's philosophy has not yet received the attention it deserves, this would be the intimate connection of Peirce and Aristotle. As I have already noted, Peirce himself expressed his admiration for Aristotle by characterizing him as "the greatest intellect that human history has to show", or as the "prince of philosophers". And, in his "Guesses at the Riddle", Peirce explained that his aim was, "...to make philosophy like that of Aristotle". So, although Peirce's commitment to scholastic realism is a topic that has been studied quite thoroughly, his connection to Aristotle has not received due attention. However, I must say that recently there is a growing interest in this aspect of Peirce's philosophy, and I think that it will give us interesting results.

**Publications on Charles S. Peirce**

1980- *Probability and Chance in the Philosophy of C. S. Peirce* (Doctoral Thesis, in Greek). Thessaloniki: Aristotle University of Thessaloniki, pp. 246.

1982-"The Dynamic Character of C. S. Peirce's Pragmatic Theory of Meaning" (in Greek). *Philosophia* (12): 359-378.

1984- *The Philosophy of C. S. Peirce's Pragmatism. How to Make Our Ideas Clear* (in Greek). Thessaloniki: Sakkoula Publications, pp. 87.

1986-"Peirce's Theory of Signs. Semeiotics, Ontology, Hermeneutics" (in Greek). *Proceedings of the 1st Philosophical Conference on Hermeneutics.*" Thessaloniki, pp. 130-39.

1991-"Towards a Potential-Pragmatic Account of C. S. Peirce's Theory of Truth." *Transactions of the C. S. Peirce Society.* Vol. 27 (1991): 27-77.

1992-"Is there a Logic of Scientific Discovery? A Pragmatic-Realist Account of Rationality in Physical Theory". In M. Assimakopoulos (et al. eds), *Historical Types of Rationality. Proceedings of the First Greek-Soviet Symposium on Science and Society.* National Technical University of Athens, pp. 239-250.

1993-"The Reality of the Unobservable in Physical Theory: An Account of C. S. Peirce's Pragmatic Realism", *Reflexao*, PUCCAMP, Campinas (57): 103-118.

1993-"The Role of Potentiality in C. S. Peirce's Tychism and in Contemporary Discussions in Quantum Mechanics and Micro-Physics". In E. Moore (ed.), *Charles S. Peirce and the Philosophy of Science: Papers from the 1989 Harvard Conference.* The University of Alabama Press, pp. 246-261.

1994-"The Character of Physical Law: A Pragmatic-Realist Account" (in Greek). *Greek Philosophical Review* (11): 134-149.

1994-"Laws of Nature. Ante Res or in Rebus?" *International Studies in the Philosophy of Science.* Vol. 8, No3: 229-242.

1995-"Peirce and Idealism: Response to Savan". In Kenneth Laine Ketner (ed.), *Peirce and Contemporary Thought. Philosophical Inquiries.* Fordham University Press, pp. 329-338.

1996-"The Reality of Thirdness: A Potential-Pragmatic Account of Laws of Nature". In R. Cohen (et al. eds), *Realism and Anti-realism in the Philosophy of Science.* Kluwer, 1996, pp. 75-97.

1997-"Peirce on Continuity and Laws of Nature", *Transactions of the Charles S. Peirce Society* (vol. 33): 591-645.

2008-"C. S. Peirce and Aristotle on Time". *COGNITIO. Revista de Filosofia.* Vol. 9 Numero 2: 261-280.

2010-*Pragmatism-Rationalism-Empiricism. Theories of Knowledge* (in Greek, 2nd edition). Thessaloniki: Ziti, pp. 231.

2012-*Pragmatism-Rationalism-Empiricism. Theories of Knowledge* (in Greek, 3rd upgraded and enlarged edition). Thessaloniki: Ziti, pp. 327.

# 31

# Sun-Joo Shin

Professor of Philosophy
Department of Philosophy, Yale University

## 1. Why were you initially drawn to Peirce?

My initiation into Peirce's thoughts is quite different from (and almost opposite from) that of other scholars. I started reading Peirce not because I wanted to figure out his deep and almost mysterious thoughts, but because I needed a (small) piece of his achievement for my (then) immediate project.

If I had known how much Peirce wrote, what a range of philosophical topics the philosopher covered, or how much was written by Peirce scholars, I might not have started getting into the world of Peirce. My meeting with Peirce took place at one of its small entrances on a narrow alley, and I did not have any intention to enter Peirce's world or even to peek through a window. Pragmatism (or pragmaticism) is one of a very few topics I associated with Peirce and that sounded like too big a landscape for me to hang onto. If I zoomed in, that grandiose scenery, I was afraid, would disappear into air. Then, what is the entrance (which I wrongly thought was small) on an alley (which, again, I wrongly thought was narrow) where I met Peirce? It was Peirce's Existential Graphs!

My work, before meeting Peirce, was to establish diagrammatic representation as a formal system. It was part of a bigger project "Heterogeneous Reasoning" initiated by Jon Barwise and John Etchemendy at Stanford University when I was a graduate student. My first book, *The Logical Status of Diagrams*, examines and challenges the common practice that diagrams have been used as a heuristic tool, but not as part of a rigorous proof. Taking up Venn diagrams, I established a formal system of Venn, by providing it with a formal syntax and semantics. What has been going on with symbolic logical systems, I showed, could be done with this specific diagrammatic system. I took it to be my main goal to formalize a well-known use of diagrams to prove that we can make a diagrammatic formal system, and I believed that mission was complete. To my surprise/dismay, some commentators concluded that my work successfully showed that Venn diagrams are symbolic (or linguistic), contrary to our naïve thought.

Facing an urgent task to clarify what makes some representation symbolic and some diagrammatic, I had to admit that using circles is neither a necessary nor a sufficient reason to call the Venn system diagrammatic. At the same time, I could not help thinking that the Venn system is not symbolic, but diagrammatic, and that maps are diagrammatic, etc. I wanted and needed to get this strong intuition clarified and justified, especially in the context of formal systems.

During my struggle to justify a naïve view of diagrams, the fact that Peirce devised two kinds of logical systems --- one symbolic and the other graphic --- suddenly occurred to me. He must have understood fundamental differences between these two kinds of representation. Otherwise, why did he have to invent two --- symbolic notation first and graphic later? I assumed that while agonizing over his Existential Graphs for years and years Peirce must have recorded why he himself took this graphical system more seriously than his own symbolic notation, even though his contemporary logicians adopted Peirce's symbolic notation over Peirce's EG and over Frege's (quasi) graphical notation. Did Peirce say anything about fundamental differences among various forms of representation? I wanted to get any useful tip from Peirce so that I might justify my original project, that is, to formalize diagrammatic systems.

I was quite surprised and disappointed not to find any theoretical justification by Peirce why his own Existential Graphs are different from his own symbolic notation, even though he had a strong conviction that the invention of Existential Graphs was one of his most significant achievements. Peirce also must have accepted the intuition that lines and cuts (i.e. quasi-circles) are non-symbolic, unlike variables, predicate letters, $\Sigma$ or $\Pi$.

My mission to find these specific clues was not accomplished, but I received an unexpected reward: While reading many pages related to Peirce's logical systems, I found myself being drawn into his thoughts and inventions further and further. It was also truly amazing to read impressive work done by Peirce scholars. The world of Peirce was so big and so inclusive that I felt thoroughly humbled.

## 2. What do you consider your contribution to the field?

As explained above, I entered Peirce's work not through a main gate but through a side door. Therefore, my work suffers from ignorance of Peirce's big body of work, which is an obvious disadvantage. However, at the same time, I would like to think that helped me to make a unique contribution to Peirce scholarship. At the risk of scratching the surface,

I avoided being submerged into a big landscape where various topics are related to one another. Instead, I zoomed in on his specific logical system and related writings, and clarified them as an outsider so that Peirce's thoughts could be more accessible to contemporary philosophers beyond the world of Peirce scholars. In order to appreciate some of Peirce's thoughts, we do not have to go through his entire system, but his main ideas are accessible to those who have limited knowledge of Peirce and Peirce's works are still full of fresh insight a century later. Of course, when we know more about Peirce, we could deepen our understanding of his thoughts, but a piecemeal approach should not be absolutely prohibited if we could get good result. (Am I too pragmatic here?) Below, I would like to illustrate my point in a more concrete way.

Even though I could not locate Peirce's own statements as to why Existential Graphs are graphic, not symbolic, working on Peirce's EG helped me to identify some unique features of diagrammatic representation. I was able to publish the work as a book titled *The Iconic Logic of Peirce's Graphs* from the MIT Press. Hence, this portion of Peirce's work has become directly related to current diagrammatic reasoning research. In the process of finding EG's distinctive properties, I was able to come up with new ways of reading and understanding EG. They are not only new but also easier and more intuitive ways of approaching Peirce's EG. I summed up these novel ways to read off Peirce's EG under the Carving-Up Principle and started applying this principle to other diagrammatic representation. Since I approached Peirce's work with a specific external agenda (rather than as a question internal to Peirce's philosophy), I was able to carve up (no pun here) certain portions of Peirce's work and to make sense out of it. I would like to think it was beneficial from both camps --- on-going Peirce scholarship and current research on diagrammatic reasoning.

It is characteristic of Peirce's writings that one and the same topic has been discussed over and over with slight modification. His discussions about reasoning, about deductive reasoning, and especially about a distinction between theorematic and corollarial reasoning, are not exceptional. Here I found Peirce's insight brilliant, not only in relation to Kant's analytic/synthetic distinction, but also for clarifying one of the mysteries involved in deductive reasoning. My paper "Kant's syntheticity revisited by Peirce" was another example of how Peirce's certain insight could be tightly and interestingly related to time-honored philosophical topics and, hence, approachable to non-Peirce scholars without being acquainted with Peirce's intricate scheme.

I would like to encourage other scholars to make a connection among Peirce's thoughts, other time-honored philosophical works, and current philosophical projects.

## 3. What is the proper role of Peirce's work in relation to philosophy and other academic disciplines?

This question is not easy to answer. My response is that there is and should be no proper role of Peirce's work defined by us: We can always be creative. Scholars have full freedom to present their ways of understanding Peirce's work so that they may persuade us that this is one way to think about Peirce's work and this another way, etc. If Peirce's work could influence other areas beyond philosophy, it would be even better.

## 4. What do you consider the most important topics and/or contributions in the field of Peirce studies?

Philosophy of Science
Logic of Relations
Pragmatism
Theory of Signs

## 5. What are the most important open problems in this field and what are the prospects/avenues for progress?

The theory of abduction, even though much work has been done on it, is one of the topics with lots of potentiality, which could guide us to new ideas and insights. Making Peirce's work and ideas – especially his theory of reasoning – more accessible to non-Peirce scholars is one of the ways to make an interesting progress in other fields.

## Bibliography

### Books

*Visual Reasoning with Diagrams*, ed. by Amirouche Moktefi and Sun-Joo Shin, Springer Basel (2013)

*The Iconic Logic of Peirce's Graphs*, Cambridge: MIT Press (Bradford) (2002)

*The Logical Status of Diagrams*, New York: Cambridge University Press (1994)

### Articles

"Preface of *Visual Reasoning with Diagrams*" (with Amirouche Moktefi), Springer Basel (2013)

"History of Diagrams" (with Amirouche Moktefi) in *Handbook of the History of Logic*, ed. by Dov M. Gabby, Francis Jeffry Pelletier, and John Woods. North-Holland. pp. 611-682. (2012)

"How do Existential Graphs show what they show?" in *Das bildnerische Denken: Charles S. Peirce*, Akademie Verlag, Germany, pp. 219-234. (2012)

"The Forgotten Individual: Diagrammatic Reasoning in Mathematics" in *Synthese* 186(1), pp. 149-168. (2012)

"Peirce's theory of representation" in *Peircean diagrammatical logic*, ed. by Joao Queiroz and Frederik Stjernfelt, de Gruyter, Berlin (2011)

"Peirce's Logic" in *Stanford Encyclopedia of Philosophy* (with Eric Hammer) (2011)

"Peirce's Two kinds of Abstraction," in *New Essays on Peirce's Mathematical Philosophy*, ed. by Matthew More, Open Court, Chicago and La Salle, Illinois (2010)

"Heterogeneous Reasoning and its Logic," in *The Bulletin of Symbolic Logic*, Vol. 10, no. 1, pp. 86-106 (2004)

"On Diagram Tokens and Types" (with Howse, Molina, and Taylor), in *Theory and Application of Diagrams* (Lecture Notes in Artificial Intelligence, Vol. 2317) pp. 146-160, Springer (2002)

"Multiple Readings of Peirce's Alpha System," in *Thinking with Diagrams*, Springer (2001)

"Diagrams," (with Oliver Lemon and John Mumma) in *Stanford Encyclopedia of Philosophy*

"Reviving the iconicity of Beta graphs," in *Theory and Application of Diagrams*, Springer, pp. 58-73 (2000)

"Reconstituting Beta Graphs into an Efficacious System," in *Journal of Logic, Language and Information* 8, pp.\ 273-295 (1999)

"Euler's Visual Logic" (with Eric Hammer), in *History and Philosophy of Logic* 19, pp. 1-29 (1998)

"Kant's Syntheticity Revisited by Peirce," in *Synthese* 113, pp. 1-41 (1997)

"Peirce and the Logical Status of Diagrams," in *History and Philosophy of Logic* 15, pp. 45-68 (1994)

# 32

# T. L. Short

Independent Scholar

---

**1. Why were you initially drawn to Peirce?**

In the 1960s, the foundationalist assumptions of logical empiricism came under attack by Quine, Popper, Sellars, Feyerabend, Toulmin, Kuhn, and others. It was shown that neither data nor methods are exempt from revision in the course of scientific inquiry. Many feared that this entails relativism, subjectivism, and irrationalism. Others eagerly embraced that supposed implication, so as to immunize their political ideology from factual refutation. Peirce had already made essentially the same critique of positivism, the ancestor of logical empiricism, but without supposing that science is any the less objective. 'Objective' is a term that seldom occurs in his writings in this sense, but it is a term I find useful. How, I wondered, was Peirce able to maintain that scientific inquiry is objective *sans* foundations?

The answer to that question has many parts, some of which, such as Peirce's use of probability theory in justifying induction, had already been discussed when I began writing on Peirce. Another part, the pragmatic maxim, was and still is wrongly assimilated to verificationist theories of meaning; it is about the growth of meaning through factual discovery. Peirce's late-blooming modal realism is essential to his view of science, but can it be defended? By his theory of signs or semeiotic, one might hope to understand how observation is both an effect of sensation and an explanatory hypothesis; thus we could understand how observation is a test of theory even while being defeasible on grounds of well-attested theory, and how rival theories, though incommensurable, may be about the same reality. Peirce's semeiotic was receiving much discussion by the 1970s, most of it erroneous. For that reason, I began to publish on this last topic, leaving aside for the nonce the other topics.

At that time, I noticed a second use of the semeiotic, that it provides a naturalistic but non-reductive account of the mind. Mind had been placed outside of nature; it was distinguished from nature on the ground that thinking has objects that sometimes are non-existent, while natural processes are to be explained wholly by events that actually occur, by objects and forces that actually exist. But animal behavior, too, cannot be fully described without citing non-existent objects: the food sought when there isn't any, the predator fled which wasn't there. The triadic structure of Peirce's semeiotic explains these facts without introducing any assumption of consciousness: real relations justify interpretation, making something a sign, but the object signified is a function of the interpretation justified, and, as justification is sometimes only probabilistic, that object may fail to exist. Thought is a special case of sign-interpretation, one that consists not immediately in such behavior as seeking or fleeing, but in the production of another sign of the same object. Consciousness is a consequence, not a presupposition, of sign-interpretation.

Consciousness is not presupposed but purposes are; and therefore it is presupposed that purpose may in some cases be independent of consciousness. It is only by being end-directed, that seeking or fleeing interpret their occasions as signs of objects – i.e., objects of a type (food, predator) which might not exist. And it is only in relation to a purpose that we can speak of relations in nature (e.g., past correlations of scents or sounds with food or predators) as justifying an interpretative response. Justification is relative to purpose. However, to say that a response or an instinct, etc. is justified is not to imply that the animal in question is aware of that fact. That animal instincts and reflexes and other organic mechanisms exist for purposes, i.e., to achieve effects of given types, is explained by the theory of natural selection. A purpose always is general: it is a type of outcome for which there is selection, natural or not. The type selected-for explains the tendency of a process toward outcomes of that type. Such types are therefore causes, albeit, as mere types, they can exert no force and are not mechanical causes; they have been called 'final causes'. (I do not feel obligated to replicate Peirce's error of supposing that the word 'purpose' refers only to those final causes that exist in someone's consciousness.) Peirce's mature semeiotic depends on his c.1902 concept of final causation, a redefinition of Aristotle's idea in light of $19^{th}$ C science.

This idea of final causation also is naturalistic but non-reductive: a tendency is an observable fact but its explanation is not reducible to the process's mechanics. Final causation, or selection for type of outcome, falls under the broader category of explanations of irreversible tendencies; such explanations always are statistical. The logical empiricists had wrongly supposed that statistical explanation always conforms to the 'covering-law' model of explanation. Mechanics and its laws are presupposed, but even in cases where irreversibility has its law (as in the Second Law of thermodynamics), its statistical explanation does not make it an instance of mechanical laws. It could not, as the latter always apply reversibly.

But final causation, as Peirce understood it, turns out to be essential not only to semeiosis and therefore to mentality but also to the objectivity of scientific method. The evolution of method consists in experience-driven changes in cognitive values and norms; such changes can be other than arbitrary only if there is a purpose that becomes clarified in the process and in reference to which those changes are justified *post hoc*. 'And what you thought you came for/ Is only a shell, a husk of meaning/ From which the purpose breaks only when fulfilled/ If at all.' Such a purpose must be real in the sense of making a difference, albeit not by force: it must determine desire, rather than desire determining it. Its reality consists in an irreversible process of selection for a type of outcome. But what applies to changes in cognitive norms might apply also to the evolution of other values, aesthetic, moral, and political (albeit the latter change also in response to changing circumstances).

I think, then, that Peirce's idea of final causation has enormous implications, not yet much noticed. But its defense is linked to that of modal realism. Both turn on issues concerning the limits of empirically meaningful language. Peirce was an empiricist not only in theory of knowledge but in philosophical method. For the latter purpose, he had to expand the idea of what is observable, which he did empirically, by a series of experimental studies of observation. The first consequence of this was to establish that experience is itself observable, making the new science – an empirical science – of phaneroscopy (phenomenology) possible. Phaneroscopy, in turn, exposes the poverty of the idea of experience that logical empiricism inherited from British empiricism. A second consequence was to show that differences of value are observable, making the science Peirce named 'aesthetics' possible. Thus he proposed that philosophy be made a set of empirical sciences, some of them normative. I don't think much of the idea of normative science or of the idea that philosophy should be made scientific; but the corollary of these ideas, that there can be knowledge, in aesthetics, ethics, and logic, that is both objective and normative, is all-important. A Peircean defense of that proposition would be three-pronged: phaneroscopic, semeiotical, and metaphysical.

You will have noticed that I have described not only what initially drew me to Peirce but what continues to draw me to him, or rather to his thought. It is his thought that matters. Peirce himself was in some respects less than admirable.

## 2. What do you consider your contribution to the field?

So far, what I have done that is of most importance is to have explicated Peirce's idea of final causation (in several articles but most fully in Chapters 4 and 5 of my 2007 book). Secondarily, I think somewhat important my explication of his idea of hypostatic abstraction – essentially, the transformation of a predicate into a subject – and its relevance to making sense of conceptual change and the growth of meaning (also in several articles and in Chapter 10 of the 2007 book), and, as well, its application to the philosophy of mind (ibid., Ch.11) and to accounting for the objectivity of science (ibid., Ch.12). I seem, however, to be most noted, so far as at all, for making some sense of Peirce's divisions of what he named 'interpretants', his idea of significance as (what I have called) grounded interpretability, and his taxonomy of signs (these topics occupy the rest of the 2007 book). Yet, I do not see that this has had much influence on what has subsequently been published about Peirce's semeiotic; distinctions, arguments, and textual evidence that I would have thought clear and compelling have been almost uniformly ignored.

Are my contributions, such as they are, now all past? I would like to think that I am still at work. I have more recently been writing on the interpretation of Peirce's writings. He is generally admitted to have been a genius, yet is seldom read with much care. Contemporary academic philosophers, whose name is Legion, may be divided into the tiny band of 'Peirceans' and all-the-others. All the others read Peirce, if at all, up to the point where he anticipated, or seems to them to have anticipated, some favorite idea of their own, and beyond that point they cast him aside as an obscurantist or a bore or a fossil. But Peirce suffers at least as much from his enthusiasts, who read him uncritically, who are bemused by grand visions of endlessly ramifying system, to which they assume that all he wrote was subordinated, and whose expository style is quotation. Digitization of texts and electronic search engines make quotation easy, but reading remains difficult.

Peirce was most artful in those essays, such as the 'pragmatic' ones of 1877-8, in which he seems most simple. His thought always featured process, relation, and structure, but it was also always itself in process, was always in flux, and therefore structures sketched in different periods, though formally similar, differ in crucial details and, indeed, in meaning. He came to conceive of philosophy itself as inquiry, not as system-building, and as empirical, not as *a priori*. If I have a contribution yet to make, it is to show that Peirce, to be understood, must be read with due attention to his use of irony (not least, in his appropriations of the ideas and/or language of earlier thinkers) and to his almost constant, but seldom announced, changes of mind. His ideas must be received, not as the finished products of ratiocination, but on the model of hypotheses in modern science, that is, as conjectures, sometimes roughly sketched, intended to guide further inquiry and to be further developed therein. Such hypotheses cannot be understood without their being applied to diverse topics and, in those applications, modified, refined, and corrected. That is what Peirce's pragmatism teaches, which, by the way, has nothing to do with 'practical' uses. The difficulty of reading Peirce is that he wrote both with literary indirection and with a research scientists' expectation that readers can work out for themselves how to apply an idea, once some technical matters have been explained, whereas the training of academic philosophers leads them to expect literalness, rigor, and attempted finality of formulation, none of which are prominent in Peirce's philosophical writings. Looking for what was not meant to be there, and not finding it, analytic philosophers wrongly condemn Peirce; his enthusiasts are still more at fault, for claiming that it is there.

## 3. What is the proper role of Peirce's work in relation to philosophy and other academic disciplines?

Presumably, this question is not about Peirce's contributions to astronomy, geodesy, mathematical logic, experimental psychology, and several other sciences, but is about what we distinguish within his writings as 'philosophical'. Is philosophy, in that vague sense, an academic discipline? Is it a discipline at all? What is a discipline? Different philosophers have had radically different ideas of the aim and method of philosophy; they do not share a discipline. Peirce, in 1902, proposed that philosophy should become a set of scientific inquiries, all of them empirical and some of them normative, each developing, as sciences do, in relation to other sciences. Philosophy's aim, even in the normative sciences, was, Peirce proposed, knowledge simpliciter, not anything practical. Among the philosophical sciences he enumerated were some of his own construction, including semeiotic. Peirce's semeiotic has been appropriated and distorted by many academics, in departments other than philosophy, who apply it in ways Peirce did not intend. Is that anything to complain of? Scientists, as Peirce knew, take from other specializations anything they think will be useful to their own. If they alter or misunderstand what they have taken, that does not matter: their thefts and mutilations will be justified if they prove fruitful. And therefore we can derive no rules from Peirce's writings about how his ideas may be used.

Peirce's 1902 classification of the sciences has been misunderstood in a way that may suggest that the forgoing conclusion is mistaken;

hence this brief digression. Peirce ordered the sciences from more to less basic, the more basic providing principles to those less basic. But (a) such judgments are retrospective and (b) it does not follow that the more basic prescribes for the less basic. As to (a): the taxonomy lists itself as a science 'of review', hence, as subject to revision as inquiry continues. Its divisions and ordering are not *a priori* but reflect the progress of science to date. And the ordering is *post hoc*: the less basic sciences often developed first. Think, in this connection, of the relation of mathematics to physics: it was the needs of the latter that drove the development of the Calculus. As to (b): even had the Calculus been developed first, in pure mathematics, it would have been physics, not mathematics, that decided whether, where, and how it could be used in physics. The principles provided are *chosen* by the less basic, not prescribed by the more basic.

Let us, then, forget what is 'proper'. And I shall leave other 'disciplines' (some of which aren't) to their own devices. What might Peirce's thought contribute to academic philosophy in its current state? (And today, unhappily, there is no philosophy worthy the name except that which flickers dimly in the academy.) Until recently, academic philosophy was divided into the Anglo-American analytic tradition and the sequence of fashions that emanated from continental Europe. Today, the situation is more fluid, unless 'crumbling' is the apt metaphor. Philosophy seems to be going nowhere. The torrential flood of publication and ceaseless conferencing prove nothing. It has gone unnoticed that Peirce's idea of philosophy, and his own manner of thinking, differ radically from all of the above. Perhaps it may suggest a way forward. Quine's idea of 'epistemology naturalized' points in Peirce's direction, but Quine himself remained analytic in method and did not see that epistemology can be naturalized only if cognitive values are subject to empirical discovery. Many today are inclined to challenge the fact/value dichotomy – but how? Gestures in that direction, e.g., by Hilary Putnam, seem to me gestures only; substance is lacking. Peirce's expansion of the empirical may be one way to put flesh on those bones. We can learn from Peirce's empiricism without adopting his entire program of making philosophy scientific.

To learn from Peirce, it is essential to do what is so rarely done, viz., to not assimilate his originality to models more familiar to us. Take, for example, his first step expanding the empirical. The non-normative science of phaneroscopy employs formal ideas drawn from the algebra of relations, much as Russell and others later employed polyadic predicate logic in conceptual analysis. But phaneroscopy is not conceptual analysis; it analyzes experience. It reveals the experiential roots of debated concepts, e.g., modal, that logical analysis has failed to illuminate. In this and in other ways, phaneroscopy offers an alternative to analytic philosophy, with which, however, it shares a scientific spirit. But phaneroscopy has also been misunderstood by being assimilated to structuralism, viz., by those who suppose that its categories, because formal, are necessary. There is no way to know that anything interesting can come from analyzing experience into monadic, dyadic, and triadic elements, other than by making the attempt. Some commentators have supposed that Peirce's early writings limn a transcendental deduction of the phaneroscopic categories; others deplore the lack of a rigorous deduction of those categories; both schools of thought are mistaken, and for the same reason.

This empirical manner of inquiry, with its sense of adventure, of trying ideas out and seeing what works (and of finding out, in the process, what 'working' means, i.e., what our purposes are), is not unique to Peirce (one thinks also of James and of Whitehead), but it is an alternative to the practices prevailing in academic philosophy today (practices that account for philosophy's being only academic).

## 4. What do you consider to be the most important topics and/or contributions to the field of Peirce studies?

There are so many topics within Peirce's work – and all of them are important! I will restrict my answer to contributions: three only, which, not being recent, are in danger of being wrongly neglected. Sometimes, they have even been disparaged.

Far and away the most important contribution to the study of Peirce that has ever been or ever will be made was the editing of the *Collected Papers* (1930-58). And the most important part of that contribution was the organization of the first six volumes, due to Charles Hartshorne (Paul Weiss was brought in subsequently, to deal with the writings in formal logic and the algebra of relations). The defects of that edition have been much complained of, and they are undeniable. Works of different periods were jostled together and sometimes even spliced together without notice. But Hartshorne was the first to bring the various facets of Peirce's philosophical thought – some highly technical, others highly speculative – together, as diverse parts of a single body of thought aspiring to unity; and he rightly made the phenomenology, or phaneroscopy, primary (despite its late development). If the *Collected Papers* had not been published, it is likely that Peirce would be almost unknown today.

Murray Murphey, in his 1961 book, *The Development of Peirce's Philosophy*, was the first to draw attention to the way that Peirce's thought changed over time: the first to examine his writings in chronological order, to mark their discrepancies, and to try to account for those discrepancies. Of course, there is much to object to in the way Murphey did this. He assumes that Peirce was always engaged in constructing a philosophical 'system', despite Peirce's own disparagement of system-building and his express preference for on-going, open-ended inquiry. Murphey assumes that a system succeeds only if there is an argument for its necessity; but such an argument would have to be *a priori* whereas Peirce espoused empiricism in philosophical method. And Murphey projected a far too simplistic scheme of how Peirce's thought evolved, where each change of 'system' was in response to a discovery in formal logic. The actual development of his thought was, as one might expect, far more complicated than that. Nonetheless, after having read Murphey, no one will reasonably deny that Peirce can be understood only by studying the way his thought developed, with due attention to the contradictions that marked its progress.

In 1967 and 1970, Karl-Otto Apel published two volumes of Peirce's writings in German translation, with extensive introductions by himself; in 1975, these introductions were republished as one book, *Der Denkweg von Charles S. Peirce*, translated into English in 1981 by John Michael Krois, as *Charles S. Peirce: From Pragmatism to Pragmaticism*. Apel locates Peirce's thought within the Kantian tradition and portrays it as a revolutionary transformation of Kant's transcendental deduction, rendering it social, pragmatic, and semeiotical. No other interpretation of that thought has been as profound or as interesting. I think that it is mistaken and that Peirce's rejection of Kant's transcendental deduction, even in his early, most Kantian days, went far deeper than Apel realized. Nonetheless, Apel's book is a brilliant example of what must be done if we are to appreciate Peirce's thought: it must be grasped, not as a system standing in splendid isolation, but as a unique way of thinking that is engaged with the great issues that have emerged from philosophy's history.

These three contributions established that Peirce's thought must be seen as a whole, studied in its development, and grasped in historical context.

## 5. What are the most important open problems in this field and what are the prospects/avenues for progress?

Every aspect of Peirce's thought remains an open problem. His philosophy is *terra incognita*. What hasn't been ignored has been mangled, e.g., its most studied aspect, his so-called pragmatism. Rather than enumerate problems, I will mention just one neglected topic.

We have not yet begun to understand what Peirce was all about. Work goes forward on what he said and what it might have meant and what it should mean for us in relation to the issues that move us, but what were the issues that moved him, why was he impelled to go in his peculiar directions, and what did he mean to achieve by those inquiries that occupied his time outside of the research in astronomy and geodesy he was paid to do? There has been little study relating Peirce's thought to the 19$^{th}$C cultural background within which his purposes were formed. The motifs that we think of as distinctively Peircean – celebration of 13$^{th}$C Scholasticism, attributing all modern ills to nominalism, embrace of probability, hypothesis, and fallibilism, the idea of inquiry as self-corrective, evolutionism and continuity of mind with matter, etc. – were, none of them, original with him. But he developed each in a distinctive way and combined them in a distinctive way. We will not appreciate his originality if we do not examine his sources. And those sources also suggest the preoccupations or underlying sense of what is problematic that he shared with others of his time. I do not mean that this topic is all-important or most important. It is trumped by what we can make out of Peirce's thought for our own purposes: a *modus operandi* that is itself Peircean. But it is a piece of the puzzle, and the one which has perhaps been most neglected. Also, as it falls outside of my own line of work, it is something that I hope someone else will study.

**Major publication:**

*Peirce's Theory of Signs*, Cambridge University Press, 2007.

**A selection of articles:**

'Teleology in Nature', *American Philosophical Quarterly*, Vol.20, No.4, 1980.

'Hypostatic Abstraction in Empirical Science', *Grazer Philosophische Studien* (Graz, Austria), Vol.32, 1988.

'Did Peirce Have a Cosmology?', *Transactions of the Charles S. Peirce Society*, Fall 2010

'Questions Concerning Certain Claims Made for the "New List"', *ibid.*, Summer 2013.

# 33
# Frederik Stjernfelt

Full Professor of Semiotics, Intellectual History, and Theory of Science

University of Copenhagen

---

**1. Why were you initially drawn to Peirce?**

As a young semiotician, I initially read Peirce as a classic of semiotics among others. Unlike a country like Finland, Denmark presented little expertise or even knowledge about Peirce in my time as a student, and much of the humanities were in a period where scientific ideas of knowledge were under attack from Marxist, poststructuralist, constructivist and other fire. What immediately appealed to me, by contrast, was Peirce's realism, both in its scientific and "scholastic" aspects, and his insistence on the close connection between semiotics, logic and philosophy of science - as against the widespread culturalism and relativism in currents of semiotics inspired by Saussurean linguistics, anthropology, etc. Within structuralism, however, Jakobson's rejection of the arbitrarity dogma led him to point in the alternative, Peircean direction. Contributing to my taking this lead was my interest in the philosophy and semiotics of René Thom and Jean Petitot who, based on the mathematical Catastrophe Theory, insisted that semiotics should form part of a rational epistemology and a basically realist, scientific approach. Thom even included Peircean notions in the eclectic "biolinguistics" (Petitot's expression), which he developed as part of Catastrophe Theory over the 1970-80s.

In 1994, together with Anne-Marie Dinesen, I edited and introduced a Danish translation of central Peirce writings in philosophy of science and semiotics; in 1996, I facilitated the publication of the physicist Peder Voetmann Christiansen's translation and introduction of the first Monist paper series including "The Law of Mind". So, I took Peirce to form a central part of the education of a skilled semiotician. What prompted my further, more specialized interest in Peirce, however, was the lightning strike of discovering Peirce's general notion of diagram. It was the Danish cognitive psychologist Michael May who pointed me in the direction of the alternative sketch for Peirce's 1906 paper "Prolegomena of an Apology of Pragmaticism" (in vol IV of NEM) known as "PAP". The general outline given there by Peirce of the process of diagrammatical reasoning struck me as a revolutionary and overlooked way of combining logic, reasoning, perception, diagrams and epistemology, potentially integrating cognitive processes often taken to be far apart. So this took me to a strong interest in the Peircean conceptions of iconicity, diagrams and continuity, the first expression of which was a *Transaction* article (2000) and which ended up in my Habilitationsschrift *Diagrammatology* some ten years later (2007) developing the idea that the notion of diagrammatic reasoning must be central in a contemporary cognitive semiotics.

These Peircean discoveries contributed to a more general suspicion that the continental-analytical split in 20 C philosophy was not only politically and geographically distastrous, but that it also tended to fossilize reductive sets of answers to basic questions, letting important earlier ideas fall into oblivion - parallel cases to that of Peirce being other pre-divide system builders integrating science and metaphysics such as Husserl and Cassirer.

During the 1990s, I had become involved in the discussions around the nascent discipline of biosemiotics through the Copenhagen biologists Claus Emmeche and Jesper Hoffmeyer and the series of annual international biosemiotic "gatherings" where an interest in applying Peircean semiotics to biological sign use was developing; this urged me to try to participate in this endeavor. Peirce's sign theory, being not confined to human beings, appears as an obvious choice for such application; less obvious, however, is the exact way of achieving its details it in a fertile way, and that discussion is far from exhausted, but it made me acutely aware of a particular strength of Peirce's thought: the integration of semiotics and logic implies a constant attention to which sign vehicles may serve the development of knowledge and reasoning.

## 2. What do you consider your contribution to the field?

My primary contributions to the field are collected in two books: *Diagrammatology. An Investigation on the Borderlines of Phenomenology, Ontology, and Semiotics* (2007) and *Natural Propositions. The Actuality of Peirce's Doctrine of Dicisigns* (2014). In the first book, I reconstruct Peirce's general conception of diagrammatical reasoning in the context of his semiotic doctrine of iconicity and his metaphysical doctrine of continuity. Here, my central argument is that diagrams form the centerpiece of Peirce's mature epistemology and form an important contribution to present-day cognitive semiotics. On top of Peirce's logic formalizations, the algebras of logic and the existential graphs, Peirce developed a general notion of diagrams covering not only formalizations of logic but also diagram use in general, across the special sciences, beginning with mathematics where diagram experiment is taken to be the central epistemological procedure. Diagrams - relational, spatial part-whole structures used to depict objects sharing parts of the same structures - are central to reasoning because facilitating the extraction of implicit information by means of diagram experiments. Peirce's diagrammatology, the book argues, may be synthesized with early, Husserlian phenomenology and ontology to a realist semiotics, which may, in turn, be taken as a basis for biosemiotics, image studies and literary studies such as indicated by the second half of the book.

In the second book, I take these ideas further by outlining and developing Peirce's theory of propositions, so-called "Dicisigns" which differs strongly in important respects from the almost exclusively linguistic notion of propositions in mainstream philosophy and logic. Peirce's purely functional definition of Dicisigns makes it independent of language, of consciousness or the propositional attitudes of human beings. This definition, highlighting the function of reference to and description of the same object by the same sign, entails important and deep ideas as to the unity of the proposition involving the self-reference of the proposition, a continuist theory of predicates and, in the semiotic surface expression of propositions in Dicisigns the crucial idea of primitive, continuous co-localization as the mother of all syntax. The purely functional definition simultaneously enlarges the extension of propositions in two directions, one in the direction of non-linguistic and composite signs in human semiotics (involving pictures, diagrams, gesture, etc.), the other in the direction of biosemiotics where a strong argument can be made that biological signs must be functionally propositional in order to be preserved by natural selection and enhance adaptation. This widely enlarges the amount of human sign vehicles capable of truth claiming, just like it makes possible to address the evolution of Dicisign use in biology. On this basis, the book develops further important Peircean themes such as antipsychologism, the status of kind universals, iconicity, and the corollarial-theorematic distinction.

### 3. What is the proper role of Peirce's work in relation to philosophy and other academic disciplines?

Peirce's philosophy is primarily a philosophy of science. The overall answer which Peirce develops over a lifetime addresses the Kantian arch question of how and why scientific knowledge is possible. In Peirce, however, this develops into an original parsing of the whole field of language, logic, cognition, perception, images, mind, knowledge, radically different from mainstream analytical and continental currents alike. Peirce's stance is alien to the linguistic turn, privileging language, as well as to the mental turn, privileging psychological explanations—and, indeed, alien to any other reduction of epistemological and ontological issues to social, historical, cultural or other levels. Logic, to Peirce, covers both the semiotic machinery necessary to express propositions, on the one hand, and the methodological strategies for discovery on the other.

Peirce's philosophy, of course, is not only relevant for philosophy of science, but its further relevance is determined by the logic-semiotic-knowledge axis which forms its center from which connections run to other parts of philosophy and to other sciences. The connection to mathematics is especially important, Peirce's philosophy of mathematics offering an important untapped potential where the double reading of diagrams (as tokens or as types) allows for an understanding of how the use of physical, causal tools (diagram tokens) is able to access knowledge about idealized, abstract relations (diagram types). From that axis, connections also run to e.g., language, art, psychology as modes of expressions related in different, particular ways to knowledge and logic; or to sociological and political issues approached from the point of view of the interacting research community as a prototype of Enlightened human collaboration and of sign meaning closely connected to possible action; or to biology as deeply motivated by the conception of organisms as semio-cognitive survival cycles.

## 4. What do you consider the most important topics and/or contributions in the field of Peirce studies?

Important topics in Peirce studies comprise: 1) the narrow connection between a general theory of signs on the one hand and logic and epistemology on the other; 2) Peirce's overlooked role in the development of modern logic and his untapped resources for its further development; 3) the central role of iconicity, of observation and experiment, in all of reasoning, particularly in mathematics and logic, more generally in all of the special sciences; 4) pragmatism and its insistence on common action as central to any concept of meaning.

## 5. What are the most important open problems in this field and what are the prospects/avenues for progress?

To begin with the more specific problems, a central want in Peirce studies is a comprehensive intellectual biography. Joseph Brent's biography collected a lot of valuable material as to Peirce's life, but Max Fisch's ambition to trace Peirce's intellectual development and its interplay with other researchers and disciplines has never been fulfilled.

In Peirce biography, of course, important questions include: 1) what were the deeper reasons behind Peirce's wide unpopularity in large parts of American Academia in general and at Harvard in particular, contributing to preventing him from a permanent academic position?; 2) Who was Juliette Froissy Pourtalai?

Practically, it is well-known among Peirce scholars how a central desideratum is electronic access to a better scanned and indexed version of Peirce's unpublished papers.

On the more general level, important open issues include: What is the metaphysical status of continuity? What is the role of continuity in the synthesis of knowledge, and in knowledge representation vehicles like diagrams and languages? What are the central subtypes of diagrams? Could there be made a typology of forms of theorematic reasoning? How is the detailed interaction between ab-, de-, and induction in the research process, in pure as well as empirical cases? How could language be reinterpreted as a special, multilevel diagrammatical reasoning tool? Can a cognition theory based on signs and action effectively bar relativism and psychologism?

The prospects for progress are promising - there has probably never been so many skilled Peirce scholars undertaking reconstructions based on the vast quarry which is Peirce's *Nachlass,* not only providing a steady stream of better and unexpected results in the understanding of Peirce's viewpoints, but also allowing for fertile interaction with present and pressing problems of philosophy and cognitive science in a period when the contintental-analytical divide finally seems to be losing its grip.

**Bibliography**

"Diagrams as Centerpiece in a Peircean Epistemology", in *Transactions of the Charles S. Peirce Society,* Summer, 2000, vol. XXXVI, no. 3, p. 357-92

*Diagrammatology. An Investigation on the Borderlines of Phenomenology, Ontology, and Semiotics,* Dordrecht et al. (2007): Springer Verlag

Special issue of *Semiotica* (186, 1-4; 2011) on "Diagrammatical Reasoning and Peircean Logic Representations", edited by Joao Queiroz and Frederik Stjernfelt

*Natural Propositions. The Actuality of Peirce's Doctrine of Dicisigns,* Boston (2014): Docent Press

# 34
# Claudine Tiercelin

Collège de France and Institut Jean Nicod, Paris

---

**1. Why were you initially drawn to Peirce?**

I was originally drawn to Peirce by a series of various circumstances: in the first place, the rather contingent discovery of his illuminating remarks on the Nominalist versus Realist views on Universals, in his Frazer's Review of the works of G. Berkeley (1871), at a time when I was myself engaged in writing a Master memoir at the Sorbonne (1974) on the philosophy of signs of Berkeley; then, a few years later, I came to read some comparisons that had been drawn between Peirce's and Wittgenstein's versions of pragmatism, by Jacques Bouveresse (a Wittgenstein scholar who then supervised my two dissertations: "Peirce's critique of intuition and metaphysics in the early papers"(1982), and "The problem of universals in C. S. Peirce"(1990)). I soon came to realize not only that Peirce had very interesting things to say on the medieval problem itself (which led me to a close study of the medievals (Duns Scotus and Ockham in particular), just as former Peirce scholars, like John Boler, had done), but also that Peirce's own reformulation of the issues related to the problem of universals, through his adaptation of scholastic realism to the modern lessons that could be drawn from logic, science and pragmatism, made it possible to erect a very insightful and new kind of both realistic and scientific metaphysics.

**2. What do you consider your contribution to the field?**

I think the right way to answer such a question would be to divide it into three aspects: First, in terms of my contribution as a French Peirce scholar, I should say that I have been one of the very few French philosophers to focus that much on Peirce's work in terms of his overall importance in all the major areas of philosophy and to try to reframe what very soon appeared to me as a rather "systematic" philosophy. Before me, Gérard Deledalle, or Gilles Gaston Granger, then Jacques Bouveresse had paid attention to Peirce's semiotics and/or logic, but no one had really attempted to see to what extent Peirce had developed a whole philosophical and metaphysical system in such a way as to be able to answer most of the important challenges raised in contemporary philosophy (philosophy of logic, philosophy of perception, philosophy of mind, cognitive sciences, general epistemology, philosophy of science, metaphysics); this is also why I have been engaged for several years in the French edition and translation of Peirce's works (three volumes published, out of ten on the program at the Editions du Cerf, Paris) together with Pierre Thibaud (a logician who had been a former student of Granger). Secondly, in terms of Peirce's scholarship, I think my main contribution has been to try and show on many of the topics I found original in Peirce (his thought-sign conception of the mind, his relations to the medieval conceptions of signs, his views on machines, self control, iconic reasoning, vagueness, abduction, his views on belief, knowledge, assertion, truth and norms, or again his views on science, metaphysics and realism), how Peirce was both very close to many authors from the tradition of the history of philosophy (which I studied in several papers relating Peirce's views with those of Aristotle, Duns Scotus, Berkeley, or Thomas Reid) but also a source of inspiration for many contemporary philosophers (Frank Ramsey, L. Wittgenstein, Isaac Levi, D.H. Mellor). This explains why –and this may be the third (and in my view most interesting) aspect of my contribution – I have always tried to show to what incredible extent we could use Peirce's writings as food for thought. In particular, I have used his analysis of knowledge as inquiry, together with his views on doubt and belief to build my own conception of knowledge and possible pragmaticist parry to scepticism (in *Le Doute en Question: parades pragmatistes au défi sceptique*, Paris, éditions de l'Eclat, 2005). In another book, more devoted to metaphysical issues, *Le Ciment des choses: petit traité de métaphysique scientifique*, Paris, éditions d'Ithaque, 2011), I have also followed Peirce's inspiration, his views on dispositions, laws and scientific realism, to try and develop my own scientific and realistic metaphysical program.

## 3. What is the proper role of Peirce's work in relation to philosophy and other academic disciplines?

Peirce's importance, in that respect, may be compared to that of an Aristotle or a Leibniz: he had original and important things to say in all the main areas of philosophy; besides, as a (formal) logician (and a semiotician), an experimental psychologist, and a practicing scientist (not only trained in chemistry but in physics and geodesy), he was able to connect philosophy to other academic disciplines. This explains why his work on logical machines, intentionality, belief, vagueness, diagrammatic reasoning, abductive inference, probabilities, scientific method, is still a very fruitful source of inspiration today in many areas outside philosophy.

## 4. What do you consider the most important topics and/or contributions in the field of Peirce studies?

I think very highly of the first generation of Peirce's scholars who have realized an amazing pioneering work on Peirce, which is still extremely valuable today (although their work is less frequently - and very unjustly - mentioned) : I feel an enormous debt towards such amazing scholars as Arthur Burks, Richard Robin, John Boler, M. Murphey, and of course, Max Fisch. Then among the Peircians who, I think, made an outstanding - both historical and philosophical - contribution, in so far as they were able to connect Peirce's views with major contemporary philosophical issues (in logic, epistemology, philosophy of mind, philosophy of science) both Susan Haack and Christopher Hookway come to the foreground.

I must say I am much more skeptical about some more recent contributions on Peirce which tend either to indulge too much into a sort of short-sighted, textual or philological veneration of Peirce's writings, or to apply Peirce's views so broadly and freely as to loose sight of the genuine philosophical import of what he wanted to say (on which I think there is still very much that needs to be clarified and may be profitably put to use).

## 5. What are the most important open problems in this field and what are the prospects/avenues for progress?

The most important problems and prospects for progress on Peirce are exactly the same as those that are at the heart of the most debated contemporary issues in philosophy. A lot of work is still needed on Peirce's analysis of epistemic norms, of his understanding of the relations between nature and norms, epistemology and ethics, or knowledge and assertion. There is also a lot to be done and benefit to be drawn from such a study, in terms of Peirce's conception of realism (e.g., the way it works, in particular, in many still untrodden areas of his philosophy of mathematics), of natural kinds (and the way they make sense within a general "evolutionary" metaphysics) and of a coherent "scientific" metaphysics.

## Bibliography

### Books:

1. *C. S. Peirce et le pragmatisme*, Paris, Presses Universitaires de France, 1993.

2. *La pensée-signe : études sur Peirce*, Nîmes, Editions Jacqueline Chambon, 1993.

**Papers:**

4. "Que signifie : "voir rouge"? La sensation et la couleur chez C.S. Peirce" *Archives de philosophie,* juil-sept. 1984, 47/3, p. 409-429.

5. "Peirce on machines, self-control and intentionality", in *The Mind and The Machine: Philosophical Aspects of Artificial intelligence,* S. Torrance (ed.), Chichester, Sussex, 1984, pp. 99-113 (translated in Japanese and Danish).

6 "Logique, psychologie et métaphysique : les fondements du pragmatisme selon C.S. Peirce", *Zeitschrift für allgemeine Wissenschaftstheorie,* XVI/2, 1985, p. 229-250.

7. "Le vague est-il réel? Sur le réalisme de C.S. Peirce", *Philosophie,* n° 10, 1986, p. 69-96.

8. "Peirce et Berkeley : l'esprit et les signes", *Cahiers du groupe de recherches sur la philosophie et le langage,* n° 8, 1987, p. 23-48.

9. "Peirce ou le courant sémiotico-sémantique de la logique formelle", *Cahiers du groupe de recherches sur la philosophie et le langage,* n° 10, mars 1989, p. 39-71.

10. "Peirce ou le projet d'une logique du vague", *Archives de philosophie,* 1989, n°4, p. 553-579.

11. "Reid and Peirce on Belief" in *The Philosophy of Th. Reid,* M. Dalgarno and E. Matthews (eds.), Amsterdam, Kluwer Akademic Publishers, 1989, pp. 209-223.

12. "La première philosophie de C.S. Peirce", *L'âge de la science, lectures philosophiques,* n°3 : La philosophie et son histoire, Paris, Editions O. Jacob, 1990, p. 71-84.

13. "Peirce's Logic of Vagueness", *IMFUFA,* Tekst NR 205, Roskilde Universitet, 1991.

14. "Le Vague de l'objet", *Cruzeiro Semiotico,* janvier 1991, p. 29-41.

15. "Peirce's semiotic version of the semantic tradition in formal logic", *New Inquiries into Meaning and Truth,* N. Cooper and P. Engel (eds.), Harvester Press, 1991, pp. 187-213.

16. "La sémiotique peut-elle être une science?", *Cruzeiro Semiotico,* juil. 1991, p. 27-47.

17. "Vagueness and the unity of Peirce's realism", *Transactions of the C.S. Peirce Society* 28 (1), 1992, pp. 51-82.

18. "Peirce's realistic approach to mathematics: or, can one be a realist without being a Platonist?", *C. S. Peirce and the Philosophy of Science* (1989 Harvard Conference), University of Alabama Press, E. C. Moore (ed.), 1993, pp. 30-48.

19. "Entre grammaire spéculative et logique terministe : la recherche peircienne d'un nouveau modèle de la signification et du mental", *Histoire, Epistémologie, Langage,* tome 16, fasc. I., 1994, p. 89-121.

20. "Dualité, Triadicité et Signification en Mathématiques", *La connaissance philosophique,* recueil en hommage à l'œuvre de G. Granger, éd. J. Proust et E. Schwartz, Paris, Presses Universitaires de France, 1994, p. 169-186.

21. "La conception peircienne de rationalité normative", *Travaux du Centre de Recherches Semiologiques,* Neuchâtel, 1994, p. 1-32.

22. "Un pragmatisme conséquent?", *Critique,* août-septembre 1994, n° spécial consacré à Jacques Bouveresse, 567-568, p. 642-660.

23. "Peirce's relevance for contemporary issues in Cognitive Science", *Acta Philosophica Fennica* 58, 1995, pp. 37-74.

24. "Peirce on norms, evolution and knowledge", *Transactions of the Peirce Society* 33 (1), 1997, pp. 35-58.

25. "Sur l'idéalisme de C.S. Peirce", *Revue Philosophique,* n° 3, 1997, p. 337-352.

26. "Die schwierige Beziehung von Metaphysik und Wissenschaft", *Deutsche Zeitschrift für Philosophie,* Berlin, 1998/1, pp. 103-117.

27. "Peirce's objective idealism: a defence", *Transactions of the Peirce Society* 34 (1), 1998, pp. 1-28.

28. "L'influence scotiste dans le projet peircien d'une métaphysique comme science", numéro spécial consacré à Jean Duns Scot et la métaphysique classique, *Revue des Sciences Philosophiques et Théologiques,* tome 83, n° 1, 1999, p. 117-134.

29. "Wittgenstein et Peirce", *La philosophie autrichienne : spécificités et influences,* Tunis, Publications de l'Université de Tunis, éd. M. Ouelbani, 2000, p. 46-74.

30. "C. S. Peirce ou l'idée d'une métaphysique scientifique évolutionnaire", *Philosophies de la Nature,* éd. O. Bloch, Paris, Publications de la Sorbonne, n° 5, nov. 2001, p. 453-463.

31. "Philosophers and the Moral Life", *Transactions of the C.S. Peirce Society* Essays in Honor of Richard S. Robin, 38 (1/2), 2002, pp. 307-326.

32. "La sémiotique philosophique de Charles Sanders Peirce", *Questions de sémiotique,* éd. A. Hénault, Paris, Presses Universitaires de France, 2002, p. 15-52.

33. "Le projet peircien d'une métaphysique scientifique", *Cent ans de*

*philosophie américaine*, éd. J.-P. Cometti et C. Tiercelin, Presses de l'Université de Pau, 2003, p. 157-182.

34. "Peirce, lecteur d'Aristote", *Aristote au XIXe siècle*, éd. D. Thouard, Presses Universitaires de Lille, 2004, p. 353-376.

35. "Le problème des universaux : aspects historiques, perspectives contemporaines", *La structure du monde : objets, propriétés, états de choses; le renouveau de la métaphysique australienne*, éd. J.-M. Monnoyer, Paris, Vrin, 2004, p. 339-353.

36. "Les philosophes et la vie morale", *L'éthique de la philosophie*, sous la direction de J.-P. Cometti, Paris, Kimé, 2004, p 15-38.

37. "Ramsey's pragmatism", *Dialectica*, special issue on F. P. Ramsey, ed. by P. Engel and J. Dokic, 58 (4), 2004, pp. 529-547.

38. "Abduction and the Semiotics of Perception", *Semiotica*, special issue on Abduction, ed. by F. Merrell and J. Queiroz, 2005, pp. 389-412.

39. "Vagueness and the ontology of art", *Cognitio* 6 (2), 2005, pp. 221-253.

40. "Le nom propre chez Peirce" in *Le Nom Propre*, éd. F. Markovits, *Corpus,* n° 50, 2006, p. 75-109.

41. "The importance of the medievals in the constitution of Peirce's semeiotic and thought-sign theory", *Semiotics and Philosophy in Charles Sanders Peirce*, R. Fabbrichesi Leo and S. Marietti (eds.), Cambridge Scholars Press (UK), 2006, pp. 158-183.

42. "Ethics and the sceptical challenge: a pragmaticist approach", *Cognitio* 8, 2007, pp. 315-340.

43. "Dispositions and essences", *Dispositions and Causal Powers*, R. Harré and M. Kistler (eds.), Ashgate, 2007, pp. 81-102.

44. "The Fixation of Knowledge and the Question-Answer Process of Inquiry", in *Knowledge and Questions*, F. Lihoreau (ed.), *Grazer Philosophische Studien* 77, 2008, p. 23- 24.

45. "Peirce on Mathematical Objects and Mathematical Objectivity", in *New essays on Peirce's Mathematical Philosophy,* Matthew Moore (ed.). La Salle, Illinois, Open Court, pp. 81-121.

46. Review of Huw Price's *Naturalism without mirrors. Metascience*, 2013.

# 35
# Fernando Zalamea

Professor of Philsophy
Universidad Nacional de Colombia

---

**1. Why were you initially drawn to Peirce?**

There were two specific moments where Peirce got my attention. First (1988), while I was doing my Ph. D. in mathematics at Amherst, I stumbled into the *New Elements of Mathematics* in a second-hand books basement. The finding was extraordinary and I got captivated by the extremely original and surprising pages on the *continuum*. Second (1993), while beginning a Seminar on the History of Logic at my University, I came across at very deceptive descriptions of Peirce's role in the discipline, particularly in respect to his outstanding *existential graphs*. Some years of study and some Peirce Seminars (1995-2000) done at Bogotá helped to put things in proper perspective, and brought me to agree with Peirce that he was really at the level of an Aristotle or a Leibniz. Further, his *grand vision* became very important for me, since at that time I was expanding my interests to philosophy and cultural studies, a trend that has become central in my development.

**2. What do you consider your contribution to the field?**

One should not answer such a question, but I may delude myself that my contribution has been bicephalous. On one hand, I have produced a mathematical, methodological and philosophical study of the continuum and the existential graphs (see reference [1]). A strong accent on *advanced mathematical* tools (particularly mathematical category theory and complex variables theory) to understand the *entanglement* of the continuum and the graphs may be the interest of that approach. I thank there my association with Arnold Oostra. On the other hand, I have fostered an appropriation of Peirce's ideas to understand Latin America [2], [3]. There, my friendship with Jaime Nubiola [4], [7] has been most illuminating. I may also be proud that our *Centro de Sistemática Peirceana* (*CSP*), directed by me in Bogotá, has already 13 active members (2014). With them we have produced five numbers (2009-2013) of our *Cuadernos de Sistemática Peirceana* [5], as far as I know the only journal in the world devoted specifically to Peirce (the *Transactions* being much more oriented to general American philosophy).

## 3. What is the proper role of Peirce's work in relation to philosophy and other academic disciplines?

Peirce is very attractive to us as a *breaker* of the disciplines. It is much more than just having some sort of "interdisciplinary" perspective. His wonderful *triadic classification of the sciences* invites to osmotic invention, to a wonderful contamination of thought, well beyond the illusory "clearness" promoted by analytical philosophy. His *pragmaticism* opens the way to enlarge our understanding through the interplay between the actual and the *possibilia*. To me, Peirce is an *instigator of life and truth*, well beyond the use of simple compartments and linguistic restraint. His *semeiotic* encompasses all the universe, and breaks the artificial segmentations of mind and nature. The mathematical *bonding* of the existential graphs is a reflection of a much more general attitude towards bonding in the continuum of intelligence. The influence for our contemporary world of such a *pragmaticist* and *synechistic* perspective should be enormous, since it will promote *creativity* [6] and will help to imagine the necessary *mixtures*, both scientific and cultural, required for a new century.

## 4. What do you consider the most important topics and/or contributions in the field of Peirce studies?

There have been many very strong contributions in the last fifty years. I consider extremely important the views of Peirce as a unitary and continuous thinker. There, the landmarks of Murphey and Fisch stand still today as unsurpassed, with other important contributions by Anderson and Parker. Other more bounded topics are also essential, where some scholars have produced remarkable works from which I have learned a lot. I mention them in approximate order along the classification of the sciences, and following a very personal perspective: Peirce's mathematics (Eisele, Havenel, Moore, Oostra), Peirce's phenomenology (Esposito, Fabbrichesi, and De Tienne's Ph. D. thesis, for me the most important contribution to Peirce's studies after Murphey), Peirce's esthetics and creativity (Barrena), Peirce's logic (Roberts, Zeman, Houser), Peirce's abduction (Niño), Peirce's classification of the sciences (Kent), Peirce's metaphysics (Mayorga, Maddalena). I have not yet found the great landmark on Peirce's semiotic that I would like to have read. It is interesting to see that many of the major contributions to the field come directly from Ph. D. theses: this underlines an *academic* status for Peirce which should hopefully be *broken* in the future (see next answer).

## 5. What are the most important open problems in this field and what are the prospects/avenues for progress?

One should begin with the availability of Peirce's own work. The fact that only in some decades we will have available a careful, chronological edition of Peirce's writings is a strong impediment for a correct understanding. It should also be clear that Harvard has to produce an *entire digital* copy of Peirce's manuscripts, to be made freely available through the web. Peirce's Centennial is an occasion to *break* the barriers of what has been a very conservative century in handling Peirce's heritage. After that, many other advances may become possible. I would think that enough work has already been done in understanding Peirce *per se*, even if much is still open, particularly in existential graphs, following Pietarinen's reconstruction of the manuscripts, or in abduction, following Niño's Ph. D. thesis. But I would think that the most important open problems will appear in the application of Peirce *per contra*, that is, in the use of Peirce's ideas to understand our contemporary world. Labeled by many as a philosopher of the XIXth century for the XXIst century, Peirce still needs his great interpreters in the new millennium. I would imagine that Peirce's scholarship will *not* be helpful there. Instead, we will have to wait for the Russell or the Wittgenstein which will be able to found –on Peirce– new perspectives for philosophy, as the young analyticians did a century ago profiting from Frege and Cantor.

## Bibliography

### Author

[1] *Peirce's Logic of Continuity. A Conceptual and Mathematical Approach*, Boston: Docent Press, 2012. 192 pp. ISBN 978-0983700494.

[2] *Signos triádicos. Lógicas – literaturas – artes. Nueve estudios latinoamericanos*, México: Mathesis, 2006. 164 pp. ISSN 0185-6200.

[3] *Ariel y Arisbe. Evolución y evaluación del concepto de América Latina en el siglo XX: una visión crítica desde la lógica contemporánea y la arquitectónica pragmática de C.S. Peirce*, Bogotá: Convenio Andrés Bello, 2000. 213 pp. ISBN 958-698-058-8.

[4] (with Jaime Nubiola) *Peirce y el mundo hispánico: lo que Peirce dijo sobre España y lo que el mundo hispánico ha dicho sobre Peirce*, Pamplona: Eunsa, 2006. 376 pp. ISBN 978-84-313-2407-0.

**Editor**

[5] (with Arnold Oostra) *Cuadernos de Sistemática Peirceana*. Number 1 (2009), ISBN 978-958-46-0619-8. Number 2 (2010), ISBN 978-958-46-0617-4. Number 3 (2011), ISBN 978-958-46-0618-1. Numbers 4 (2012) and 5 (2013) in print.

[6] (with Giovanni Maddalena) *European Journal of Pragmatism and American Philosophy* 5 (2013): *Pragmatism and Creativity*, Milano: Associazione Culturale Pragma, 2013. 252 pp. ISSN 2036-4091.

[7] (with Jaime Nubiola) *Anthropos* 212 (2006): *Charles S. Peirce. Razón e invención del pensamiento pragmatista*, Barcelona: Anthropos, 2006. 224 pp. ISSN 1137-3636.

# About the Editors

**Francesco Bellucci** (b.1983), Ph.D. in Semiotics (Università degli Studi di Siena, 2012). Research fellow at the Tallinn University of Technology and Università di Bologna, his research focuses on Peirce's logic and the theory and history of semiotics. His publications include "Peirce's Continuous Predicates", "Diagrammatic Reasoning. Some Notes on C. S. Peirce and F. A. Lange", "Peirce, Leibniz, and the Threshold of Pragmatism".

**Ahti-Veikko Pietarinen** (b.1971), Professor of Semiotics at the University of Helsinki, Finland and Professor and Head of Chair in Philosophy at the Tallinn University of Technology, Estonia. Publications include *Signs of Logic: Peircean Themes on the Philosophy of Language, Games, and Communications* (Springer 2006); *Logic of the Future: Peirce's Writings on Existential Graphs* (Indiana University Press, 2014).

**Frederik Stjernfelt**, professor of semiotics, intellectual history, and theory of science at the University of Copenhagen. Critic at *Weekendavisen*, Copenhagen. Editor of the journal KRITIK 1993-2013. Has published, among other things, the books *Diagrammatology* (2007), *The Democratic Contradictions of Multiculturalism* (with J.M.Eriksen, 2012), *Natural Propositions* (2014). Member of the Royal Danish Society of Sciences and Letters.

www.ingramcontent.com/pod-product-compliance
Lightning Source LLC
Chambersburg PA
CBHW021835220426
43663CB00005B/253